G000112192

Managing Finance and Information

Managing Finance and Information

by:

Alan Jennings
Howard Senter

Copyright © Open Learning Foundation Enterprises Ltd 1995

First published 1995

Blackwell Publishers Ltd
108 Cowley Road
Oxford OX4 1JF, UK

238 Main Street
Cambridge, Massachusetts 02142, USA

Every effort has been made to trace all copyright owners of material used in this book but if any have been inadvertently overlooked the publishers will be pleased to make necessary arrangements at the first opportunity.

British Library Cataloguing-in-Publication Data
A CIP catalogue record for this book is available from the British Library

Library of Congress Cataloging-in-Publication Data
A catalogue record for this book is available from the Library of Congress

ISBN 0-631-19668-4

Printed in Great Britain by Alden Press

This book is printed on acid-free paper

273137

Contents

Introduction   1

SECTION ONE: MANAGING FINANCE

Session one: Types of business organisation   13
                    Unincorporated businesses   14
                    Incorporated businesses   19
                    Company growth and the structure
                    of groups   25
                    Other business organisations   36

Session two: Sources and types of finance   43
                    External providers of finance   44
                    Overdrafts, bills of exchange,
                    creditors and factoring   50
                    Hire purchase, credit sales and
                    finance leases   56
                    Bank loans, mortgages and debentures   61
                    Share capital   67

Session three: Published accounts   75
                    Published accounts requirements   76
                    Profit and loss account theory   77
                    Profit and loss account format   81
                    Balance sheet theory   86
                    Balance sheet format   93
                    Cash flow statement theory   99
                    Cash flow statement format   104

Session four: Analysis and evaluation   113
                    Users of accounting information   114
                    Methods of analysis   118
                    Profitability   125
                    Solvency and liquidity   130
                    Capital gearing   137
                    Investment ratios   143
                    Control of working capital   148

Session five: Analysis of costs   157
                    Ascertaining costs   158
                    Direct and indirect costs   162
                    Functional analysis of costs   166
                    Behavioural analysis of costs   169
                    Absorption costing and marginal costing   176
                    Marginal cost applications   179
                    Break-even analysis   188

Session six: Budgetary control   197
                    The nature and purpose of budgeting   198

Contents

	Application of budgetary control	205
	Flexible budgets	211
	Cash budgets	220
Session seven:	Capital investment appraisal	231
	Capital expenditure	232
	Payback methods	235
	Accounting rate of return	244
	Net present value and yield	250
	Interest rates, weighted average cost of capital	260

SECTION TWO: MANAGING INFORMATION

Session one:	Why organisations need information	269
	The information age	270
	Information and decision-making	275
	What kind of information is useful?	284
	Hard and soft information	286
	Different functions, different needs	295
Session two:	From data to information	301
	What do we mean by data?	302
	What do we mean by information?	306
	Computers and information management	317
	Processing data into information	320
	Information technology	329
	Methods of data capture	335
	Information overload	338
Session three:	Meeting an organisation's information needs	343
	The bulging in-tray	344
	Information management in organisations	350
	Management information systems	355
	Decision support systems	369
	Personal information systems	374
	Information flows	376
Session four:	Using information technology	387
	Databases	388
	Spreadsheets	403
	Acquiring data	413
	Presenting information effectively	418
Session five:	Quality and reliability	427
	How reliable is the data?	428
	Hardware and software problems	433
	How information can mislead	437
	Evaluating forecasts	448
	Errors of analysis	454
	Evaluating written reports	461
Resources		469

Foreword

BTEC is committed to helping people of any age to acquire and maintain the up-to-date and relevant knowledge, understanding and skills they need for success in current or future employment.

These aims are greatly enhanced by this series of open learning books for the new BTEC HND and HNC in Business Studies.

These books will provide more students with the opportunity to achieve a widely recognised national qualification in business by allowing flexible study patterns combined with an innovative approach to learning.

Our active involvement in a partnership with the Open Learning Foundation and Blackwell Publishers ensures that each book comprehensively covers the specific learning outcomes needed for a module in this Higher National programme.

Acknowledgements

Authors
Alan Jennings and Howard Senter

Open Learning Editor: Fiona Carey

For the Open Learning Foundation:
Director of Programmes: Leslie Mapp
Design and Production: Stephen Moulds
Co-ordinator: Jane Edmonds
Text Editor: Paul Stirner
Academic Co-ordinator: Glyn Roberts (Bradford & Ilkley
                             Community College)
Academic Reviewers: Martin Gibson (University of Central
                          Lancashire)
                          Bob McClelland (Liverpool John Moores
                          University)

The Open Learning Foundation wishes to acknowledge the support
of Bradford & Ilkley Community College during the preparation of
this workbook.

For BTEC
Diane Billam: Director of Products and Quality Division
John Edgar: Consultant
Françoise Seacroft: Manager of Futures Department
Mike Taylor: Deputy Head of Department of Service Sector
                 Management, University of Brighton

For Blackwell Publishers
Editorial Director: Philip Carpenter
Senior Commissioning Editor: Tim Goodfellow
Production Manager: Pam Park
Development Editors: Richard Jackman and Catriona King
Pre-production Manager: Paul Stringer
Sub-editorial team: First Class Publishing
Reviewers: Mary Banfield (Highbury College)
               Steve Culliford (West Herts College)
               Noel Meaney (University of Central Lancashire,
               Preston)

Introduction

Welcome to this workbook for the BTEC module Managing Finance and Information.

This is a book specifically designed for use by students studying on BTEC Higher National programmes in Business, Business and Finance, Business and Marketing and Business and Personnel. However, it can be also used by people who wish to learn about this aspect of business.

How to use the workbook

Please feel free to:

- write notes in the margins

- underline and highlight important words or phrases.

As you work through this module, you will find activities have been built in. These are designed to make you stop to think and answer questions.

There are four types of activities.

Memory and recall These are straightforward tests of how much text you are able to remember.

Self-assessed tasks (SATs) These are used to test your understanding of the text you are studying or to apply the principles and practices learnt to a related problem.

Exercises These are open-ended questions that can be used as a basis for classroom or group debate. If you do not belong to a study group, use the exercises to think through issues raised by the text.

Assignments These are tasks set for students studying at a BTEC centre which would normally require a written answer to be looked at by your tutor. If you are not following a course at college, the assignments are still a useful way of developing and testing your understanding of the module.

There are answer boxes provided below each activity in this module. Use these boxes to summarise your answers and findings. If you need more space, use the margins of the book or separate sheets of paper to make notes and write a full answer.

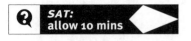

SAT: allow 10 mins

Managing tasks and solving problems ✔

EXAMPLE ACTIVITY

As an 'icebreaker' try this exercise.

What are the advantages of debt factoring to a company that relies heavily on credit sales?

Commentary...

Debt factoring firms take responsibility for collecting money owed to their clients, so the seller does not have to worry about slow payment or defaulting customers. This improves cash flow and reduces the resources needed for administration and collection. In turn, this means the company can concentrate on its principal activity – selling its products.

The emphasis of the workbook is to provide you with tasks that relate to the general operating environment of business. The work that you do on these tasks enables you to develop your BTEC common skills and a skills chart is provided at the end of this introduction for you to note your practice of each skill. One sheet is probably not enough, so cut this sheet out and photocopy it when you require new sheets.

Aims of the workbook

This workbook looks at managing finance and information systems within organisations. The emphasis is on the management process, giving an understanding of the concepts, theories and systems, and thereby developing the skills needed to manage financial resources and handle information in a way that improves decision making ability.

The book has two sections which are designed to cover the learning outcomes (as shown in bold in the boxes below) for this core module. These are as given in the BTEC publication (code 02–104–4) on the Higher National programmes in Business Studies. Where appropriate, BTEC's suggested content may be reordered within the sections of this book.

SECTION ONE: MANAGING FINANCE

On completion of this section, you should be able to:

> ◗ **identify and analyse organisational financial resources**

> ◗ **identify and evaluate alternative sources of finance**

> ◗ **use financial information and procedures to support decision making**

> ◗ **evaluate the financial performance of organisations.**

Content

Types of business organisation: the financing, legal standing and operation of incorporated/unincorporated businesses; how a company's status affects its options to attract external finance; growth by absorption, amalgamation and acquisition; the identities and operation of corporate groups; other types of business organisations.

Sources and types of finance: providers of external finance; overdrafts, bills of exchange, creditors and factoring for short-term finance; hire purchase, credit sales and finance leases for medium-term financing; mortgages and debentures for longer term finance; preference and ordinary shares, the main source of permanent finance in a company.

Published accounts: the financial statements that incorporated businesses must publish; the theory and format of profit and loss accounts, balance sheets and cash flow statements; how to draft financial statements from a list of transactions and balances.

Analysis and evaluation: analysis of financial reports and the interested parties; the methods of measuring profitability, solvency and liquidity; capital gearing and the calculation of investment ratios; the role and control of working capital.

Analysis of costs: how to ascertain and analyse costs; the nature of direct and indirect costs; functional and behavioural analysis of costs; absorption and marginal costing for financial reporting and decision making; calculating break-even points.

Budgetary control: the nature and purpose of budgeting; how to construct a master budget, compare actual and budgeted results, interpret variances and identify corrective action; the principles, construction and analysis of flexible budgets; monitoring businesses with cash budgets.

Capital investment appraisal: the characteristics of capital expenditure and its role in budgeting; how to undertake appraisals using the payback, discounted payback, accounting rate of return, net present value and yield methods; how to apply the principles of discounting; choosing an appropriate interest rate for capital projects.

SECTION TWO: MANAGING INFORMATION

On completion of this section, you should be able to:

> ▶ **evaluate the scope, key areas within and purposes of a management information system**

> ▶ **use information technology to store, retrieve and analyse information**

> ▶ **review systems for monitoring and providing management information**

> ▶ **evaluate the relevance and appropriateness of information generated from a management information system.**

Content

Why organisations need information: the key role of information in managerial decision-making; what kind of information is useful and the management processes that are dependent on it; the qualities of information necessary to make it useful; hard and soft information and the different needs of different business fucntions.

From data to information: how to distinguish data from information; using computer processing to turn data into information; information technology and methods of inputting data; a costs–benefits analysis of computerising information processing.

Meeting an organisation's information needs: maintaining information quality and avoiding information overload; the six sub-systems in a management information system; spreadsheets, modelling, databases and planning software in decision support systems; the criteria for developing a management information system; tracing and managing information flows.

Using information technology: the key factors of database and spreadsheet software; the principal methods of data acquisition; how to present information visually.

Quality and reliability: how to identify likely sources of data errors and ways of reducing them; minimising the impact of hardware and software errors; recognising misleading information; evaluating forecasts and errors of analysis; assessing written reports.

In working through the BTEC Higher National programme in Business Studies, you will practise the following BTEC common skills:

Managing and developing self	✔
Working with and relating to others	✔
Communicating	✔
Managing tasks and solving problems	✔
Applying numeracy	✔
Applying technology	✔
Applying design and creativity	✔

You will practise most of these skills in working through this module.

Recommended reading

SECTION ONE

Dyson, J.R., Accounting for Non-Accounting Students, 3rd edition, Pitman.

Jennings, A.R., Financial Accounting, 2nd edition, D P Publications.

Jennings, A.R., Accounting and Finance for Building and Surveying, Macmillan.

Lacey, T., Costing, 4th edition, D P Publications.

Millichamp, A.H., Finance for Non-Financial Managers, 2nd edition, D P Publications.

Samuels, J., Wilkes, F. and Brayshaw, R., Management of Company Finance, 5th edition, Chapman and Hall.

SECTION TWO

Carter, R.J., 1982, Stores Management and Related Operations, Pitman.

Clemen, R.T., 1986, Making Hard Decisions: an introduction to decision analysis, Boston; PWS Kent Publishing Co.

Drucker, P.F., 1964, Managing for Results, Harper & Row.

Francis, D., 1991, Effective Problem Solving: a structured approach, Routledge.

Kroenke, D. and Hatch, R., 1994, Managing Information Systems, Mitchell/McGraw-Hill.

Rothwell, D.M., 1993, Databases: an introduction, McGraw-Hill.

Secrett, M., 1993, Mastering Spreadsheet Budgets and Forecasts, Pitman Publishing/Institute of Management.

Sutcliffe, G.E., 1988, Effective Learning for Effective Management, PrenticeHall.

Wagner, S.F., 1992, An Introduction to Statistics, HarperCollins College Outlines.

Woodcock, J. and Salkind, N.J. (rev.), 1994, Running Microsoft Works for Windows, Microsoft Press.

Name

Module

BTEC Skill	Activity No./Date	Activity No./Date	Activity No./Date	Activity No./Date	Activity No./Date	Activity No./Date
Managing and developing self						
Working with and relating to others						
Communicating						
Managing tasks and solving problems						
Applying numeracy						
Applying technology						
Applying design and creativity						

Managing Finance

Types of business organisation

UNINCORPORATED BUSINESSES

INCORPORATED BUSINESSES

COMPANY GROWTH AND THE STRUCTURE OF GROUPS

OTHER BUSINESS ORGANISATIONS

Objectives

After participating in this session, you should be able to:

- ▶ understand the financing, legal standing and operation of unincorporated businesses

- ▶ understand and describe the implications of corporate status

- ▶ compare and contrast the status and financing of a private company with that of a public company

- ▶ explain the meaning and implication of company growth by absorption, amalgamation and acquisition

- ▶ list and identify the roles of the various members of corporate groups

- ▶ describe other types of business organisations.

In working through this session, you will practise the following BTEC common skills:

Managing and developing self	✔
Working with and relating to others	
Communicating	✔
Managing tasks and solving problems	✔
Applying numeracy	
Applying technology	
Applying design and creativity	

Unincorporated businesses

All businesses can be classified legally as either 'incorporated' or 'unincorporated'; we look first at unincorporated businesses.

LEGAL STATUS

The significance of an unincorporated business is that the legal status of the business is not in any way separate from that of its owner or owners, even if the business trades under a name different from that of its owners. The owner (or 'proprietor') and the business are not distinguished from each other, and so for instance the owner can sue, or be sued, in a personal capacity in all matters relating to the affairs of the business.

Unincorporated businesses are simpler, more flexible, less formal and less legally constrained than incorporated businesses.

The most commonly encountered unincorporated businesses are:

- sole proprietorships
- partnerships.

SOLE PROPRIETORSHIP

This is the name given to a business owned by one person: a sole trader. The term 'trader' in this context is used in a wide sense to cover activities other than buying and selling or making and selling. A sole trader could, for instance, be a designer, a window cleaner, a consultant engineer, a self-employed electrician, or a freelance journalist. Many professionals, such as accountants, barristers and veterinary surgeons offer their services on the basis of sole proprietorships. In all these cases, the defining factor is that the all these people will be operating as the sole, i.e. only, owner of their businesses.

This one person owns and manages the business and, at the same time, carries out the activities of the business. However, this limit of one on ownership does not mean that the owner is barred from engaging employees. Neither is there any limit on the number of employees, although there is a practical ceiling on the number of employees that a sole owner can manage effectively. In a thriving sole proprietorship, the owner often employs someone to manage the office and the administration so as to free him or her to concentrate on the main activity of the business.

A sole proprietorship may trade under the name of the owner or of the business. Thus, for example, Helen Ralph, who makes curtains and soft furnishings, could trade under her own name, or choose an unconnected business name, such as Futura Fabrics. Likewise, Nick Burge, who runs a burger van, could trade simply as Nick Burge, or he could invent a name under which to trade, e.g. Burge's Burgers.

A sole proprietorship is financed mainly by the owner's capital. Capital is used to acquire the assets needed to start up and run the business, items that vary according to the nature of the business. The assets of a hot food take-away would be held in the form of cash and bank balances, the premises (if owned), cooking and sterilising equipment and food; a painter and decorator would require a van, ladders and a stock of paint as well as cash and bank balances.

Later in this module, we look at the precise nature of capital and other forms of finance.

Partnership

A partnership is a business owned by several individuals; effectively, it is a group of sole traders working with a common aim because legally each and every partner is liable in an individual, personal capacity, to meet all the debts of the partnership out of their private resources, if the partnership should default. For obvious reasons, a partnership cannot consist of less than two partners but the law restricts the upper limit to 20 (except in the cases of accountants and solicitors, where it is 50, and bankers, where it is 10).

Partnerships are most commonly found in areas of business where the operators' major assets are their skills or expertise, rather than, say, buildings or productive equipment. Architects, opticians and accountants are typical examples of people whose skills and value lie in what they personally can do – i.e. in their training and expertise – rather than in what they physically bring into the business. In short, partnerships are very often the way that professionals operate.

A partnership enables a successful sole trader to expand the business beyond the limits of his or her personal resources. It enables individuals to combine their different strengths.

One partner may have good business contacts and outlets, another may have more skill and experience, another may have none of these but is able to contribute the bulk of the capital. It is a matter for the partners to decide how the capital should be put into the business (or 'subscribed'), and how the partnership's profits and losses should be shared. Profits and losses may well be shared in proportions that differ from the capital contributions. In this case, it is not unusual for the partners to agree that interest on the capital balances should be charged before calculating their shares of profit or loss, as illustrated below.

Account 1.1 shows the position of partners A and B, who share profits and losses equally, and have subscribed capitals of £10,000 and £20,000 respectively; interest is charged at (the statutory rate) of 5 per cent p.a. before the profit is divided up.

	£	£
Profit		18,500
less interest on capitals:		
A (5% on £10,000)	500	
B (5% on £20,000	1,000	
		1,500
Residual profit		17,000
A's share (50%)	8,500	
B's share (50%)	8,500	
		17,000

ACCOUNT 1.1: Profit shares of partners A and B.

Partner B receives a total of £9,500, as opposed to A's £9,000, in recognition of their different capital subscriptions. These and other matters affecting the conduct of the partnership are contained in the partnership agreement which prudent partners would put in writing. A verbal agreement, though still legally valid, is much harder to enforce should disputes arise at a later stage.

A business can be constituted as a partnership from the outset, but often results from the amalgamation of several sole traders. Like a sole proprietorship, the partnership may trade under the names of the partners or under a business name. If Helen Ralph, referred to earlier as a sole trader, should go into partnership with Rebecca White and Cathy Oldham, they might trade as Ralph, White and Oldham, or as Helen Ralph and Partners, or they could retain the name Futura Fabrics, a name which gives no indication that the business is operated as a partnership.

The capital of a partnership is recorded in separate accounts in the names of the individual partners who contributed it. Apart from contributing capital, partners may also lend money to the partnership.

Two implications follow from this:

1. Such loans may be interest-free, but if they are not, then loan interest is charged against the profits or losses of the business and consequently reduces the amount of profit available (or increases the loss) to be shared out.

2. Should the partnership be terminated for any reason and is dissolved (i.e. ceases to exist), partnership loans are repaid in priority to partnership capitals.

If, on dissolution, any one or more (or indeed all) of the partners' capital accounts is overdrawn, then those partners who are solvent must contribute sufficient funds from their private resources to eradicate their own balances and those of any other insolvent partners.

 **RECALL:**
allow 10 mins

Describe briefly how the operation and financing of a sole proprietorship differ from those of a partnership.

UNINCORPORATED BUSINESSES

Communicating ✔

Managing tasks and solving problems ✔

ACTIVITY 1

A friend intends to open a shop and to run it as a sole proprietorship. She has now been invited to do so in partnership with three other people instead. She has sought your advice as to the advantages and disadvantages that are involved in operating as a partnership, rather than going it alone.

Make a note of the main points that you would include in a letter to her.

Commentary...

There are both advantages and disadvantages arising from operating as a partner, rather than as a sole trader. Advantages include:

- more time available to devote to actual selling
- greater prospects of successful establishment because of greater access to money and expertise
- increased opportunities for expansion (opening branches)
- greater number of contacts with potential clients and customers.

Disadvantages include:

- loss of independence
- greater exposure to risk, because of personal liability to make good losses if any partner becomes bankrupt.

Incorporated businesses

A business that is incorporated is regarded in law as an entity in its own right. The business is said to be a corporate body or corporation. Although we are concerned with corporate businesses, which we call companies, many other forms of corporate bodies also exist, e.g. universities, district and county councils, the Post Office, Area Health Authorities and many others.

The key characteristic of an incorporated body is that, because it has a legal 'personality' of its own, all its affairs are conducted by the business in its own capacity. This is the crux of the distinction between the legal status of unincorporated and incorporated businesses.

- In an unincorporated business – a sole proprietorship or partnership – all legal matters are conducted by or against the individual owners who can sue or be sued in their own names. If you are run over by one of Burge's vans, you will sue Nick Burge himself.

- By contrast, in an incorporated business, the legal affairs are conducted in the name of the business without the involvement of individual owners. If you are run over by a van belonging to Burge's Burgers Ltd, you will sue the company.

LIMITED LIABILITY

From now on, we deal with that form of business corporation which is most common: companies. The term company is shortened from its full name 'limited liability company'. The significance of the words limited liability is that the owners of a company are liable to contribute only the nominal amount of their capital to cover any debts of the business. In contrast, sole traders and partners are liable to the full extent of their private resources for any financial deficiencies of their businesses.

The capital of a company is divided into shares of a stated denomination, most commonly £1, 50 pence, 25 pence or 5 pence, but in theory the shares could be of any value. Thus the initial owner of 2,000 shares with a nominal or face value of 50 pence per share is liable to pay £1,000 for them to the company.

In most cases, this sum is paid all at once, but if some of it remains outstanding because of the terms under which the shares were sold, then the owner of the shares (called the shareholder) remains liable for the remainder. However, even if the company has sustained heavy losses, the shareholder cannot be required to contribute any amount in excess of this nominal value: the shareholder's liability is thus limited.

Limited liability encourages investment from people who do not have the funds or the inclination to run their own businesses. Because the financial risk is limited, more people are prepared to subscribe for shares than would otherwise be the case. Unless they are also directors, these shareholders are not involved in the day-to-day running of the company and know in advance the full extent of the financial risk which they are undertaking. The position of shareholders, therefore, contrasts sharply with that of sole traders and partners.

Disregarding the relatively uncommon form known as 'company limited by guarantee', there are two types of limited company:

- private limited companies
- public limited companies.

PRIVATE LIMITED COMPANIES

Usually called simply 'private companies', these businesses must indicate their legal status by including the word 'limited', or its shortened form 'Ltd', in their business names. The shareholders of a private company are usually friends, relations or business associates who form a close circle. This is because the Companies Act (1985) does not allow a private company to offer its shares (and other forms of finance that we cover later on) to anyone outside the company.

One implication of private company status is that, because there is an embargo on the issue of shares to the public, access to large amounts of share capital is somewhat curtailed, being restricted to the amounts that the private shareholders (called 'members') can raise.

This access to share capital can be further hindered because, although technically the liability of the members is limited to the nominal value of their shareholdings, in practice the institutions that make loans to private companies usually attach very demanding conditions that extend the liability beyond the nominal value of shareholdings. Directors of the company – often themselves the major shareholders – are usually required to provide 'personal guarantees' or securities for the loan, and have to undertake 'joint and several liability' for any debts, so that any one director can be made responsible for the entire loan. In essence, this can put the directors in much the same position as partners find themselves, carrying the risk that business difficulties might lead to the loss of their largest assets, which in most cases is their homes.

Another implication is that it is relatively difficult for the members of private companies to dispose of all or part of their shareholdings: because they cannot be offered for sale publicly, the only option is to sell them privately to other members of the company. Failing that, the company itself could buy them back and cancel them. Once cancelled the shares cannot be re-issued, thereby permanently reducing the company's issued, called up and paid up share capital. This leaves fewer shares to receive dividends, and alters the relative holdings of the remaining shareholders in the now-reduced capital.

Private companies are managed by directors elected by the members.

Reporting requirements

Although a private company has to file an Annual Report and Accounts (which we will also examine in depth later on) with the Registrar of Companies, the reporting requirements are not so onerous as for a public company, thus enabling a private company to conduct its affairs with a reasonable degree of confidentiality. Some very large businesses elect to remain as private companies, e.g. Macmillan Press Ltd, the Mars company (reputedly Britain's largest private company) and KwikSave Stores Ltd, the retail grocery chain.

Managing and developing self ✔

Managing tasks and solving problems ✔

ACTIVITY 2

Look through your local Yellow Pages and identify five business categories where a high proportion of the businesses describe themselves as 'limited'. Then find five categories where few, if any, do so.

List both groups below.

Many limited companies	Few limited companies
1	1
2	2
3	3
4	4
5	5

What conclusions can you draw from a comparison of the two groups?

Commentary...

There are scores of categories to choose from, but in general you probably found that skill-based businesses, operated by one or two people, possessing few major assets and incurring few substantial liabilities (such as osteopaths, plumbers, florists and 'home-tune' businesses) tended not to be limited companies. Bigger operations, where assets, liabilities and payroll are substantial (examples range from large car dealerships to chemical manufacturers) are much more likely to describe themselves as limited companies.

PUBLIC LIMITED COMPANIES

These are usually called public companies, and contain the words 'public limited company' or its abbreviation 'plc' in their business names. In contrast to the limitations imposed on a private company, the shares of a public company can be sold to individual members of the general public and, indeed, to other unincorporated and incorporated bodies. This wider access to funds is the main incentive most private companies would cite for their decision to 'go public'.

The shares of public companies are sold initially by the companies themselves, but most are subsequently bought and sold through the Stock Exchange.

Companies may be incorporated as public companies at the outset or can be converted from (or indeed to) private companies:

- Sainsbury's, the national grocery supermarket chain, was for many years a private company but has changed its status to that of a public company.

- Virgin Retail is a rare example of a private company which converted to a public company and subsequently reverted to its private status.

When a company makes a new issue of shares, the issue price can be at the nominal value (a par issue) or in excess of nominal value (a premium issue). Any premium has to be accounted for separately because there are stringent legal restrictions on ways in which it can be utilised. Once shares have been issued to shareholders they can be sold at whatever market price they command, and the proceeds go to the shareholder rather than to the company.

The management of a public company is the responsibility of the board of directors, members of which are elected by the shareholders.

Reporting requirements

A public company, like a private company, must prepare and publish its Annual Report and Accounts and lodge a copy with the Registrar of Companies. The reporting requirements of a public company are much more demanding than for a private company, and are covered later.

RECALL:
allow 10 mins

Explain the distinction between:

1. **incorporated and unincorporated status**

2. **a public company and a private company.**

Explain the principle of limited liability.

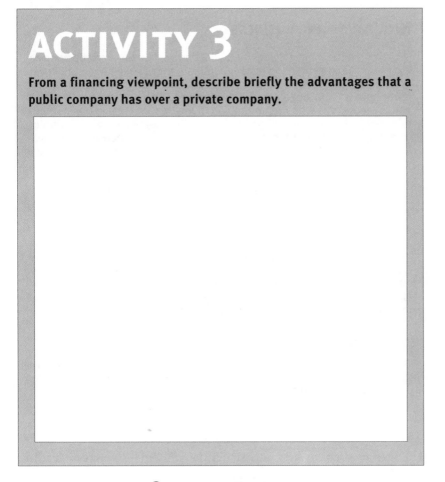

ACTIVITY 3

From a financing viewpoint, describe briefly the advantages that a public company has over a private company.

Commentary...

It is much easier to raise capital as a public company, because a greater number of individuals are eligible to become shareholders. In addition, institutional investors, including insurance companies, pension funds and other companies, tend to acquire large tranches (blocks) of shares. The shares of public companies are an attractive investment proposition because they can be bought and sold by investors with the minimum difficulty. Private company shareholders may have difficulty valuing and disposing of their shares.

Company growth and the structure of groups

One measure of the success of a business is its growth. With growth, tends to come a change in structure. The growth route of a particularly successful small business may be illustrated by the following case study.

COMPANY GROWTH AND THE
STRUCTURE OF GROUPS

NICK'S CATERING BUSINESS

Nick's burger trailer, a sole proprietorship, grows from its small beginnings. Nick initially did everything himself, but he has gradually acquired seven trailers. He still plans and buys stocks for them, manages them on a day-to-day basis, and does regular paperwork, but now has a number of employees: some who prepare and load the trailers early in the morning; operators who pick up the vans early in the morning and return them, cleaned, at the end of the day; and he employs a trainee accountant to keep his accounts. Nick now has a successful business, but lacks the substantial amount of capital he requires to enlarge the business further.

He considers forming a partnership with a friend, Rob, in the same line of business. They have talked about pooling resources and splitting responsibilities: Nick is good at figures and at buying, while Rob excels at the operational side.

In the meantime, however, Nick is approached by Valerie and Peter Cameron, who own a public house and also supply 'beer tents' for large outdoor events, such as fêtes, exhibitions and concerts. They want to be able to offer an overall catering package to event organisers, and need resources and know-how in the catering area.

Nick and the Camerons decide to set up a limited company that will be able to raise the capital necessary to start up the catering business (they will need assets such as marquees, furniture and trailers, as well as catering equipment), and in order to manage the cashflow required for extra employees and bigger supplier contracts.

This case study shows how the momentum of growth necessitates changes in organisation and structure of a small business, leading eventually to the formation of a limited company. (But note that there is no compulsion on a small business either to expand or to change its status: many small traders wish to stay that way, avoiding the extra responsibilities and work that expansion inevitably involves.)

Large organisations need to react in much the same way: success leads to growth, and growth requires change. So how does an established company cope, structurally, with the challenge of growth?

There are a number of strategies, but they fall roughly into two categories:

1. to issue more share capital

2. to combine with other businesses.

Issuing more share capital is considered later; first we look at the options of combining with other businesses.

COMBINING WITH OTHER BUSINESSES

A common means of growth for a strong company is for it to expand by absorption (take over): by acquiring and absorbing the resources of a weaker company, the empty shell of which then ceases to exist under a process known as liquidation, or winding up.

An alternative is for one or more businesses of similar size to join forces in what is termed an amalgamation or merger. This involves the formation of a new company that takes over the resources of each of the two combining companies, which are then wound up.

Both these two courses of action involve some or all of the original businesses ceasing to exist. A third method works by enabling a number of business to continue to operate, but with varying degrees of influence and control over each other – the formation of groups.

GROUPS AND THEIR FORMATION

A company can acquire control or exercise a degree of influence over other businesses, both incorporated and unincorporated, by various means:

1. It can acquire a majority of voting shares in another business.

2. It can acquire a shareholding (which could be quite small) that is coupled with the right to appoint or remove directors holding majority voting rights at board meetings.

3. It can exercise control or influence without any shareholding, by means of:

   - a control contract

   - provisions contained in the company's constitution

   - by agreement with the other company's shareholders.

In law, the companies that exercise control and/or influence over other businesses, together with the businesses that are subject to that control or influence, are termed groups. Each business within the group retains its separate legal existence and identity but, for accounting purposes, these businesses are regarded as a single economic entity.

CONSTITUENTS OF A GROUP

In dealing with groups, the following descriptive labels are used:

- parent

- subsidiary

● sub-subsidiary

● associate.

A group consists of one parent and any number of subsidiaries, sub-subsidiaries and associates. The various elements within the group are described below. Their relationships are represented graphically in figure 1.1.

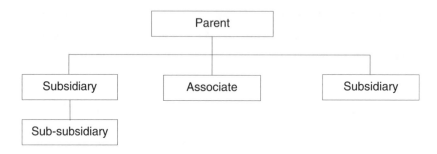

FIGURE 1.1: Structure of a business group.

Parent

The parent is the company that exercises control or influence. This need not necessarily be by means of a shareholding, though this is very common. The investment in shares in another company under these circumstances is called a participating interest, and this is defined as an investment, intended to be held in the long term, for the purpose of securing a contribution to the activities of the parent company through the exercise of control or influence. There is a presumption that the holding of 20 per cent or more of the equity voting shares of another company constitutes a participating interest, unless there is evidence to the contrary.

The parent company, in other words, expects to gain in some way from having control or influence over the other undertakings.

ACTIVITY 4

Give two examples of the ways in which Greenhouse Ltd, a publisher of children's books, might expect to gain from its control of Lithart, a printing firm.

Commentary...

As the parent company, Greenhouse has a means of controlling some (though not necessarily all) of its printing costs and may benefit from any profits made by the printing business. Greenhouse would also be able to smooth its own production schedules by ensuring that the printer gave priority to Greenhouse's work.

Depending on the degree of control or influence exercised by the parent, the company in which a participating interest is held is either an associate or a subsidiary of the parent.

Under the Companies Act (1985), the parent company is responsible for preparing, publishing and filing with the Registrar of Companies, the Annual Report and Accounts of the group, i.e. of the parent and all subsidiaries, sub-subsidiaries and associates, as though they were a single company.

Associate

Where a parent has a participating interest in a second company, the parent is assumed to have 'significant influence' over that company's operating and financial policies, unless this assumption can be rebutted by evidence to the contrary. This second company is called an 'associate' or an associated company.

Subsidiary

The company is said to be a 'subsidiary' when the parent has acquired full effective control of that company (by one of the three means described above).

It is also a subsidiary if the parent has a participating interest in it (i.e. at least 20 per cent of the equity voting shares) when this participating interest is coupled with either one of the following:

- a dominant influence, which arises when the wishes of the parent can secure the desired results in major decisions, even in the absence of legal control rights

- unified management of the two companies, which occurs when the operations of the two companies are integrated and managed as a single unit.

Thus Linguarama Ltd, a language training company, is one of the many subsidiaries of BPP Holdings plc, a group of companies which provides professional education and training. BPP Holdings' share holding is 100 per cent of the equity share capital.

Sub-subsidiary

It is possible for a subsidiary itself to be the parent of a subsidiary. This last company is termed a sub-subsidiary of the main parent and must be included as a member of the group for accounting purposes.

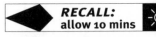

RECALL:
allow 10 mins

Write down what you
understand by the following
terms:

1. absorption

2. amalgamation

3. acquisition of control by
   shareholding

4. parent

5. participating interest

6. subsidiary

7. associate.

ADVANTAGES OF GROUP STRUCTURE

There are several reasons why a company might choose to acquire
control of other companies by becoming a parent rather than by other
means.

Financing

It is usually requires less outlay to acquire shares than to acquire the
total resources of another company under an absorption or
amalgamation scheme.

Flexibility

The shares can be bought and sold at any time. This would not be
possible with an absorption or amalgamation.

Diversification

The financing and flexibility implications mean that the investing
company can spread risk by acquiring control of dissimilar
businesses.

Vertical integration

Control can be gained over a number of companies, forming a chain from raw-material producer to manufacturer, and through to wholesaler and retailer.

Horizontal integration

A company can capture a large share of businesses operating in the same market.

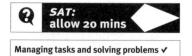

Managing tasks and solving problems ✔

ACTIVITY 5

Glenhorn Ltd (the parent company) has shareholdings in three other companies: it owns 29 per cent of the shares of Moonshine Distillery Ltd, 62 per cent of those of Thompson Malting Ltd, and 24 per cent of Baxter Bros Ltd.

At Moonshine, three of the four directors are related to Glenhorn's Chairman, Richard Littlechild, and they effectively take their lead in decision-making from him.

Thompson, in turn, owns 33 per cent of Billings Growers Ltd.

Moonshine Distillery Ltd owns 54 per cent of the shares in Fielding Cox Ltd.

Draw a diagram showing the relationships between the six companies. State whether the companies in the group are subsidiaries, sub-subsidiaries or associates. Give your reasons.

Commentary...

The relationships between the companies are shown in figure 1.2 which illustrates the following:

- Glenhorn has full effective control of Thompson Maltings, by way of its majority shareholding, so Thompson is a subsidiary of Glenhorn.

- Glenhorn's participating interest in Moonshine, 29 per cent of its shares, would not on its own constitute full control, but the relationships between Moonshine's directors and the board of Glenhorn would suggest that a 'dominant influence' exists, so Moonshine would assume the status of a subsidiary of Glenhorn.

- Glenhorn's shares in Baxter Bros constitute a participating interest with a significant interest, and Baxter would be designated an associate of Glenhorn.

- Thompson's participating interest in Billings Growers does not constitute full control, but its holding would constitute 'significant influence' (unless there was evidence that this was not the case), and Billings would be deemed an associate of Thompson Maltings.

- Moonshine's holding in Fielding Cox is a majority shareholding, so Fielding Cox is a subsidiary of Moonshine, and a sub-subsidiary of Glenhorn.

These companies retain their separate legal and trading identities but, for accounting reporting purposes, have to be regarded as though they were a single company. Each company prepares its own separate, final accounts but, for statutory reporting purposes, Glenhorn is obliged to bring them all together as consolidated accounts. These treat the whole group as if it was one company.

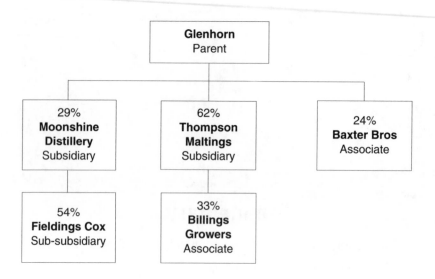

FIGURE 1.2: Structure of Glenhorn's business group.

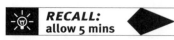

RECALL:
allow 5 mins

List the principal means by which a company can acquire control over another company.

ACTIVITY 6

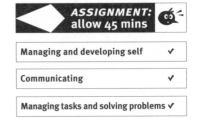

ASSIGNMENT:
allow 45 mins

Managing and developing self	✔
Communicating	✔
Managing tasks and solving problems	✔

Helen Ralph and her associates, Rebecca and Cathy, have established a legal partnership and trade under the name of Futura Fabrics. From an initial annual turnover £60,500 the business has grown to £180,000, with trading profits (in addition to a modest salary for the partners) of £24,000.

The partners, who now employ around 15 part-time homeworkers, see the opportunity to expand, through supply contracts with various retailers. This will involve taking on some full-time staff, renting larger premises, acquiring vehicles, equipment and so on. It will require a larger 'capital base' and loan facilities.

Your task is to write a short report advising the partners on the benefits and implications of launching a limited company. You should arrange your report under four headings:

1. Explain what steps need to be taken in dissolving the partnership and forming a company. (You may need to consult a text book on company law for the company formation details.)

2. Explain the legal status of a limited company, and the statutory obligations for record-keeping and reporting.

3. Explain what limited company status may do to help the business obtain more finance.

4. Explain what differences, if any, the change will make to the partners' individual obligations, rights and circumstances, assuming that all three become directors with an equal shareholding.

Write your report on separate paper. Summarise your findings in the box below.

Other business organisations

Apart from the types of organisations dealt with already (i.e. sole proprietorships, partnerships, and private and public companies), and the groups to which these entities may belong, there are several other important forms of organisation:

- joint ventures
- consortia
- public bodies
- not-for-profit organisations.

JOINT VENTURES

A joint venture consists of two or more businesses which act together in a formal way to achieve a common objective of specified duration or purpose.

This is an increasingly common way for a business to undertake work it would not otherwise have the resources to do, by operating in concert with another business or businesses, either on a specific project or for a specific period of time. The joint venture avoids the need for the permanent arrangement that is part and parcel of a partnership, absorption or amalgamation.

To set up a joint venture, an agreement is drawn up setting out the rights and responsibilities of each of the parties involved (co-venturers), including the manner in which the profits and losses are to be shared. These are two important characteristics of this type of venture:

1. At no time, do the co-venturers lose their independence or surrender their separate identities.

2. The venture is wound up when the objectives for which it was formed have been achieved.

In similar fashion to the partners in a partnership, co-venturers contribute different resources to the common enterprise – finance, skills, expertise, contacts and physical facilities.

Recording transactions in joint ventures

All joint venture transactions are recorded as transactions of the joint venture, so that the profits and losses of the venture can be found out periodically and shared out between the respective co-venturers.

Scale of operations in joint ventures

This may vary from small to very large and may involve businesses internationally. They can consist entirely of incorporated or unincorporated companies, or can be a mixture of the two.

- At the small end of the scale are agricultural joint ventures where several co-venturers are involved in the separate operations of growing produce, packing it, transporting it, marketing it and administering and financing all these operations.

- At the other end of the scale is the channel tunnel link, which was constructed by a joint venture, TransManche Link (TML), which consisted of such well-known names as Wimpey, Costain, Balfour Beatty, Tarmac and Taylor Woodrow, together with five French contractors, a total of ten co-venturers in all.

- Another multi-billion dollar international joint venture is engaged on a landfill project in Hong Kong, and involves companies from the UK, China and Hong Kong.

CONSORTIA

A consortium is, in many respects, similar to a joint venture, in that it involves the collaboration of a number of businesses on a project that no individual business could undertake alone. As with a joint venture, each business retains its own identity and independence. However, whereas in a joint venture all transactions are those of the joint venture and the resultant profits and losses are shared out between the co-venturers, the members of a consortium:

- account for their own transactions

- discharge their own liabilities

- retain their own profits or bear their own losses.

None of these transactions is pooled.

A consortium arrangement is therefore particularly appropriate if the various parties to the project are expecting to achieve different sorts of objectives. While one business sees the project as a high-risk/high-return investment opportunity, it may suit another to be making losses on the project, while yet another may be investing heavily in non-profit-generating activity such as research.

In the UK some years ago, local authorities formed a development consortium called CLASP (Consortium of Local Authorities Special Programme) to build school and college buildings in areas affected by mining subsidence.

PUBLIC BODIES

Public bodies are organisations that provide utilities or services to the public, and whose operations are the responsibility of officers appointed by (and ultimately responsible to) the government. Examples of public bodies, at the time of writing, are:

- the British Broadcasting Corporation (BBC)
- the Post Office
- the Bank of England.

Some public utilities, including those for gas, electricity and water, began life as private companies, then became nationalised public bodies, and have subsequently been re-privatised as public limited companies.

NOT-FOR-PROFIT ORGANISATIONS

These are operated primarily to provide a service to members rather than to make a profit. This does not mean that they cannot or do not make a profit, but that the main aim is to avoid a loss while covering the cost of providing such services as are offered. In the process, many such organisations make a small profit.

Typical of this type of organisation are the non-commercial bodies that cater for leisure pursuits. Amateur sports clubs for athletics, football and cricket fall into this category, and so do amateur dramatic, operatic and debating societies. Some businesses sponsor a social club for their employees. The club is nevertheless an entity in its own right, legally separate from the business from which it receives its subsidy. The day-to-day running of the club is the responsibility of a club secretary under the control of a management committee or board of trustees. The trading activities will vary according to the nature of the club: a musical society may stage concerts and festivals, while a cricket club's trading may amount only to selling food and drink to their members.

RECALL:
allow 10 mins

What are the distinguishing characteristics of the following?

1. Joint ventures

2. Consortia

3. Public bodies

4. Not-for-profit organisations

ACTIVITY 7

Reese Services is considering making an approach to Kalik Enviroplast Ltd about working together on a large recycling project. The management at Reese is trying to establish the financial implications of the options available for organising, financing and running the project. They have asked you to explain the advantages and disadvantages of entering into a consortium as opposed to a joint venture.

Write your answer in the form of a detailed memorandum, and summarise the key points below.

SAT:
allow 20 mins

| Communicating | ✓ |

| Managing tasks and solving problems | ✓ |

Commentary...

The main advantages for a company entering into a consortium, rather than into a joint venture are as follows:

- It maintains independent control over all aspects of its activities.

- It can raise capital independently of the financial means of the other participants; this might be a disadvantage if the company's financial means are weak relative to the other participants.

- It does not have to pool the profits that it makes. This is particularly important for a company that is expecting to make relatively more profit than the other businesses involved in the consortium. These may even be making losses or be engaged on a non-profit generating activity such as research.

The disadvantages include lack of access to pooled resources. For example, the involvement in the consortium has to be financed entirely from within itself. If a loss arises on operations, it has to be borne in full and cannot be shared.

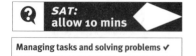

SAT:
allow 10 mins

Managing tasks and solving problems ✔

ACTIVITY 8

Say whether the following statements are true or false:

	True	False
(a) Sole traders are not allowed to employ other people full-time.	☐	☐
(b) By forming a limited liability, a sole trader can escape responsibility for a business's trade debts and borrowings.	☐	☐
(c) A joint venture resembles a partnership in that the co-venturers share the risks and the profits.	☐	☐
(d) A shareholder in a private limited company can only sell his or her shares to other members of the company or to the company itself.	☐	☐
(e) Private limited companies are not required to deposit an Annual Report and Accounts with Companies House.	☐	☐

	True	False
(f) 'Not-for-profit' organisations are not allowed to make a profit.	☐	☐
(g) 'Groups' are usually formed when two or more companies combine in order to enjoy economies of scale.	☐	☐
(h) When a local garage chain buys a similar business in a neighbouring town, this is an example of 'horizontal integration'.	☐	☐

Commentary...

Statement (a) is false; no such restriction exists. Statement (b) is true. However, although in theory a limited company is legally separate from its directors as individuals, it is not possible for the individual trader to escape responsibility for liabilities already incurred before the company was set up. In practice, even after setting up a company, most small business people will be required to give personal guarantees.

Statements (c), (d) and (h) are true. Statements (e), (f) and (g) are false. Groups exist primarily for the benefit of the parent; the arrangement described here is an amalgamation or merger.

In the sessions that follow you will occasionally be asked to examine a published company Annual Report and Accounts. Preferably you should obtain reports from companies operating in three different business sectors, such as manufacturing, services (transport, insurance, banking), and healthcare.

Ensure that you will have access to this material. Your tutor should be able to help you identify suitable sources.

summary

▶ Businesses may be incorporated or unincorporated. Unincorporated business consist of sole proprietorships (sole traders) and partnerships. The latter are legally constituted but, in both cases, the business and the owners are inseparable for legal purposes, and there is no limit on the owners' liability for the business's debts.

▶ Unincorporated businesses are usually small, and their main 'product' is usually the skills and experience of the owners.

▶ Incorporation identifies the business as a separate legal entity from its owners, the shareholders, who are not liable for its debts.

▶ Almost all incorporated business are either private limited companies (Ltd) or public limited companies (plc). The private limited companies are not allowed to sell shares to the public, and thus are generally restricted in the amount of external finance they can attract.

▶ There are several means by which one business can acquire control of other businesses: outright purchase (take-over), amalgamation and acquisition of a controlling interest.

▶ Groups consist of a parent company and any number of subsidiary, sub-subsidiary and associated undertakings. Within a group, each entity retains its legal and trading identity but, for accounting purposes, all are treated together as a single entity.

▶ Other types of business organisations include joint ventures, consortia, public bodies and not-for-profit organisations.

Sources and types of finance

EXTERNAL PROVIDERS OF FINANCE

OVERDRAFTS, BILLS OF EXCHANGE, CREDITORS AND FACTORING

HIRE PURCHASE, CREDIT SALES AND FINANCE LEASES

BANK LOANS, MORTGAGES AND DEBENTURES

SHARE CAPITAL

Objectives

After participating in this session, you should be able to:

- ▶ identify the internal and external sources of finance available to businesses

- ▶ describe four common types of short-term finance, and their suitability to particular situations or transactions

- ▶ describe the characteristics of hire purchase, credit sale and finance lease contracts, bank loans, mortgages and debentures, and their suitability to particular situations or transactions

- ▶ list the different main types of share capital.

In working through this session, you will practise the following BTEC common skills:

Managing and developing self	✔
Working with and relating to others	✔
Communicating	✔
Managing tasks and solving problems	✔
Applying numeracy	✔
Applying technology	
Applying design and creativity	

External providers of finance

Businesses need finance in order to operate; they obtain it from internal sources (which means shareholders, whose role we examine in a later session) and/or external sources.

There are several external sources that businesses can turn to in order to raise finance. The main external sources are:

- banks

- venture capitalists

- finance houses

- debt factors

- central and local government departments.

Later, we look in detail at many of the specific types of finance mentioned here.

BANKS

A range of finance and financial services are offered by commercial banks (i.e. high street clearing banks that process huge quantities of cash transactions, as opposed to merchant banks which typically offer fee-based advisory and investment services in areas such as takeovers, mergers and large investment projects). The types of finance that commercial banks provide can be categorised, according to their time span. (These are described in more detail in the next section.)

- Short-term finance can last for as much as two years but is usually for much shorter periods, includes overdrafts and the discounting of bills of exchange.

- Medium-term finance is usually granted for a period of between two and seven years. Thus bank finance would be a loan with a fixed or variable interest rate, and would be repayable either in instalments or as a single lump sum at the end of its term.

- Long-term finance is granted for periods in excess of seven years. Typically, it would be for the development and expansion of the business, or it may be a mortgage on the business premises.

VENTURE CAPITALISTS

These institutions do not involve themselves in small-scale operations; they are willing to provide finance above a £100,000 threshold, in the form of shares and loans. The finance may be used by existing businesses wanting to expand and new businesses to become established. Venture capital is characterised as a high-risk/high-return form of finance; it will be granted only where high returns are expected. It is usually available for no more than a period of about three years and is subject to demanding conditions. For example, it is a common requirement of the lender that a director is nominated to serve on the board of the borrowing company.

One venture capital company with a fairly high profile is Investors in Industry (3i).

FINANCE HOUSES

These organisations provide finance in the form of:

- credit sale finance

- hire purchase

- leasing.

Many finance houses are independent operations, although many of the clearing banks also run subsidiary companies dedicated to providing these forms of finance. These types of finance contracts are short-term, mostly with terms of two or three years, and they are commonly available to private consumers, as well as to businesses.

Lease contracts with finance houses usually have a term of five to seven years and so are regarded as a medium-term source of finance. Hire purchase and finance leasing are frequently used to finance the acquisition of plant, equipment and vehicles.

DEBT FACTORS

These firms take on the responsibility for the collection of money that is owed to their clients for goods bought by business customers on normal credit terms. They may both issue invoices and collect payment, or collect payment only.

The main role of debt factoring in the provision of finance is in ensuring the smooth flow of income arising from those credit sales. The seller of the goods does not have to worry about slow-paying or, under certain conditions, defaulting customers.

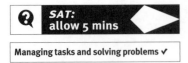

SAT:
allow 5 mins

Managing tasks and solving problems ✔

ACTIVITY 1

List three advantages that debt factoring could offer to R D Hatley, a stationery company with a large proportion of credit sales.

Commentary...

Some of the advantages of debt factoring are:

- ⊙ the business need not worry about irregular payments and can reduce the incidence of bad debts

- ⊙ Hatley can concentrate on its principal activity, which is selling

- ⊙ Hatley can reduce overheads because it will need to dedicate fewer resources to the administration and collection of credit payments

- ⊙ the regular nature of the payments will lead to a more reliable cashflow, and better financial planning.

Later in this session, we consider factoring in more detail, alongside some other forms of short-time finance.

CENTRAL AND LOCAL GOVERNMENT

Funds of various sorts are available to businesses at both local and national level:

Local government financial assistance is geared mainly towards helping businesses to start up, and to nurturing them until they become firmly established. Typically finance takes the form of

- enterprise grants, which are not repayable

- loans, which are repayable but at lower rates of interest and on easier repayment terms than could be obtained from commercial sources.

Central government has provided finance to industry and commerce for many years through the Department of Trade and Industry (DTI). This type of funding is usually part of a strategic plan to assist those regions of the UK where the traditional industries have disappeared and, as a consequence, unemployment is relatively high. (Further funds may be available from the EU for schemes on this scale.)

The finance is in the form of loans and grants (which do not have to be repaid). Where grants are used to finance day-to-day running activities they are, in effect, subsidies. Other grants are awarded for specific projects, to enable premises, plant and equipment to be acquired. For example, this type of government funding made possible the building of the Nissan car assembly plant in Washington in north-east England.

ACCESS TO FINANCE

Although there are many types of finance providers (and this is by no means an exhaustive list), with each provider filling a particular niche, whether or not any one business can obtain these types of finance depends on a number of factors:

- the amount of finance required

- the size of the business

- the length of time for which the money is to be borrowed

- the degree of risk to which the lender will be exposed.

EXTERNAL PROVIDERS

OF FINANCE

RECALL:
allow 10 mins

List the five main providers
of business finance and
briefly describe the type of
finance they offer.

SAT:
allow 10 mins

Managing tasks and solving problems ✓

ACTIVITY 2

Think about the different types of finance that are available. Consider
the requirements of the businesses below. For each business
situation, decide which providers would typically offer the
appropriate finance (there may be more than one for each business),
and say why.

1. An international building contractor is entering into a
   consortium to build a large suspension bridge across an
   estuary. The project is scheduled to last for eight years.

2. A sole-trader needs £550 to buy a fax machine.

3. A plastics moulding company is looking to provide a company
   car for its new account executive, Louise Buisson.

Commentary...

The engineering construction company is likely to look for funding from banks and perhaps from government, depending on the nature and perhaps on the geographical location of the building scheme. Because of the duration of the project, funding is unlikely to be forthcoming from a venture capitalist.

The sole trader's most appropriate source of funding is likely to be a bank overdraft, agreed at a given rate for a given period of, say, a few months. Alternatively, it could acquire the fax machine on hire purchase. If the trader is just starting out, it may be possible to look to local government for help with expenses involved in establishing the business.

The plastics company probably already has a leasing arrangement, but may also consider acquiring the vehicle through a credit sale contract. Either way, it is likely to look to a finance house to raise the money and manage the transaction.

There is a wide variety of providers for finance because a variety of businesses require finance. Each business has its own needs, and not all forms of finance are appropriate for all businesses. The right sort of finance depends on the size of the business, its state of development, the amount of finance it requires, its geographical location, the nature of the business, its financial stability, and its future prospects.

Overdrafts, bills of exchange, creditors and factoring

All businesses rely on short-term finance. We now look at four types that are commonly used in business:

- bank overdrafts

- credit purchase transactions

- bills of exchange

- debt factoring.

BANK OVERDRAFTS

An overdraft is a very common form of finance for businesses; the bank allows more money to be drawn out of the business's account than it actually contains. Banks usually impose severe financial penalties on customers, both private and business, who overdraw their accounts either without prior authority from the bank, or in excess of the agreed overdraft limit.

By formulating its plans in detail and preparing cashflows for the coming months, a business can predict whether an overdraft facility will be needed or not. (We look at cashflow forecasting later in this module.) The bank usually wants to see the business's plans; if the bank regards the plans as reasonable and the anticipated income as realistically achievable, it will usually grant the request. A business without detailed plans to back up its request will usually be turned down.

Bank overdrafts can be arranged with relative ease if the proper procedures are followed by the applicant business. Overdraft interest is geared to bank base lending rate, but the precise rate charged varies according to circumstances. In general, an unauthorised overdraft is charged at a much higher rate than an authorised one. The actual number of percentage points above the base rate that a bank charges varies between individual customers. Other factors taken into account when establishing these rates include:

- the size of the overdraft

- the authorised period

- the financial standing of the business

- general demand for, and availability of, overdraft finance

- the perceived risks of default and the general economic climate.

In theory, at least, overdrafts are regarded as a very short-term (and indeed expensive) form of finance. However, in practice, overdraft arrangements tend to be treated by the borrowers as semi-permanent even though, technically at least, they are repayable on demand or at short notice. The amounts will usually be repaid fairly quickly, but the arrangement itself – usually referred to as 'the overdraft facility' – tends to remain in place, and to be used in the long term as a means of financing seasonal or fluctuating cash shortfalls: the business dips in and out of 'the red' as cashflow falls and rises. This situation applies particularly in small and medium-sized businesses, many of which are perpetually short of cash resources.

Some banks may require some form of security or guarantee before granting an overdraft facility, much as they would with a medium- or long-term loan – see page 62.

CREDIT PURCHASE TRANSACTIONS

Credit purchase transactions use the most common form of short-term finance; it is known simply as 'trade credit'. The trade credit period, i.e. the interval of time between the goods and services being acquired and their being paid for, can vary between three and six weeks. Different arrangements are negotiated with each supplier, but all businesses obtain goods and services through credit purchase transactions as a matter of course.

With credit purchase transactions, the business retains the use of the money for the credit period. The main features of this form of finance are that it is:

- a generally accepted way of financing purchases

- cost free.

As an inducement for businesses to pay their accounts as soon as possible, some suppliers give an 'early settlement discount': customers pay 'less' for settling on time, or are penalised for paying late, depending on your point of view.

BILLS OF EXCHANGE

Sometimes a business needs a period of credit that is longer than the usual trade credit, but less than would be involved in hire purchase. The most suitable form of finance to span this gap is a bill of exchange – in effect, an arrangement for a delayed single payment – the currency of which can be from about eight weeks to nine months. Bills of exchange are used mostly for financing trading transactions, both within the UK and internationally.

The details of the financing arrangement are agreed in advance of the transaction by the supplier and customer. A bill of exchange is a written order, somewhat similar in form to an ordinary cheque – indeed, a cheque is a specialised form of bill of exchange – and the bill works as follows.

1. The supplier sends the goods to the customer and, either at the same time or shortly afterwards, draws up and sends a bill of exchange. The details on the bill include: the name and address of the drawer (i.e. the supplier); the name and address of the customer (the drawee); and the financing arrangements. These state that an agreed amount of money (the purchase cost of the goods) should be paid to the payee, who is either the supplier (the drawer) or the supplier's banker, on a certain date.

2. When the bill is received by the customer, the word 'accepted' is written across the face of it, together with the customer's signature and the date; it is then sent back to the supplier, who can then discount it with their bank. (This means that the bank gives the supplier the agreed amount minus interest for the period over which the bill is outstanding.)

3. When the agreed date is reached, the bill is described as having matured. The customer pays the amount due and the bill is discharged and cancelled. In the intervening period between acceptance and discharge, the goods bought by the business have been financed by the bill of exchange.

DEBT FACTORING

Debt factors are providers of finance and factoring is a mechanism by which sales to customers on credit can be financed. Otherwise, waiting for credit customers to pay for goods bought on normal trade credit terms can cause cash flow problems and difficulties in financing the purchase of stock. Without some form of finance, the supplier is unlikely to be able to meet its cash outgoings and debt factoring is one way of overcoming this problem: the debts owed by customers who have bought goods on credit are factored.

A debt factor, which is a specialist business, enters into an agreement with the supplier, whereby the factor in effect 'buys' the book debts, i.e. the amounts owed by the supplier's customers, and pays the amount concerned to the supplier, usually within two days. An administrative fee of between 1 per cent and 3 per cent is charged by the factor, as well as an interest rate of about 3 per cent above base lending rate. When the customers subsequently settle their accounts, it is the factor who receives the money and retains it, so recouping the initial outlay paid to the supplier.

Bad debt protection can be included in a variety of ways. Sometimes the whole of the book debt is factored, but more commonly only a proportion of it, say 80 per cent. Usually the factor collects the whole amount due and retains the amount that is factored. This has the effect of spreading the risk of default.

In both cases, the supplier has in effect received a loan, to cover the period of credit allowed to customers, and in return pays an interest rate above base lending rate.

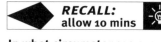

RECALL:
allow 10 mins

In what circumstances are the following forms of credit appropriate?

o **Bank overdrafts**

o **Credit purchase transactions**

o **Bills of exchange**

o **Debt factoring**

**OVERDRAFTS, BILLS OF
EXCHANGE, CREDITORS
AND FACTORING**

ACTIVITY 3

Obtain from your bank a copy of the terms and conditions for granting:

- personal banking overdrafts

- corporate business overdrafts.

The information may be contained in leaflets and brochures available on the counter, failing which you should obtain it verbally from the enquiry desk.

Compare the two sets of terms and conditions, and note down how they differ in respect to:

1. amount

2. period

3. interest rate chargeable

4. restrictions on purposes for which the loan may be used

5. security required.

Where you find significant differences, explain why you think they exist. Summarise your findings briefly in the box below.

Commentary...

Your answer will depend on which bank(s) you visited and when.

- The amount of the overdraft will depend on the borrower. Usually individual customers are likely to require (and be granted) smaller overdrafts than businesses, which usually have much larger cashflows than individuals.

- The period for which an overdraft is required may vary greatly. Individuals who are granted overdrafts are likely to have regular incomes and may use the overdraft only to tide them over the 'end-of-the-month' syndrome. The facility may be offered for long periods in the expectation that it will be used only for a few days each month. A business may use the overdraft quite differently, to smooth out seasonal fluctuations in cashflow.

- The interest rate is likely to be higher for a private individual than for a business user, although banks often charge an extra fee to businesses for arranging overdraft facilities. On the whole, rates are lower for businesses because they are borrowing larger amounts (historically cheaper) and because the banks want to attract business custom.

- The purpose to which it is being put may be restricted since the bank may be unwilling to finance an overdraft for certain purposes.

- The availability of security is likely to be required on any large overdraft, whether this is for a private or commercial client, but the forms of security may differ.

- Differences in terms of the length of time the current account has been open will be taken into consideration. Established customers are likely to be looked on more favourably than are new ones with no track record.

- Evidence will be required by the bank of proposed transactions, e.g. the bank will want to see business plans, and it may require evidence of salary details for private customers.

- The previous conduct of the account is an important factor. Customers, both private and business, that have repaid previous overdrafts in accordance with agreements are the customers most likely to be granted further overdraft facilities. Private customers who have always kept their accounts 'in the black' might be surprised at the heavy conditions placed on them when they ask for an overdraft: the fact is that they have no track record in repayment!

Hire purchase, credit sales and finance leases

As a general rule, medium-term finance implies a period of between two and seven years. The types of finance which fall within this span include:

- hire purchase

- credit sale agreements

- finance leasing.

HIRE PURCHASE

This is a very popular method of financing transactions when a buyer is unable or unwilling to pay the full purchase price at the outset. It might be used by a business to finance the acquisition of plant, equipment, vehicles or indeed any other item that has a life longer than the term of the hire purchase contract, which is usually two or three years.

The hire purchaser pays an initial deposit to the supplier or to the finance house and in return receives the item. Subsequently, the hire purchaser pays regular monthly or quarterly payments for the duration of the contract. Each instalment (like the instalments on credit sales contracts and on finance leasing, both discussed below) contains two elements:

- an element of hire purchase interest

- an element of repayment of the principal sum.

The final instalment contains an option to purchase fee, a purely nominal amount. This is for technical reasons: up to that point, although the hire purchaser has had possession and use of the item, the legal ownership has remained with the supplier or finance house, and the option fee is the legal device which transfers ownership to the hire purchaser. From the start of the contract, up to the point when the option fee is paid, the item has in law only been on hire. This is why hire purchase contracts cannot be used for acquiring goods that are to be disposed of before the contract expires; the disposal of the hired goods would constitute theft.

Hire purchase interest rates tend to be high, making hire purchase a relatively expensive option, but for some businesses it may be the only way of acquiring items they need.

CREDIT SALE AGREEMENTS

The label 'credit sale agreements' can be confusing. It refers not to goods sold by the business but goods sold to it, in other words, purchases. These agreements are structured very like hire purchase contracts. Both run for the same duration, two or three years typically, and involve the payment of a deposit followed by a series of regular instalments each of which contains elements of both interest and principal.

The major point of difference is that in a credit sale agreement, the legal ownership of the item passes to the acquirer at the outset, when possession of the item changes hands after the deposit has been paid.

FINANCE LEASING

Finance leasing is another means by which businesses can acquire high value items without having to meet the full outlay at the outset. A common example is when businesses acquire vehicles on finance lease contracts. Such contracts typically run for periods of five or six years.

The parties to the contract are the lessor (the supplier or a finance house) and the lessee, who acquires the goods. Although the items legally belong to the lessor (i.e. the supplier or finance house), it is the lessee who is contractually responsible for all maintenance and insurance costs during the life of the contract.

In certain respects, finance leasing contracts resemble hire purchase contracts, because the lessee has to make regular payments (termed finance lease rentals) to the lessor. The terminology here, though, reflects the fact that the items concerned do not, and will not, belong to the lessee (unless a completely second, separate transaction is entered into at the end of the lease term).

As the finance lease contract is, in effect, a loan (allowing the lessee the use of goods it would otherwise have had to buy or forego) then like the repayments discussed above, the leasing rental is a combination of two elements:

- interest, called the finance charge

- principal, i.e. the reduction in the outstanding obligation.

SALE AND LEASEBACK ARRANGEMENTS

As well as acquiring new items under finance lease contracts, businesses can also use their existing assets to raise finance under what are known as sale and leaseback arrangements. Premises, plant or equipment can be sold to a finance house for a lump sum and immediately be leased back under a finance lease, so that the items concerned never leave the possession of the lessee. The advantage to the lessee is that the business receives a cash injection from the sale proceeds.

Obviously, from the beginning of the leaseback contract, the leased items belong to the lessor (although during the period of the leaseback arrangement the lessee will be responsible for their upkeep).

ACTIVITY 4

SAT:
allow 10 mins

Managing tasks and solving problems ✓

Consider the range of medium-term financing arrangements discussed above. Then fill in the table to identify the distinguishing features of each.

	duration of contract	owner during contract	owner after contract ends	drawbacks/ limitations?
hire purchase contracts				
credit sale agreements				
finance leases				

Commentary...

	duration of contract	owner during contract	owner after contract ends	drawbacks/ limitations?
hire purchase contracts	2 - 3 years	finance house or supplier	hire purchaser	goods only disposable at contract end
credit sale agreements	2 - 3 years	buyer	buyer	
finance leases	5 - 6 years	lessor	lessor	lessee never owns goods

HIRE PURCHASE,

CREDIT SALES

AND FINANCE LEASES

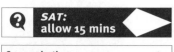

Communicating   ✓

Managing tasks and solving problems ✓

ACTIVITY 5

A friend manages a sizeable company offering contract cleaning and maintenance services. She is thinking about the finance options that will be available to her when she needs to replace various expensive items of equipment over the next year. The choice is between hire purchase, credit sales and finance leasing, but she is wondering about the main factors she should consider in relation to each acquisition. What would you tell her?

Write a short memo (around 100 words) and summarise your key points in the box below.

Commentary...

To a very great extent the circumstances would dictate the most appropriate means, but for each acquisition she should consider the following points.

Ownership

If she wants the business to own the equipment eventually, that would rule out a finance lease.

Payments

Under a hire purchase or credit sale contract, the size of the regular payments would be larger in amount than with a longer finance lease, but they would run for a shorter period. The amount of cash that the business can afford to pay will be an important consideration here.

Disposal

If it were likely that the business might want to dispose of the equipment during the life of the contract (i.e. while instalments are being paid), then the only option would be a credit sale agreement.

There are also taxation implications which are beyond the scope of this workbook.

Bank loans, mortgages and debentures

BANK LOANS

Banks are prepared to provide short-, medium- or long-term forms of finance and the basic arrangements are the same; only the details differ. The bank advances the loan, either all at once or in a series of progressive payments, which the borrower repays with interest.

The terms of the loan may require repayment of the amount borrowed either:

- as a lump sum paid on or by a specified date, or

- as a series of instalments throughout the period of the agreement.

Interest payments may also have to be made on regular monthly, quarterly, half yearly or yearly dates; alternatively they may be 'rolled up', which means that they are deferred until the end of the loan period.

Short-term bank loans are relatively rare because under most circumstances it is usually more appropriate to obtain an overdraft, particularly if the borrower is unable to estimate how long the loan is likely to be needed for. One advantage of an overdraft, in comparison to a loan, is that with an overdraft, interest is charged only for the number of days for which the account is overdrawn, whereas interest

BANK LOANS,
MORTGAGES AND DEBENTURES

on a bank loan is charged for the whole period for which the loan has been granted. Even if the borrower repays early, a stipulated minimum amount of interest still has to be paid.

Medium-term bank loans are commonly used to enable a business to become established, or to expand an already existing business. Once the business is up and running, or the expansion has been achieved, the business should be generating cash under its own steam, and the need for loan finance decreases or disappears altogether. Some form of security or guarantee is required before a loan of this type is granted.

Some businesses may decide that they wish to rely on loan finance as a permanent feature. This would make commercial sense particularly if the business can lock into substantial borrowings at fixed interest rates when these rates are low. Banks that lend money on these terms include both the clearing banks and specialist banks. The latter tend to concentrate on long-term lending.

Long-term bank loans of large amounts for lengthy periods of, say, up to 25 years are frequently granted only if backed by guarantees or other securities. Security may take the form of either

- a fixed charge, or

- a floating charge.

A fixed charge involves depositing the legal documents of title to the property of the business with the lender. The idea is that the property represents the bank's security, and it cannot be disposed of by the business as long as the bank holds the deeds. At the end of the term of the loan, after it has been repaid, the documents are returned to the borrower. In the event of default, the lender can have a receiver appointed to seize the secured property, sell it and recoup the amount owing.

Domestic mortgage arrangements use this form of fixed charge, with the title documents being held by the mortgage provider until the mortgage is finally paid off. Until then, the building society always has (and may well exercise) the option of selling the property in order to recoup the money it has loaned if the borrower defaults.

If the security takes the form of a floating charge on all assets, there are no legal documents to be deposited but if the borrower defaults, the charge crystallises, which means that it becomes effective, and a receiver is appointed to sell the assets of the business, the proceeds of which enable the loan to be discharged.

The rates of interest on bank loans differ, depending on:

- prevailing economic conditions

- the amount borrowed

- the period of the loan

- the status of the borrower

- the risk involved

- the absence, or presence of, security.

Banks are not the only institutions which grant loans. Other lenders include insurance companies, finance houses and pension funds, but the same considerations apply to these sources as have been stated for banks.

MORTGAGES

A mortgage is a specialised form of loan. It is usually large in amount and is secured on property by the deposit of legal documents with the lender. Its characteristics are similar to those of a bank loan secured by a fixed charge. Traditionally, the amount of loan advanced is less than the value of the property on which it is secured. However, for a period during the property boom in the late 1980s, lending institutions, anxious to compete for business, often granted '100 per cent mortgages'. As property values have fallen, many mortgage holders are now caught with negative equity, with a mortgage that exceeds the value of the property against which it is secured.

DEBENTURES

Debentures are a specialised form of borrowing that is written up in the form of a legal deed. The borrowing company 'issues' debenture stock, which is bought or held by debenture holders (lenders). In return, the borrower pays interest to the lender at a rate that is specified at the time of issue.

The whole sum borrowed by a company may be the subject of a single debenture, but it is frequently broken down into fractional amounts, when it is termed debenture stock (hence 'stocks and shares'). This has the effect of widening the lending base since smaller private investors can combine to provide the requisite sum.

Debenture stock is quoted in nominal units of £100, but it is usual for the stock to be issued at a discount. Thus if the price is stated to be £94, it means that the investor (the lender) has to pay £94 for every £100 nominal debenture stock acquired, but will receive interest at the rate applicable to the nominal amount. So, if the interest rate is 8 per cent, 8 per cent is paid on the full nominal amount of £100, not on the £94 cost price.

There are two kinds of debentures: perpetual debentures and redeemable debentures.

Perpetual debentures can be held by the investor (the lender) for as long as required, or can be disposed of (through the Stock Exchange) to another investor. Redeemable debentures are sold subject to the condition that the issuer (the borrower) can buy them back, i.e. redeem them, at some specified date, or more commonly, during some specified period, in the future.

Redeemable debentures give the borrower a degree of flexibility. By providing a wide period during which the redemption can occur, the business has a higher chance of being able to do so at a time when its cash resources are adequate. The price at which the debenture would be redeemed is stipulated in the terms of issue. Once the amount has been repaid (redeemed), the debenture certificate is cancelled by the issuing company.

If debentures are described as '9 per cent redeemable debentures 2019-2025', this signifies that they will be redeemed by the borrower at some unspecified date within that six-year period; in the meantime, the borrower will pay 9 per cent interest on the nominal value of each investor's holding. Like the holder of perpetual debentures, the holder of redeemable debentures is free, in the period before the redemption date or period arises, to dispose of the holding, or any part of it, to another investor on the open market.

The borrower can, like any other investor, buy and sell debentures on the open market. The price paid would simply be the prevailing market price, which might be at the nominal price, below the nominal price (at a discount) or above it (at a premium). If the borrowing business buys back its own debenture stock, it can either cancel it, or hold it for future re-issue, but any buy-back on the open market would be at the prevailing market price. A borrower might choose to do this if it finds itself unexpectedly cash-rich.

If the debentures are redeemable, the business will have to find the cash to redeem them at some stage anyway: if it has the cash earlier than anticipated, then in the absence of a more attractive investment proposition, the borrower may well decide to 'strike while the iron is hot'. By buying the debentures, the business will be able to reduce the level of outgoings it would otherwise be committed to, either for a specified period in the case of redeemable debenture stock, or in perpetuity for perpetual debentures.

Debentures, like bank loans, may be either secured by a legal charge, or unsecured. Unsecured debentures will bear a higher interest rate to compensate for the risk of loss.

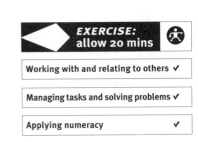

EXERCISE:
allow 20 mins

Working with and relating to others ✔

Managing tasks and solving problems ✔

Applying numeracy ✔

ACTIVITY 6

In groups of four, consider the following problem.

Connolly Ltd has a long-term strategy of raising finance via debenture issues. The company made an issue of 10 per cent redeemable debenture stock fifteen years ago and is now six months into the five-year redemption period. Commercial interest rates have just fallen and, in the opinion of the finance director, are unlikely to fall further in the foreseeable future. In order to redeem the debentures, Connolly would have to borrow.

1. Should Connolly redeem/buy back the debentures now, or should it wait?

2. What are the main factors and considerations the company needs to take into account in reaching a decision?

Summarise your conclusions and the main points you made in arriving at your answer in the box below.

BANK LOANS,

MORTGAGES AND DEBENTURES

Commentary...

As debentures are usually a long-term financial vehicle it is, of course, impossible to predict, at the time they are originally issued, whether interest rates will be high or low in, say, 20 years' time – hence the need for flexibility. By including a five-year redemption period in the terms and conditions of issue of the debentures, Connolly has given itself considerable flexibility – it has another four and a half years before it is forced to redeem. However, at some point during this period it will have to find the cash to do so.

The interest payable on debentures is fixed, so at points during the redemption period when commercial interest rates are lower than the debenture interest, it will be to Connolly's advantage to redeem the stock, even if it has to borrow to do so. However, in the longer term, since interest rates go up and down, it is better for the company to make a fresh issue of debentures that reflect the current low interest rate, to replace the finance used for the redemption or buy back.

It may also choose to redeem the debentures when interest rates are higher, if it has the necessary cash in hand.

The principal considerations are therefore as follows:

- What are commercial interest rates at present?

- Are they likely to change in the short-term future?

- If we redeem, do we borrow or use cash, if it is available?

- Do we issue new debenture stock at today's interest rates, assuming they are lower?

SAT:
allow 5 mins

Managing tasks and solving problems✔

ACTIVITY 7

Fill in the blanks to check that you have understood the key points about bank lending and debentures.

1. Bank loans have a role to play in the _____, _____ and _____-term financing of a business.

2. Mortgages are _____-term loans for the specific purpose of financing _____ acquisitions.

3. Debentures enable a company to _____ large sums from a large _____ of lenders to which it would not otherwise have access. Terms and _____ can be imposed at the time of issue which make debentures a very _____ financial instrument.

Commentary...

The missing words are: (1) short, medium, long; (2) long, property; (3) borrow, group (number), conditions, flexible.

Share capital

All the sources of finance considered so far have been external in the sense that their providers have not been members (owners) of the businesses. But the owners of businesses do play an important role in the financing of those businesses, and the finance that they provide – as we saw when we looked at sole proprietorships and partnerships – is called capital. In the specific instance of limited companies, both private and public, this finance is called share capital.

When a new company is being formed, the people setting it up (termed 'promoters') have to assess the amount of share capital that will be needed to enable the company to operate on the scale they envisage. The amount that they decide on must then be included in the legal document called the Memorandum of Association, which must be prepared and filed with the Registrar of Companies before the company can be registered and legally come into existence.

Authorised share capital

The share capital shown in the memorandum is termed the company's authorised capital, and this is the maximum share capital that the company is allowed to issue. It can be altered subsequently only by the due observance of certain legal procedures and the approval of the High Court. Details of the authorised capital must include the number, denomination and class of each share that the company can issue.

The amount of authorised share capital is fixed at a figure sufficiently high to meet the company's estimated future needs. Only rarely, therefore, does a company issue the whole of its authorised capital at the outset. The usual procedure is to issue shares progressively as need arises with the passage of time.

Even when shares are issued, the company may not require the full nominal value to be paid all at once. We saw earlier that a company can call up the amounts of nominal share capital in a series of instalments.

Some special terms relate to the various stages of issue and payment of these shares.

- The nominal value of the shares that have been issued is termed issued capital.

- That part of the issued capital on which instalments have been requisitioned is termed called-up share capital.

- Called-up share capital on which the instalments have all been paid is called paid-up share capital.

There are various rules surrounding the amount and frequency of instalments. The first instalment is known as the application, the second is the allotment and any subsequent instalments are known as calls.

SAT:
allow 10 mins

Managing tasks and solving problems ✔

Applying numeracy   ✔

ACTIVITY 8

Global County Resources Ltd has an authorised share capital of £160,000.

- **In May 1993, when the company began, 80,000 £1 shares were issued, payment for which were made outright.**

- **In May 1994, a further 20,000 £1 shares were issued, with the application representing 60 per cent of the shares' nominal value.**

- **By May 1995, further calls had been made on the remaining 40 per cent of the May 1994 issue.**

Identify the issued share capital, the called-up share capital, and the paid-up share capital at various stages in time, by filling in the table below:

	May 1993	May 1994	May 1995
Authorised share capital	160,000	160,000	160,000
Issued share capital			
Called-up share capital			
Paid-up share capital			

Commentary...

The issued share capital will be £80,000 in May 1993, £100,000 in May 1994 and £100,000 in May 1995. The called-up capital will be £80,000, £92,000 and £100,000 respectively. The paid-up share capital will be £80,000, £92,000 and £100,000.

THE ISSUE PRICE OF SHARES

The minimum price at which a company can issue its shares is at their par (nominal) value, but it can be set higher. It is illegal for a company to issue its shares at below par value. However, this restriction applies only to the issuing company, and it does not in any way affect shareholders when they trade their shares. A shareholder who wants to sell shares, usually through the medium of the Stock Exchange, at less than their nominal value (below par) is perfectly free to do so.

The principle of limited liability, coupled with the small nominal value of each share, typically ranging between 20 pence and 100 pence per share, means that they are both attractive and readily accessible to large numbers of private and institutional investors. If either of these conditions were absent, companies would have great difficulty in raising capital.

TYPES OF SHARE

There are several types of share. Here, we discuss:

- preference shares
- ordinary shares
- bonus shares
- rights shares.

Preference shares

Preference shares are so called because they are preferential in several respects. First, they carry a fixed dividend, expressed as a percentage of their nominal value, the payment of which takes priority over that of ordinary shareholders.

Of course, a company can only pay a dividend if it has profits available for distribution according to legal rules. Shareholders therefore take the risk that, in any particular year, there may be no dividends available for any of the shareholders, preferential or otherwise. However, if the shares were issued as cumulative preference shares, then the dividend rights will accumulate in the absence of profits until such time as there are sufficient profits to meet the preference dividend, including the arrears.

Second, when a company goes out of existence, the preference shareholders receive up to the nominal amount of their holding, depending on availability of cash, before the ordinary shareholders receive anything.

Preference shares, therefore, appeal to those cautious investors who require a degree of security and certainty, and who are prepared to accept a lower return on their investment in exchange for this reduced risk. As a result, the fixed dividend rate is less than that which ordinary shareholders would expect. The voting rights of preference shareholders are very restricted, being limited to matters which affect their rights.

Ordinary shares

All companies must issue some ordinary shares, and indeed the share capital of many companies consists solely of ordinary shares. They are also known as equity shares and equity capital.

Ordinary shareholders have one vote for each share they hold and as a body are able to reach decisions on matters such as the election of directors. The dividends on ordinary shares are not fixed: the amount is recommended by the board of directors, and the ordinary shareholders can accept the recommendation or have it reduced, but not increased. (If they are unhappy about the directors' decision they can vote to remove them.) The dividend income of the ordinary shareholders therefore fluctuates with the fortunes of the company and the dividend policy of the directors.

Despite these apparent drawbacks, ordinary shares are popular with investors, partly because good dividends are paid when the company is prospering, and partly because all the surveys indicate that, ignoring temporary fluctuations, the underlying values of equity shares increase at a greater rate than inflation and in many instances, substantially so.

Bonus shares

When a company has accumulated a large amount of profit which it has not distributed as dividend and which it wishes to retain permanently within the company, it may make a bonus (scrip) issue. This involves converting the profit into ordinary share capital and distributing it to shareholders on a proportionate holding basis. This manoeuvre does not result in any cash coming into the company but has the effect of watering down its share prices on the Stock Exchange and consequently of making them more marketable.

Rights shares

When a company wishes to raise more cash, one alternative is for it to make a rights issue. The shares are made available to existing shareholders, on a proportionate holding basis, at a concessionary price sufficiently below open market price to be an attractive investment proposition.

ACTIVITY 9

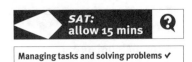

SAT: allow 15 mins

Managing tasks and solving problems ✓

State whether the following statements are true or false.

	True	False
(a) A company can issue debentures at a discount, but not shares.	☐	☐
(b) 'Equity capital' describes a situation in which a company's shares are divided equally between the shareholders.	☐	☐
(c) Debt factoring is mainly designed to help a business to recover bad debts.	☐	☐
(d) A bill of exchange resembles a cheque except that it is issued for payment on a particular day in the future.	☐	☐
(e) Banks may charge extra fees to penalise a company which exceeds its overdraft limit without authorisation.	☐	☐
(f) Unsecured debentures usually pay a higher interest rate.	☐	☐

Commentary...

Statements (a), (d), (e) and (f) are true. Statement (b) is false; statement equity capital is simply another term for ordinary (voting) share capital; (c) is false. Factoring may help recover bad debts, but those debts are no longer the original company's – they now belong to the factor; the main reasoning for using factoring is to improve the flow of cash from customers.

SHARE REDEMPTION AND BUY BACK

Many companies take powers enabling them to redeem and buy back their own shares. In a redemption, the shares are acquired direct from the shareholders but, in buy-back, they are bought on the open market. When acquired by the company by either of these methods they are cancelled. This facility is very useful to a company engaged in restructuring its capital.

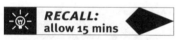

RECALL:
allow 15 mins

Distinguish between:

1. the two elements that form the repayments on an HP loan or finance lease

2. permanent and redeemable debentures

3. fixed and floating charges

4. authorised share capital and issued share capital

5. preference shares and ordinary shares.

ACTIVITY 10

ASSIGNMENT:
allow 40 mins

Managing and developing self ✔

Managing tasks and solving problems✔

A substantial new private company is being formed to exploit opportunities in the domestic security field. Its directors hope to use the issue of shares and (in due course) debentures as a means of raising capital.

Write a report advising them what options they have under the following headings.

1. Share issues:

   (a) total share capital

   (b) types of shares

   (c) the proportion to be issued

   (d) arrangements for payment

   (e) the par price of the shares, and the actual price that can charged

   (f) who can buy shares

   (g) dividend policy.

2. Debentures:

   (a) advantages and disadvantages

   (b) types of debenture

   (c) typical terms and conditions

   (d) arrangements for redemption/buy-back.

You may wish to do some further research on some of these issues, in which case, ask your tutor for suitable reading references.

summary

Finance is the lifeblood of any business organisation. The finance comes both from within the business and from external sources.

▶ Externally, there are established providers of finance which cater for the specialised needs of individual businesses. The most commonly encountered providers are: banks, venture capitalists, finance houses, debt factors, and central and local government.

▶ Bank loans have a role to play in the short-, medium- and long-term financing of a business. Mortgages are long-term loans for the specific purpose of financing property acquisitions.

▶ Debentures enable a company to borrow large sums from a large group of lenders to which it would not otherwise have access. Terms and conditions can be imposed at the time of issue which make debentures a very flexible financial instrument.

▶ For finance required for a period of up to one year, the four commonly available types of finance are: bank overdrafts, credit purchase transactions, bills of exchange and debt factoring.

▶ Medium-term finance includes hire purchase contracts and credit sale agreements, whereby items are acquired on deferred payment terms, and finance leases where the use, but not the ownership, of items is secured by a series of rental payments.

▶ The main source of permanent finance in a company is its share capital. Each company has an authorised capital, in terms of numbers and types of shares, which it must not exceed. A company is not obliged to issue the whole of its authorised capital; it may issue it as it is needed.

▶ The two main types of share are preference and ordinary, each of which have their own characteristics. It is the ordinary shareholders who benefit financially from the success of the company and suffer from its poor performance, while the preference shareholders are protected to a certain degree.

Published accounts

PUBLISHED ACCOUNTS REQUIREMENTS

PROFIT AND LOSS ACCOUNT THEORY

PROFIT AND LOSS ACCOUNT FORMAT

BALANCE SHEET THEORY

BALANCE SHEET FORMAT

CASH FLOW STATEMENT THEORY

CASH FLOW STATEMENT FORMAT

Objectives

After participating in this session, you should be able to:

▶ identify and briefly describe the three financial statements that an incorporated business must publish

▶ explain the derivation of the various items in the financial statements

▶ describe the main financial accounting principles that apply to the preparation of financial statements

▶ prepare simple draft financial statements from a list of transactions and balances.

In working through this session, you will practise the following BTEC common skills:

Managing and developing self	✔
Working with and relating to others	✔
Communicating	✔
Managing tasks and solving problems	✔
Applying numeracy	✔
Applying technology	
Applying design and creativity	✔

Published accounts requirements

All businesses need to prepare annual accounts, which detail the effects of their numerous financial transactions. Apart from the fact that those who own or manage a business need to have details of how it has fared and what the financial position is, properly prepared accounts are an essential prerequisite to settling the tax affairs of the business with the Inland Revenue. In the case of limited companies, however, there is an additional legal requirement that all companies publish their accounts as part of the Annual Report and Accounts, copies of which go to all shareholders and to the Registrar of Companies where anyone can inspect them.

The Annual Report and Accounts contain the following:

- a review of the last year and an assessment of future prospects by the Chairman of the company

- the directors' report, covering certain matters prescribed by the Companies Act (1985)

- three major financial statements:

  (a) the profit and loss account

  (b) the balance sheet

  (c) the cash flow statement.

In this session, we look at the nature, theory, terminology and format of these three financial statements. For the purposes of illustration, we use a fictitious company called Stokkit Ltd, a wholesaler of non-perishable goods including craft goods, novelties, gifts and toys. Demand for individual lines from the large and diverse range stocked varies on a seasonal basis. Stokkit's suppliers also vary widely, from manufacturers, to importers of foreign goods (mainly from outside the EU), to individual artists who make craft jewellery, pottery, etc. Stokkit's customers are mainly, independent retailers, cash and carry warehouses, and the central buying departments of national retail chains.

Profit and loss account theory

MEASURING PROFIT

In its simplest terms, within a trading business such as Stokkit, profit arises when the total value of sales is greater than the total of all expenses incurred directly and indirectly in producing those sales. The reverse situation results in a loss. Revenue is the term used to describe the sales value of goods and services supplied (this is also commonly referred to as turnover) and so we say that:

revenue - expenses = profit

We shall use the notation R for revenue, E for expenses and P for profit. If expenses are greater than revenue, then the result is a loss (L).

REVENUE

In any trading business, such as Stokkit, almost all revenue is earned from the sales of goods. This is called trading revenue (R_t) to distinguish it from other revenue that arises from minor sources, incidental to the main objective of the business (in this instance, wholesaling). An example of an 'other source' of revenue is the rent earned by Stokkit from sub-letting an unused part of its warehouse to a sole trader. We can label the rent received as other revenue (R_o).

Thus, total revenue is given by:

$R = R_t + R_o$

It is normal trading practice for businesses to buy and sell goods and services on credit, so there is a time lag between buying (or selling) goods, and paying (or being paid) for them. When we talk about revenue, we ignore this time lag. Revenue means the total value of goods or services supplied, so the revenue arises when the goods are sold, not when they are paid for. This is known as the accruals basis.

This is important, because if Stokkit is preparing its accounts for the year to 31 December Year 6 and allows its customers six weeks in which to pay for the goods after they have been despatched, then goods sold in December Year 6 will not have been paid for until January or February in Year 7. In view of what we have said above, however, the trading revenue (R_t) is deemed to have occurred in Year 6 when the sale took place, not in Year 7 when the money is received. As a consequence, this revenue will be reflected in the profit (or loss) for Year 6.

The same principles apply to expenses. We can identify trading expenses (E_t) and other expenses (E_o):

- Trading expenses (E_t) are the expenses that relate directly to goods sold. This is the cost of goods bought in from manufacturers and other suppliers, and usually constitutes the list price plus carriage charges (if any), less trade discount.

- Other expenses (E_o) are incurred in connection with the business, such as running vehicles, paying for electricity and buying stationery.

ACCRUALS

Expense is determined in the same way as revenue: an item is treated as an expense when it is incurred, not when payment is made. This is known as the accruals basis. Most payments are made after the item has been acquired or after the service has been performed. For example, wages and salaries are usually paid in arrears, so that salaries earned by Stokkit's staff in December Year 6 would be an 'other expense' in Year 6 when they were earned, not in January Year 7 when they were paid.

Some payments, like insurance premiums, have to be paid in advance. Where this happens, only the element that is used up in the accounting period is allocated to the period, and the remainder is held over and treated as an expense in that forthcoming period. So, if an annual insurance premium is paid on 1 October Year 6, only three-twelfths of it (the October to December portion) would count as an 'other expense' in Year 6, and the remaining nine-twelfths would be allocated to Year 7.

When goods are bought to be held in stock for resale or use, the E_t and E_o arise, not when the purchase itself is made but, when the goods are issued from stock for resale or consumption.

REFINING THE EQUATION

As we saw earlier, profit arises from revenue less expenses. Having looked in more detail at how revenue and expenses are allocated, we now refine this simple formula to produce a more specific figure for the profit (or loss) that arises from trading activities:

trading revenue - trading expenses = gross profit (GP)

When other revenue and other expenses are also taken into account, we can calculate a net profit (NP), or a net loss (NL):

gross profit + other revenue - other expenses = net profit

Using the notation, this equation becomes:

$GP + R_O - E_O = NP$ (or NL)

MATCHING

Profit measurement can therefore be described as a process of matching. Overall total expense is matched against total revenue on a time basis to produce total profit or loss. Within this framework, revenue arising from trading activities is offset by the corresponding expense incurred in generating that revenue, to produce a figure of gross profit. Gross profit is augmented by ancillary items of revenue and reduced by all other expenses, resulting in a figure of net profit or loss.

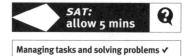

SAT:
allow 5 mins

Managing tasks and solving problems ✓

ACTIVITY 1

Fill in the missing words, to make sure that you are clear about the nature of gross and net profit.

1. _____ profit (or loss) takes account of all the direct and indirect costs and revenues of the business.

2. _____ profit (or loss) relates directly to income from goods or services sold and to the costs of producing or acquiring those goods and services.

3. $R_t + R_O =$ _____ _____.

4. $GP + R_O - E_O =$ _____ _____.

Commentary...

The missing words are 'net', 'gross', total revenue and net profit (or net loss) respectively.

DEPRECIATION

Most expenses, both trading expenses and other expenses, result in a cash payment to employees or outsiders, but one important exception is an expense called depreciation, which we consider later on. For the

PROFIT AND LOSS

ACCOUNT THEORY

moment, you should note that depreciation is a measure of the loss in value of the permanent resources of the business due to wear and tear, passage of time and several other factors. Although it counts as an expense, depreciation does not require any form of cash payment.

? *SAT:*
allow 20 mins

| Managing tasks and solving problems | ✔ |
| Applying numeracy | ✔ |

ACTIVITY 2

Apply your knowledge of the principles of profit measurement to identify:

(a) whether the items in the first column of the table below should be classed as R_t, R_o, E_t or E_o

(b) how much should be allocated to the profit and loss account for the year ended 31 December Year 6.

Write your answers in the appropriate box in the table below.

Revenue and expense items	R_t	R_o	E_t	E_o
Wages earned and paid, £36,000				
Wages earned but paid in year 7, £1,000				
Insurance premium paid on 1 September for one year, £300				
Stationery bought for £120, of which £25 still remaining at 31 December Year 6				
Interest on borrowings, paid in Year 7, £175				
Sales: cash sales of £41,000, and credit sales of £92,000, of which £34,000 is received in Year 7				
Interest received on bank deposit account £29				
Cost of goods sold, £77,000				

Commentary...

The following should be placed in the E_o column:

- Wages earned and paid (£36,000)

- Wages earned but paid in Year 7 (£1,000)

- Insurance premium paid on 1 September for one year (but only £100, i.e. four-twelfths of £300)

- Stationery, but excluding the £25 still remaining at 31 December Year 6, i.e. £95 only

⦿ Interest on borrowings, paid in Year 7 (£175).

The 'Sales' items, totalling £133,000, should be in the R_t column. Interest received should be in the R_o column, and cost of goods sold (£77,000) should be in the E_t column.

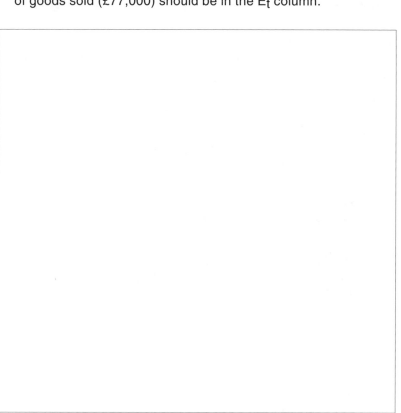

RECALL:
allow 10 mins

Give three reasons why companies need to maintain accurate financial records

Briefly explain the accountancy terms:

(a) depreciation

(b) accruals

(c) matching.

Profit and loss account format

Businesses produce a schedule of the profit or loss they have made, in the form of a statement, known as a profit and loss account. This gives a detailed breakdown of the individual items of revenue and expense which have given rise to the profit or loss during the period. In the profit and loss account for Stokkit (see account 3.1), items are labelled R_t, E_t, R_o and E_o. These symbols are included so that you can link the items to what you have been learning, but they would not normally be shown.

Look carefully through the account, bearing in mind that the figures in the second of the four columns often explain the figures in the third column. Note that the heading is essential; without the heading, a reader attempting to use the account would not know which period it covers or to which business it relates, making the figures useless. Certain items need further explanation.

- Cost of sales is a derived figure which represents the cost price of the goods whose selling price produces the revenue (or turnover).

- Gross profit (GP) and net profit (NP) have been calculated in the way we described above.

- Sundry expenses contains a whole number of smaller items, which do not warrant a line in their own right.

Stokkit Ltd
Profit and loss account for the year ended
31 December Year 6

	£000	£000	Symbol
Turnover		2,898	R_t
Opening stock	477		
Purchases (for resale)	1,996		
	2,473		
Closing stock	592		
Cost of sales		1,881	less E_t
Gross profit		1,017	equals GP
plus			
Rent received for sub-letting		16	plus R_o
		1,033	
less			
Wages and salaries	406		
Power heat and light	79		
Postage and telephones	47		
Vehicle running expenses	44		
Audit and accountancy fees	11		
Stationery	29		
Debenture interest	27		
Business rates	53		
Depreciation	58		
Sundry expenses	5		
		759	less E_o
Net profit before tax		274	equals NP
Taxation		49	
less			
Net profit after tax		225	
Proposed dividends		70	
Retained profit: for the year		155	
brought forward		113	
carried forward		268	

ACCOUNT 3.1: Stokkit's profit and loss account.

EXPENSES AND APPROPRIATIONS

As you can see, the profit and loss account does not stop at the calculation of net profit. The items that occur after net profit has been derived, are taxation and dividends. These are termed appropriations. They are not expenses (which reduce profit), but represent how the profit itself is shared out. Of course, unless the company makes a profit, there can be no tax levied on it nor can any be given to shareholders as dividend.

Profit left over after appropriations have been made for taxation and dividends is retained profit. This can:

- arise in the year

- be brought forward from the previous year

- be carried forward to the next financial year.

Financial years can be any period of twelve months. Many companies' financial years end on 31 March or on 31 December, but can end on any month end.

The profit and loss account (account 3.1) was designed to show the various elements and how they relate to each other, and it would certainly be a useful tool to the managers of any company. However, it could not be published in this format. The published profit and loss account must conform with one of the four formats specified by the Companies Act (1985). The most commonly used format is shown in account 3.2.

Company name
Profit and loss account for the year ended
XXXX

	£000	£000	
Turnover		X	
Cost of sales		(X)	
Gross profit		X	
Distribution costs	X		
Administrative expenses	X		
		(X)	
[Trading profit]		X	
Other operating income		X	
[Operating profit]		X	
Income from other fixed asset			
investments	X		
Other interest receivable	X		
		X	
		X	
Interest payable		(X)	
Profit on ordinary activities before tax		X	
Taxation		(X)	
Profit on ordinary activities after tax		X	
Extraordinary items		X	or (X)
Profit for financial year		X	
Dividends		(X)	
Retained profit for the year		X	

ACCOUNT 3.2: Standardised format for profit and loss account
conforming to Companies Act (1985).

Items shown in square brackets [ ] are non-statutory labels, and the curved brackets ( ) indicate figures to be deducted. The profit and loss items of Stokkit Ltd, which we have already discussed, can now be rewritten in statutory format (see account 3.3). We have assumed the total 'other expenses', break down as follows:

	£000
Distribution costs	416
Administrative expenses	316
Interest paid	27
Total other expenses	759

Stokkit Limited
Profit and loss account for the year to
31 December Year 6

	£000	£000
Turnover		2,898
Cost of sales		1,881
Gross profit		1,017
Distribution costs	416	
Administrative expenses	316	
		732
Trading profit		285
Other operating income (rent received)		16
Operating profit		301
Interest paid		27
Profit on ordinary activities before tax		274
Taxation		49
Profit on ordinary activities after tax		225
Dividends		70
Retained profit for the year		155

ACCOUNT 3.3: Stokkit's profit and loss account
in a format conforming to Companies Act (1985).

In the presentation of Stokkit Ltd's figures, the statutory format has been adapted to suit the circumstances. For example, if there is no amount for a statutory item, it is completely omitted and not recorded as a nil. Additionally, the law requires that the figures be supported by copious notes, which give detailed breakdowns and explanations of the main figures. These have been omitted from this simple example.

ACTIVITY 3

SAT:
allow 10 mins

Managing tasks and solving problems ✓

Explain briefly what counts as an appropriation (as opposed to an expense). Mark with a highlighter pen the items in the profit and loss account (account 3.2) that fall into this category.

Commentary...

The appropriated items represent what happens to the profit, rather than how it has been derived. They appear after the profit figure in the profit and loss account and, in this case, they are taxation and dividends.

ACTIVITY 4

SAT:
allow 10 mins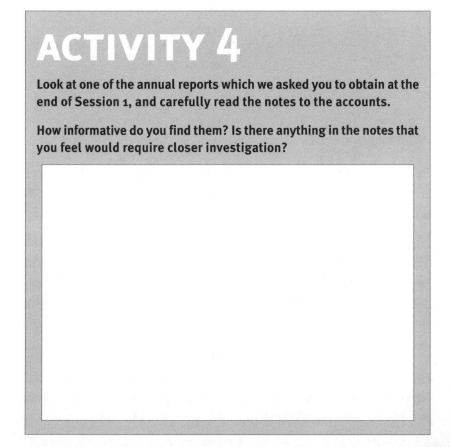

Managing tasks and solving problems ✓

Look at one of the annual reports which we asked you to obtain at the end of Session 1, and carefully read the notes to the accounts.

How informative do you find them? Is there anything in the notes that you feel would require closer investigation?

Commentary...

The notes should have helped you understand the accounts a little better, by stating the purpose of special reserves, 'provisions', etc. However, some of them are probably of a highly technical nature, and you may feel that they were included because it was necessary to do so, and not out of a strong desire to be informative to readers.

Balance sheet theory

In contrast to a profit and loss account, which records the effect of transactions over a period of time, a balance sheet gives a statement of the financial position of the business at a specified point in time. It has been likened to a snapshot of the financial standing of the business. A balance sheet records financial values for those resources which it is holding at the time and which are capable of being expressed in monetary terms, and shows them together with (and 'balances' them against) the finances that were used in acquiring the resources.

The resources referred to are items that a business owns and uses in order to achieve its aims. The nature of the business concerned will determine what resources are needed. At one end of the scale:

- a self-employed plumber needs a van, an extending ladder, tools, equipment, various materials and cash

- a manufacturing company needs premises – factory, warehouse, garage and offices – plant, equipment, tools, vehicles, stocks of raw materials, cash and other items.

Resources of the sort so far described are termed assets. Only those resources which have resulted from a financial transaction are classed as assets. So, the skills of a trained workforce, the loyalty of employees and the team spirit of the directors – although all factors that contribute to the success and prosperity of the company – are not assets because they have not been acquired as the result of a transaction. Machinery is, however, an asset because it has been bought at a stated price.

A balance sheet does not show the value of a business, as this can only ever be a subjective decision. Instead, balance sheets are designed to be as objective as possible, and the values of the assets are based on actual cost, or modified cost.

The assets of a business are acquired out of the finance available to it. In a balance sheet, the various sources of finance are labelled liabilities, to reflect the fact that the business owes these amounts to their providers. A company will obtain finance from various sources, both outside and within the company, and these are known as external and internal liabilities respectively.

External liabilities include creditors (trade and hire purchase), lenders (banks) and debenture holders. Internal liabilities include share capital and reserves (undistributed profits which belong to shareholders and will be explained later).

These facts are expressed in the accounting equation which states that, at all times within a business:

total assets = total liabilities

Note that this balance exists at all times, not just at the end of the year when the balance sheet is drawn up. In fact, it could be drawn up at the end of every working week or day, or even after every single transaction that the business makes. The total value of the assets and liabilities are in a state of constant flux, and could therefore change after every transaction, but they would nevertheless remain at all times equal to each other.

The balance sheet is simply a formal end-of-year statement of these classified assets and liabilities.

FIXED ASSETS

Some assets are permanent (e.g. land) or semi-permanent, such as buildings, or otherwise long-lived as in the case of equipment and vehicles. Assets such as these are called fixed assets and, because they have a physical existence, they are often called tangible (literal meaning: touchable) fixed assets. They represent the productive, revenue-earning capacity of the business. They are valued on the basis of their original cost which is then reduced by a suitable amount, known as depreciation, to reflect their loss in value over time due to usage and obsolescence brought about by technological advances.

Depreciation can be calculated in various ways, but a common approach is to take the difference between what the asset cost and what it is likely to be worth by way of scrap or resale value at the end of its useful life, and to charge a proportion of this total loss in value as depreciation in each year of its life.

For example, if a piece of machinery is bought for £40,000 and is expected to have a useful life of ten years at the end of which it can be sold for a replacement at a trade-in value of £5,000, then the total loss in value, or depreciation, is £35,000. This would be divided over the ten years of its expected useful life, and charged to the profit and loss account at the rate of £3,500 per annum, for ten years. Its balance sheet value would be reduced cumulatively.

SAT:
allow 5 mins

Applying numeracy ✓

ACTIVITY 5

Stokkit brought a a packing machine for £40,000 when the business started. It is expected to have a useful working life of ten years. In Year 10, the company can expect to receive £5,000 in trade-in or scrap value for the machine.

What depreciation charge for this machine should be shown in the profit and loss account? What value should be placed on the machine in the balance sheet in Year 4?

Commentary...

The packing machine reduces in value from £40,000 to £5,000 over its 'lifespan', depreciating £35,000 over ten years. So, the depreciation charge for this item in the profit and loss account would be £3,500. In year 4, the balance sheet should disclose a figure of £26,000 (i.e. £40,000 less four years' depreciation at £3,500 per year). This £26,000 is labelled the net book value (NBV) or written down value (WDV) of the machinery.

Depreciation is not always assumed to occur evenly; many assets (vehicles, for example) lose value more quickly in the first year or two than in subsequent years, and it may be more realistic to reflect this in the balance sheet and profit and loss account. However, depreciation is a matter of accounting policy, and no company is obliged to track the exact change in its assets' market value.

As time passes, the values of some assets increase rather than reduce. This is particularly true of land and buildings. Some businesses have these assets professionally valued and substitute the revaluation figure for the cost. The resultant profit is only notional (it has not been realised at this stage) and it is kept as a special account until the asset concerned is sold.

Fixed asset investments and intangible assets are valuable legal rights for which the company has had to pay and include trademarks, licences, copyrights and patent rights. We have briefly discussed a number of items that would be considered fixed asset investments although we considered them, as it were, from the other side of the fence, when we were looking at sources of finance. For example, a company that is providing finance to another one, may hold fixed asset investments in one of two ways:

- it might have a shareholding in another company

- it might hold debentures issued by another company, and which earn regular interest as well as having saleable value of their own.

CURRENT ASSETS

All businesses have current assets. These are resources which a business must have at all times but which, unlike fixed assets, are constantly changing in composition, i.e. are turned over.

Managing tasks and solving problems ✔

ACTIVITY 6

Think about the assets listed in a balance sheet (see account 3.4 on page 93 for an example). Which are current assets, according to the definition above?

Commentary...

Trading stock is a current asset; it is constantly changing as items are taken from it for sale, while others are brought in to replenish it. In most businesses, cash is an even more obvious example, changing its composition many times each working day as money is received and paid out. Debtors – i.e. the amount owed to the business by customers who have obtained goods on credit – is a current asset for the same reason.

CURRENT LIABILITIES

The same principle applies to items which the business owes in the short-term. Creditors, amounts owed to suppliers of goods and services on credit, are paid regularly as more items are bought on credit.

As we will see more clearly when we look at the format of the balance sheet, there is a relationship between current assets and current liabilities, which recognises that current assets should be sufficient in amount to meet the current liabilities. The term given to this excess is working capital, or net current assets.

These items are also known as circulating capital, because of the way the individual items flow. Figure 3.1 shows that the business acquires stock on credit from suppliers and sells it, again on credit, to customers who become debtors. When the customers (debtors) pay their accounts, cash balance is increased, but is reduced when the suppliers' (creditors) accounts are settled.

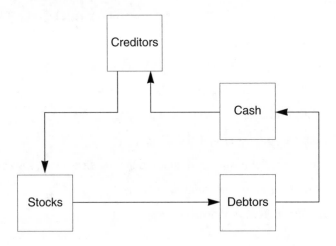

FIGURE 3.1: The working capital cycle.

LONG-TERM LIABILITIES

Long-term liabilities are fixed or semi-fixed external liabilities (such as debentures) that the company has issued, and loans of longer than one year before repayment date.

RECALL:
allow 10 mins

What is the distinction between assets and liabilities?

What is meant by the following terms?

○ **Fixed assets**

○ **Fixed asset investments**

○ **Current assets**

What is 'the accounting equation'?

SAT:
allow 10 mins

Managing tasks and solving problems ✓

ACTIVITY 7

Apply the principles you have just learned to classify the following items as fixed assets, current assets, long-term liabilities, or current liabilities.

(a) A loan to the company repayable in five years time, £50,000.

(b) A car bought for the managing director's use, £16,000.

(c) A car bought for resale, £9,000.

(d) Cost of an extension to the office buildings, £37,000.

(e) Amount owed for electricity used, £1,770.

(f) Balance of cash at the bank, £19,600.

(g) Cash held in the shop tills, £810.

(h) 11 per cent debenture, redeemable in ten years' time, £80,000.

(i) Amount owed by a customer, £650.

(j) Stock of cleaning materials, £95.

Commentary...

Items listed in (b) and (d) are fixed assets; (c), (f), (g), (i) and (j) are current assets; (a) and (h) are long-term liabilities; (e) is a current liability.

Work through any errors carefully; if you are still unable to understand why an item has been classified in the way it has, consult your tutor.

Balance sheet format

Businesses produce a statement of assets and liabilities, in the form of a balance sheet, at the end of each period for which a profit and loss account has been prepared. This invariably means at the end of each financial year, but additional 'interim' balance sheets may also be prepared. For reporting internally for management purposes, the format of the balance sheet can be in any style, but it will always conform to the basic accounting equation: the assets and the liabilities equal each other.

BALANCE SHEET LAYOUT

Like the profit and loss account you have seen, the balance sheet has a proper heading, consisting of the name of the business and the date at which it has been prepared. The purpose of this information is the same as for a profit and loss account; its absence would render the document useless.

			Stokkit Limited		
			Balance sheet as at 31 December		
Year 5				Year 6	
£000	£000			£000	£000
	926		Fixed assets		1,021
			Current assets		
477			Stock – trading	592	
35			– other	47	
286			Debtors	370	
41			Bank and cash	53	
	839				1,062
	1,765		Total assets		2,083
			Long-term liabilities		
	200		9% debentures		300
			Current liabilities		
380			Creditors – trade	401	
47			– other	65	
40			Taxation	49	
55			Dividends	70	
	522				585
	800		Called up share capital		800
			Reserves		
70			Share premium	70	
60			Fixed asset replacement	60	
113			Profit and loss	268	
	243				398
	1,765		Total liabilities		2,083

ACCOUNT 3.4: Stokkit's balance sheet.

You can see that at both dates the aggregates of assets and liabilities are the same, but certain other items may need explanation:

- Fixed assets have been inserted as a single figure in the balance sheet and the figure was derived from the following details:

	Land £000	Buildings £000	Plant £000	Vehicles £000	Total £000
Cost					
Cost 1/1/Year 6	390	400	157	132	1,079
Additions Year 6	–	70	64	46	180
Disposals Year 6	–	–	(43)	(22)	(65)
Cost 31/12/Year 6	390	470	178	156	1,194
Depreciation					
Balance 1/1/Year 6	–	40	72	41	153
Disposals Year 6	–	–	(21)	(17)	(38)
Charge Year 6	–	9	18	31	58
Bal: 31/12/Year 6	–	49	69	55	173
Net book value					
:at 1/1/Year 6	390	360	85	91	926
:at 31/12/Year 6	390	421	109	101	1,021

ACCOUNT 3.5: Stokkit's fixed assets.

- Net book value, shown in the bottom two lines of account 3.5, is calculated as cost minus the accumulated depreciation at each of the dates, and appears on the main balance sheet as the value of 'fixed assets'. All disposals were at net book value.

- Taxation is shown as a current liability because the company does not have to pay it until nine months after its financial year end. Thus, the £49,000 is payable in September Year 7.

- Dividends are only proposed at this stage. They have to be approved at the Annual General Meeting to be held in about April or May Year 7. While awaiting payment, the £70,000 is a current liability.

- Reserves are undistributed profits.

- Share premium is the amount above par (nominal) value at which Stokkit issued shares. This surplus has to be held in a share premium account until it is utilised by one of the few purposes permitted by law.

- Fixed asset replacement reserve is profit that is set aside rather than distributed as dividend, for use when fixed assets need to be replaced at prices higher than their initial cost. It is an attempt to account for the effect of inflation and the tendency of machinery costs in many sectors to increase over time as technical complexity increases.

- Profit and loss is the same figure as in Stokkit's profit and loss account (account 3.1).

Like the first profit and loss account (account 3.1), this balance sheet is intended to illustrate the terms you have just encountered, and to show their relationship to each other: it is not in one of the formats prescribed by the Companies Act (1985). The Act allows two versions, only one of which is ordinarily used in the UK. The layout in account 3.6 shows the commonly used format.

	£000	£000
Company name		
Balance sheet as at XXX		
Fixed assets		
Intangible	X	
Tangible	X	
Investments	X	
		X
Current assets		
Stock	X	
Debtors	X	
Cash at bank and in hand	X	
	X	
Creditors: amounts falling due within one year		
Bank loans and overdrafts	X	
Trade creditors	X	
Bills of exchange payable	X	
Other creditors (including taxation, dividends etc.)	X	
	(X)	
Net current assets		X
Total assets less current liabilities		X
Creditors: amounts falling due in more than one year		
Debentures	X	
Loans (long-term)	X	
		(X)
Provisions for liabilities and charges		
Deferred taxation		(X)
		X
Capital and reserves		
Called up share capital		X
Reserves		
Share premium	X	
Revaluation reserve	X	
Other reserves	X	
Profit and loss account	X	
		X
		X

Figures in ( ) indicate deductions.

ACCOUNT 3.6: Standardised format for balance sheet conforming to Companies Act (1985).

'Provisions' means amounts charged against the profit and loss account to meet a known liability of uncertain amount. The actual addition and subtraction processes involved are shown in figure 3.2; you can see that the figures arrived at in the two halves of the balance sheet do match.

1.	Fixed assets
	plus
2.	Current assets
	minus
3.	Creditors: amount falling due in less than a year
	minus
4.	Creditors: amount falling due in more than one year
	minus
5.	Provisions for liabilities
	------------------
	matches

6.	Called up share capital
	plus
7.	Reserves

FIGURE 3.2: The processes shown on a balance sheet.

The balance sheet of Stokkit Ltd can now be rewritten in statutory format, but adapted to suit its circumstances. As with the profit and loss account, if there is no actual item corresponding to a statutory item, it is completely omitted. There are also usually lengthy supporting notes, but we have omitted them from this simple example.

Remember that for internal management purposes, businesses are free to produce a balance sheet in any format, but for published purposes, the law is prescriptive. The labelling, sequence and format is laid down in the Companies Act (1985). The internally useful figures of Stokkit have been re-orientated into a form suitable for publication.

Stokkit Limited
Balance sheets as at 31 December

Year 5			Year 6	
£000	£000		£000	£000
		Fixed assets		
	926	Tangible		1,021
		Current assets		
512		Stock	639	
286		Debtors	370	
41		Cash at bank and in hand	53	
839			1,062	
		Creditors: amounts falling due within one year		
380		Trade creditors	401	
40		Taxation	49	
55		Dividends	70	
47		Other	65	
522			585	
	317	Net current assets		477
		Total assets less		
	1,243	**current liabilities**		1,498
		Creditors: amounts falling due in more than one year		
	(200)	Debentures		(300)
	1,043			1,198
		Capital and reserves		
	800	Called up share capital		800
		Reserves		
70		Share premium	70	
60		Fixed asset replacement	60	
113		Profit and loss	268	
	243			398
	1,043	Shareholders' funds		1,198

ACCOUNT 3.7: Stokkit's balance sheet in a format conforming to Companies Act (1985).

ACTIVITY 8

Working in small groups, compare the original balance sheet shown for Stokkit Ltd (account 3.4) with that produced in line with the statutory format (account 3.7). Make sure that you can see how each of the figures in the latter is derived.

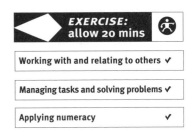

EXERCISE: allow 20 mins

Working with and relating to others ✔

Managing tasks and solving problems ✔

Applying numeracy ✔

Commentary...

It is apparent that these are the same figures as in the original version but differently arranged and, in some cases, differently labelled:

- ● 'current liabilities' are now described as 'creditors: amounts falling due in less than one year';

- ● 'long-term liabilities' are described as 'creditors: amounts falling due in more than one year;

- ● 'shareholders' funds' is a non-statutory label applied to the aggregate of share capital and reserves.

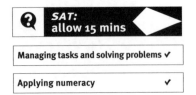

Managing tasks and solving problems ✔

Applying numeracy ✔

ACTIVITY 9

Look again at the Annual Report and Accounts that you used in activity 4. Study the balance sheet and see how it coincides with the format illustrated in this session. Raise any queries with your tutor.

Cash flow statement theory

So far we have looked at two accounting statements:

- the profit and loss account, which is a classified list of revenues and expenses for a period of time

- the balance sheet, which is a classified list of assets and liabilities at a particular point in time.

The third financial statement required to be published in the Annual Report and Accounts is the cash flow statement. Its preparation and publication is a Financial Reporting Standard requirement, a mandatory pronouncement of the accounting profession, the effect of which is the same as if it had statutory force.

A cash flow statement reports actual inflows and outflows of cash and of what are termed cash equivalents, in the time span between two accounting period dates for which balance sheets are available. Cash equivalents include:

- borrowings, including bank overdrafts, which need to be repaid, within three months

- items that can be converted quickly into cash, such as marketable securities (investments) that are within three months of maturity when they are acquired.

The cash flow statement is important because business survival depends on the adequacy of cash resources; it provides valuable management information by reporting on the activities (a) from which the cash has originated, and (b) on which it has been expended, under five classifications:

1. operating activities

2. returns on investments and servicing of finance

3. taxation

4. investing activities

5. financing.

Under each of these heading, we can examine cash flow in more detail looking at inflows (sources from which the cash has originated) and outflows (sources on which cash has been expended).

OPERATING ACTIVITIES

For operating activities, inflows are mainly cash payments received from cash sales and from credit customers, in each case excluding the value added tax (VAT) component; other inflows include patent royalties received, mineral royalties received, copyright royalties received and rent received from sub-letting.

Outflows consist of cash paid to suppliers of goods and services and these, like the inflows, should exclude the VAT component, provided that it is recoverable. If the VAT paid out is not recoverable, it is treated as a cash outflow. Royalties paid for patent and mineral rights and copyright are examples of other outflows.

The net result of these inflows and outflows within the operating activities heading is that they show the net increase or decrease in cash that has resulted during the period from the operations to which the item operating profit in the profit and loss account relates. It is a common mistake to assume that these figures will be the same, but you will remember that not all of these activities have resulted in a cash flow. We saw earlier, for instance, that depreciation is a non-cash expense, so although it is charged as an expense in arriving at operating profit, there has been no corresponding outflow of cash. (The cash outflow occurred when the assets, to which the depreciation relates, were first paid for in cash.) Consequently, the net cash inflow (or outflow) is not identical in amount to operating profit (or loss) but is different by an identifiable amount. This amount appears on the cash flow statement (illustrated later), and 'reconciles' operating profit to net cash inflow from operating activities.

RETURNS ON INVESTMENTS AND SERVICING OF FINANCE

As the name suggests, this heading covers revenues and expenses that arise from the investments and borrowings that the company holds, together with dividend distributions to shareholders.

- Inflows consist of dividends received and interest received.

- Outflows include dividends paid and interest paid. Included also is the interest element of any hire purchase instalments and finance lease rental payments, discussed earlier.

TAXATION

Under this heading are included cash flows in connection with taxation levied on the business, but VAT on sales and purchases is excluded because the business is merely acting as a collector.

- Inflows include tax rebates and overpayments refunded. In the case of unincorporated businesses this relates to refunds of income tax on their taxable profits. For companies the refunds would be of corporation tax on their taxable profits.

- Outflows consist of payments of income tax on the taxable profits of unincorporated businesses and of corporation tax on the taxable profits of companies. Also included are payments of advance corporation tax and purchases of tax deposit certificates (a form of settling taxation liabilities by means of pre-bought certificates).

INVESTING ACTIVITIES

This heading covers flows from the acquisitions or disposal of investments in fixed assets, investments in shares in other businesses and of loans to other businesses, excluding investments classed as cash equivalents.

- Inflows include cash received from the sale or disposal of fixed assets and investments, together with cash received by way of repayment of loans made as investments.

- Outflows include payments to acquire fixed assets and investments and to make loans to other businesses.

FINANCING

There are two criteria for inclusion within this classification. First, that the flows are to or from external providers of finance. Second, that the flows are in respect only of the principal amounts being provided by the provider to the company. The interest element of hire purchase instalments and of finance lease contracts is included within 'returns on investments and servicing of finance'.

- Inflows include amounts received from the issue of shares of all classes and of debentures and other loans.

○ Outflows are payments to buy back or to redeem shares and debentures and to repay borrowings, as are the principal elements of hire purchase instalments and of finance lease rentals.

RECALL:
allow 10 mins

Give an example of an inflow and an outflow for each classification heading. Refer to the descriptions of classifications above to check whether your examples are appropriate.

	Inflows	Outflows
Operating activities		
Returns on investments and servicing of finance		
Taxation		
Investing activities		
Financing		

SAT:
allow 30 mins

Managing tasks and solving problems ✔

Applying numeracy	✔

ACTIVITY 10

Apply the principles you have learned in this session to classify the transactions in the first column of the table below to their correct cash flow classification, using brackets to denote an outflow:

1. **for operating activities**

2. **for returns on investments and servicing of finance**

3. **for taxation**

4. **for investing activities**

5. **for financing.**

	1	2	3	4	5
Dividend received, £120					
Royalty received, £800					
Corporation tax paid, £8,700					
Cash sales, £705, including £105 VAT					
Purchase of new vehicle for cash, £12,800					
Dividend paid, £21,000					
Interest paid, £1,750					
Issue of new shares, £100,000					
Redemption of debentures, £70,000					
Payment of hire purchase instalment, £8,300 including £900 interest					

Commentary...

Your classification should look like this.

	1	2	3	4	5
Dividend received, £120		£120			
Royalty received, £800	£800				
Corporation tax paid, £8,700			(£8,700)		
Cash sales, £705, including £105 VAT	£600				
Purchase of new vehicle for cash, £12,800				(£12,800)	
Dividend paid, £21,000		(£21,000)			
Interest paid, £1,750		(£1,750)			
Issue of new shares, £100,000					£100,000
Redemption of debentures, £70,000					(£70,000)
Payment of hire purchase instalment, £8,300 including £900 interest		(£900)			(£7,400)

Note that:

- outflows are shown in brackets

- that the VAT element should be excluded in the fourth item

- that the final item consists of two parts which are classified separately.

Cash flow statement format

An accounting directive, called Financial Reporting Standard 1, which makes the publication of cash flow statements compulsory, also specifies their content, format, and the nature of the accompanying notes.

There are two ways of showing the cash flows from operating activities. In the version shown in account 3.8, they appear in the cash flow statement in a summarised form (the other categories are covered in detail), and an accompanying note called a 'reconciliation' provides the details.

Company name
Cash flow statement for the year ended
XXXX

	£000	£000
Net cash inflow/(outflow) from operating activities		X or (X)
Returns on investments and servicing of finance		
Interest received	X	
Dividends received	X	
Interest paid	(X)	
Dividends paid	(X)	
Interest element of hire purchase and finance lease contract payments	(X)	
Net cash inflow/(outflow) from returns on investments and servicing of finance		X or (X)
Taxation		
Corporation tax paid	(X)	
Advance corporation tax paid	(X)	
Tax paid		(X)
Investing activities		
Payments to acquire tangible fixed assets	(X)	
Payments to acquire investments (other than cash equivalents) in other entities	(X)	
Receipts from sale of tangible fixed assets	X	
Net cash inflow//(outflow) from investing activities		X or (X)
Net cash inflow/(outflow) before financing		X or (X)
Financing		
Receipts from issue of shares	X	
Receipts from issue of debentures	X	
Payments to purchase/redeem:		
own shares	(X)	
own debentures	(X)	
Principal element of hire purchase and finance lease contract payments	(X)	
Net cash inflow/(outflow) from financing		X or (X)
Net cash increase/(decrease) in cash and cash equivalents		X or (X)

ACCOUNT 3.8: Standard cash flow statement format.

An accompanying note (as in account 3.9) shows how the operating activities have produced the net cash flow. It is called a reconciliation because it reconciles the difference between the profit and the net cash flow.

Reconciliation of operating profit to net cash inflow/(outflow) from operating activities

	£000
Operating profit	X
Depreciation charges	X
(Profit)/loss on disposal of tangible fixed assets	X or (X)
(Increase)/decrease in stocks	X or (X)
(Increase)/decrease in debtors	X or (X)
Increase/(decrease) in creditors	X or (X)
Net cash inflow/(outflow) from operating activities	X or (X)

ACCOUNT 3.9: Reconciliation of operating profit to cash flow statement.

You will note that depreciation is added back because, as explained earlier, although it is charged as an expense, it does not represent a cash outflow.

An alternative version of the statement replaces the single line showing net cash inflow/outflow from operating activities by a whole section disclosing receipts and payments. The reconciliation shown above is not then needed. The appropriate section of this alternative format, which is otherwise the same as that shown previously, is shown in account 3.10.

	£000	£000
Operating activities		
Cash received from customers	X	
Cash payments to suppliers	(X)	
Cash paid to and on behalf of employees	(X)	
Other cash payments	(X)	
Net cash inflow/(outflow) from operating activities		X or (X)

ACCOUNT 3.10: Alternative standard format for cash flow statement.

The cash flow statement of Stokkit Ltd can now be prepared in the stipulated format. Supporting notes are omitted, except for the reconciliation statement which is essential when the first of the alternative versions is employed.

Stokkit Limited
Cash flow statement for the year ended
31 December Year 6

	£000	£000
Net cash inflow from operating activities		187
Returns on investments and servicing of finance		
Interest paid	(27)	
Dividends paid	(55)	
Net cash (outflow) from returns on investments and servicing of finance		(82)
Taxation		
Corporation tax paid	(40)	
Tax paid		(40)
Investing activities		
Payments to acquire tangible fixed assets	(180)	
Receipts from sales of tangible fixed assets [65 – 38]	27	
Net cash (outflow) from investing activities		(153)
Net cash (outflow) before financing		(88)
Financing		
Receipts from issue of debentures [300-200]	100	
Net cash inflow from financing		100
Increase in cash and cash equivalents [53 – 41]		12
Reconciliation of operating profit to net cash inflow from operating activities	£000	£000
Operating profit	301	
Depreciation charges	58	
Increase in stocks [639 – 512]	(127)	
Increase in debtors [370 – 286]	(84)	
Increase in creditors [466 – 427]	39	
Net cash inflow from operating activities		187

ACCOUNT 3.11: Stokkit's cash flow statement.

The figures in the statement have been obtained from the Stokkit profit and loss account (account 3.1) and the balance sheet (account 3.7) presented earlier. In particular, note that:

- the item 'Payments to acquire tangible fixed assets' is the total fixed asset acquisitions in the detailed schedule of fixed assets

- the item 'Receipts from sales of tangible fixed assets' is equal to the net book value (cost minus depreciation) of fixed asset disposals.

In the alternative version of the statement, the single line entry for net cash inflow from operating activities would be replaced by those given in account 3.12 (all figures have been assumed).

	£000	£000
Operating activities		
Cash received from customers	2,830	
Cash paid to suppliers	(1,975)	
Cash paid to and on behalf of employees	(398)	
Other cash payments	(270)	
Net cash inflow from operating activities		187

ACCOUNT 3.12: Alternative presentation of Stokkit's cash flow arising from operating activities.

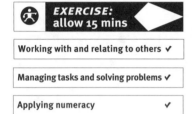

EXERCISE:
allow 15 mins

Working with and relating to others ✔

Managing tasks and solving problems ✔

Applying numeracy   ✔

ACTIVITY 11

Return to the group you worked with in an earlier activity, and look again at the Annual Report and Accounts that you have been examining.

Which of the two alternative ways of showing cash flows from operating activities does it use (i.e. a fully detailed statement, or a summary line plus attached reconciliation note)?

Trace each individual item in the cash flow statement back to the profit and loss account and the balance sheet until you are all completely clear about how the cash flow statement is constructed. The accounts should contain explanatory notes to help you do this; otherwise, consult your tutor.

ACTIVITY 12

ASSIGNMENT:
allow 1 hour

Managing and developing self	✓
Communicating	✓
Applying numeracy	✓
Applying design and creativity	✓

Your assignment is to prepare notes for a presentation on published company accounts. The notes should take the form of 'pages' for a flipchart or overhead projector slides, i.e. you should minimise the amount of text, turn your key statements into 'bullet points', and use graphics (diagrams, etc.) where this will help your potential audience to follow your argument. You can refer to any of the accounts used in this session as examples.

The content of the presentation should cover:

- who is obliged by law to publish financial statements

- what the three financial statements are intended to show.

You should then provide a little more detail on the profit and loss account and balance sheet, covering:

- their principal contents

- how they relate to each other

- the rules for their format and layout.

Prepare your presentation on separate sheets of paper. Jot down the main points you intend to make in the box below.

summary

All businesses are required to keep proper records of their transactions. This session has covered the three financial statements which incorporated businesses must publish.

▶ Companies are legally required to produce an account of the profit or loss they have made during the financial year. This involves matching expense with the revenue which it has generated on an accruals basis: revenue counts on goods sold whether it has actually been received or not, and expense which has been incurred is counted, whether paid or not.

▶ The published accounts must also contain a balance sheet for the last day of the financial year. The balance sheet provides a snapshot, in classified form, of those resources owned and used by a business which have resulted from a financial transaction, and shows the sources from which they have been financed.

▶ The cash flow statement is a non-statutory but mandatory statement (with accompanying notes) that must be published in the Annual Report and Accounts. Its purpose is to disclose the net movement for the period in cash and cash equivalents. It records and reports the cash flows coming into and out of a business under five specific headings: operating activities; returns on investments and servicing of finance; taxation; investing activities; and financing.

Analysis and evaluation

USERS OF ACCOUNTING
INFORMATION

METHODS OF ANALYSIS

PROFITABILITY

SOLVENCY AND LIQUIDITY

CAPITAL GEARING

INVESTMENT RATIOS

CONTROL OF WORKING
CAPITAL

Objectives

After participating in this session, you should be able to:

▶ identify the various parties interested in the financial reports published by a business, and explain their interests

▶ explain the role of ratio analysis and the main techniques for performing it

▶ apply profitability-measuring techniques to actual figures and interpret the results

▶ explain the meaning and significance of capital gearing

▶ calculate the commonly used investment ratios

▶ describe the role of working capital, and the ways in which it can be measured and controlled.

In working through this session, you will practise the following BTEC common skills:

Managing and developing self	✔
Working with and relating to others	✔
Communicating	✔
Managing tasks and solving problems	✔
Applying numeracy	✔
Applying technology	
Applying design and creativity	

Users of accounting information

The main users of any accounting information are the managers at the various levels of the business, from section supervisors to board directors. The particular aspects in which they are interested will differ according to who they are and what work they do.

These individuals have access not only to the published accounting reports (with which we have already dealt), but also to many other internal documents: accounting reports, schedules, statistics and other information.

EXTERNAL USERS

For outside users, the only readily available financial figures are those published in the Annual Report and Accounts; the profit and loss account, the balance sheet and the cash flow statement, plus the notes and written reports that accompany them.

We now examine various external groups and establish the particular aspects of their interest. They include actual and potential creditors, debtors and shareholders, plus:

- employees and their representatives

- local and national government departments

- investment analysts and advisers

- competitors.

Creditors are those who supply goods and services on credit and those who make short-term and long-term loans to the business. Creditors for goods and services expect to be paid for the goods supplied or the services rendered within a few weeks – typically four to six weeks after they have submitted their invoice. Before creditors will supply goods or services they need to be reasonably sure that their customer will be able to pay for them on the due date. This information could be vital, because the financial failure of a business's main customer could result in its own financial collapse if it was owed substantial amounts.

Similar considerations apply in the case of lenders, banks and other short-term and long-term lenders. Lenders need to be assured that the business:

- has the ability to pay interest on the due dates

- will be in a position to repay the principal amount loaned, either in instalments or at the end of a stated length of time.

Debtors also have an interest in the financial affairs of the business. This may seem less obvious, but the failure of a business can have serious consequences for its customers.

Customers suddenly faced with a total stoppage of vital supplies may well have extreme difficulty in obtaining suitable alternative supplies at short notice. Their own operations could be drastically disrupted and even their continued survival jeopardised, so debtors too have an interest in the business.

Shareholders, as investors in the business, are usually interested in:

- whether the business is profitable

- how much of the profit is being paid to shareholders (and how much is being retained or 'ploughed back')

- whether this situation is likely to be maintained or improved in the future.

Taking a longer-term view, shareholders are interested in the underlying growth in the value of their investment.

Employees and their representatives have an interest in the financial affairs of the business for which they work which is centred on job security and their remuneration package. Employees and their representatives use financial information about the business when formulating wage and salary claims. They are also interested in the long-term stability and prospects of the business from the viewpoint of their careers and job security.

Local and national government departments and various government agencies are concerned with business financial matters:

- The Inland Revenue is responsible for assessing and collecting income tax (from unincorporated businesses) and corporation tax from companies.

- HM Customs and Excise collects value added tax (VAT).

- Local authority departments assess and collect business rates.

Investment analysts and advisers will look at the investment potential of companies so that they can advise their clients on whether to buy, sell or retain their holdings. Their sphere of interest is similar to that of shareholders. They also act in an interpretative role when clients are formulating or reviewing their investment strategy.

Competitors, not surprisingly, try to gain as much financial information as possible, about other businesses in their sector.

RECALL:
allow 10 mins

What groups have an interest in the financial reports of businesses? Why?

EXERCISE:
allow 20 mins

Managing and developing self	✔
Working with and relating to others	✔
Managing tasks and solving problems	✔
Applying numeracy	✔

ACTIVITY 1

Move into groups of three or four, so that you can pool your ideas, particularly about presentation.

Imagine that you work in the personnel department of Stokkit Ltd. The manager has asked you to prepare a brochure explaining to employees the financial information contained in the Annual Report and Accounts. Referring to the financial information about Stokkit that was given in session 3, decide:

- **what the purpose/objective of this exercise would be**

- **the nature of the information you would include in the brochure (not the actual figures)**

- **ways of communicating the information effectively to a non-expert audience.**

You should assume that you have access to the figures for each of the years 1 to 5 as well as for Year 6.

Complete this exercise using separate sheets of paper. Summarise the main points of your answer below.

Commentary...

Some companies are reluctant to give financial information to employees. But, since this information is available anyway, it makes sense to issue it in a controlled way rather than leaving staff to discover it piecemeal and perhaps to place incorrect interpretations on it. The objective would therefore be to help staff to gain a better (and positive) understanding of the financial working of the company in which they are 'stakeholders'.

It would be useful to include the following information, provided for each of the years, which highlights growth and progress:

- sales growth
- the uses to which profit after tax was put
- growth in the net assets
- investment in the business.

To communicate the information effectively, you could use various graphic devices:

- bar charts could represent, say, the growth of profit

- pie charts could show market share if this information is available

- the growth of net assets could be represented imaginatively by, say, a growing warehouse building.

Methods of analysis

The analysis and evaluation of financial figures involves calculating the relationships between various items and interpreting the results.

By analysing published results, a user can determine not only whether a business can generate an adequate profit, but also whether it can meet its financial obligations in the long-term as well as in the short-term. The terms used to measure and describe these aspects of business life, and which we will examine next, are:

- profitability

- liquidity

- solvency.

Profitability

The figure of profit before and after tax, obtainable from the profit and loss account, is in itself informative, but its usefulness is greatly increased if a user also knows the value of the resources used to generate it. This relationship is called profitability and is expressed as a percentage.

For example, it would be useful for a business, and those parties interested in the business, to know that it had made a profit of £16,000 in the financial year, but the adequacy of this figure, in terms of the performance of the business, could be judged by its profitability. For example, if this absolute figure of £16,000 represented 10 per cent of the value of the net assets employed (£160,000) it would probably be regarded as good, or at least, satisfactory; but if it worked out at 0.4 per cent – i.e. if the net assets used to generate it were worth £4,000,000 – then the £16,000 profit would be thought of as very poor.

We return to the subject of profitability later in this session.

Liquidity

Liquidity is the ability of a business to pay its bills on the due dates, which means having sufficient cash resources or, alternatively, items which, though not actually cash themselves, can be converted into cash when the need arises.

Solvency

As well as being able to meet its financial obligations in the period immediately ahead, a business must also have sufficient assets to meet external liabilities or, in other words, its financial obligations to parties other than shareholders. This is what is meant by solvency. The opposite situation, an inability to discharge financial obligations, is insolvency. If this applies to individuals, including sole traders and partnerships, they are said to be bankrupt. When a company is in this situation, it is termed insolvent.

Sometimes an insolvent business is put under the control of an administrator and/or a receiver who runs the business and may be able to restore it to a position of solvency. If this fails to happen the business is put into liquidation, its assets are sold, the creditors are paid whatever is available and the business is wound up, i.e. it ceases to exist. Solvency measures are covered later on.

RECALL:
allow 10 mins

Define:

1. profit

2. profitability

3. liquidity

4. solvency

5. insolvency.

RATIO ANALYSIS

It should now be apparent that a number of significant relationships exist between various items within the balance sheet (such as assets and net assets) and within the profit and loss account (such as sales and profit).

There are also relationships between items in different statements. There is, therefore, a relationship between assets (or net assets) and the sales they generate, and another between sales and the profit they produce. This being the case, there must also be a relationship between assets (or net assets) and profits. These relationships are measured numerically by what we term ratio analysis.

Ratio analysis is the calculation of financial relationships. The ratios may be expressed:

- as a 'number of times' (e.g. '12.6 times earnings')

- as a ratio of 1 (e.g. 3:1, or 4.2:1)

- as a percentage.

The three main approaches to ratio analysis are:

- horizontal analysis

- base period analysis

- vertical analysis.

Horizontal analysis

Here the items in each line are compared (year to year) and the difference is expressed as a percentage change. Table 4.1 is an example from Stokkit's profit and loss account, which uses actual figures for Year 6 and assumes them for Year 5.

	Year 5	Year 6	Difference	Change
	£000	£000	£000	
Sales	2,100	2,898	+798	+ 38.0%
Gross profit	876	1,017	+141	+ 16.1%
Net profit before tax	245	274	+29	+ 11.8%

TABLE 4.1: Horizontal analysis – growth in sales, gross and net profit at Stokkit.

ACTIVITY 2

What questions do you think shareholders and analysts might want to ask about these results, and matters relating to them?

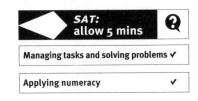

Commentary...

The most obvious question is why the handsome 38 per cent increase in sales was only partly reflected in gross and net profit. Related questions include: Can the company continue to expand sales at this rate? Does it have the capacity to do so without a major increase in investment (for more warehouse space, delivery vehicles, systems, etc.)? Investors may be concerned that the sales increase has been exceptional (perhaps achieved by fierce discounting, which competitors will soon match, and which thus cannot be repeated in future years). Alternatively, they may feel that costs have not been adequately controlled, and that this is a sign of weak management.

Base period analysis

Base period analysis is similar to the horizontal analysis in that it is also carried out on a line by line basis; this time a base period is selected and then each item in it is given a base of 100. Figures for subsequent years are expressed in relation to the base. Table 4.2 uses the previous figures for Stokkit and assumes that the base year was Year 1.

	Year 1		Year 5		Year 6	
	£000	Base	£000	Index	£000	Index
Sales	934	100	2,100	225	2,898	310
Gross profit	211	100	876	415	1,017	482
Net profit	53	100	245	462	274	517

TABLE 4.2: Base period analysis – growth in sales, gross and net profit at Stokkit.

By comparing Year 6 with the base year a user can see that sales have trebled, gross profit is almost five times greater and net profit just over five times greater. This puts the results of horizontal analysis in a slightly different light, in that gross profit and net profit look healthier in comparison with Year 1. This shows why it pays to use several methods of ratio analysis.

Vertical analysis

In vertical analysis, one figure within the statement is used as a base figure and the other items are shown as a percentage of this base. Table 4.3 is presented using the sales figure in each year as the base for that year.

	Year 5		Year 6	
	£000	%	£000	%
Sales	2,100	100.0	2,898	100.0
Gross profit	876	41.7	1,017	35.1
Net profit	245	11.7	274	9.5

TABLE 4.3: Vertical analysis – Stokkit's gross and net profit as a percentage of sales.

These results express, in a different way, what we discovered using horizontal analysis, i.e. gross and net profits have both deteriorated by comparison with Year 5.

RATIO COMPARISON

As you have now seen, ratio comparisons are of limited value when used in isolation, but when different methods are combined and compared with base period and previous period figures, they can provide useful information.

There are two further areas in which ratio comparison is useful:

1. Comparison of actual figures with forecast or with target (budgeted) figures can be made, so that divergences from

estimates and plans can be identified and corrective action taken to remedy any unsatisfactory performances revealed.

2. Comparisons can be made with the published results of competing businesses, for which figures can be obtained through Trade Association sources.

RECALL:
allow 10 mins

What are the three ways in which a ratio can be expressed?

Briefly explain the following analysis methods:

1. **horizontal analysis**

2. **base period analysis**

3. **vertical analysis.**

ACTIVITY 3

Suppose that Stokkit has offered the business for which you work a regular monthly contract for the supply of goods. You have no previous experience of trading with Stokkit. Write a short memo to your purchasing manager, outlining the nature of the investigations that should be made into Stokkit's financial position, based on information that is obtainable from its published accounts.

Your answer should be in proper memo form and contain the names and titles of the sender and the recipient. The subject matter should be clearly stated and there should be a short introduction, followed by the advice and ending with a proper conclusion.

Draft out the memo on a separate sheet of paper, and summarise the key points here.

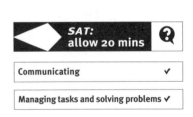

SAT:
allow 20 mins

Communicating	✓

Managing tasks and solving problems ✓

Commentary...

The advice should centre on investigating the short-term liquidity and long-term solvency of Stokkit Limited. The key points are made in the memorandum shown in figure 4.1.

Memorandum

From: Mark   To: Heather
Date: 5/7/95

Subject: **Financial investigation re. contract to supply Stokkit.**

You have asked me to outline the nature of the investigation we ought to make about Stokkit's financial standing, before proceeding with the supply contract.

1 We need to be confident about Stokkit's liquidity, that is, that invoices will be paid, and done so in a timely manner.

This means reassuring ourselves about the amount of cash and near-cash shown in the financial statements, and the level of immediate outgoings (short-term liabilities) to which Stokkit is committed.

2 We also need to look at its long-term prospects for survival, in other words, is Stokkit solvent? We will need to look at Stokkit's loans and borrowings, the size of its assets and at its ability to discharge its financial obligations.

We can ourselves investigate Stokkit's financial position based on:

● *its current and previous Annual Report and Accounts*
● *its competitors.*

We can also request bank and trade credit references. If we are satisfied on all counts, then we can proceed. If there are any questions or doubts, we will need to seek and obtain reassurance on these issues before signing contracts.

FIGURE 4.1: Memorandum on Stokkit's financial position.

Profitability

Profitability means relating profit to the resources employed in earning it. We now look at the calculations which enable us to do this. Unfortunately, there is no general agreement on which profit figure should be used or what should constitute the resources to which the profit is to be related.

Profit can mean:

- net profit before tax
- net profit before interest and tax
- operating profit
- net profit after tax.

Resources, i.e. capital employed, can be interpreted as:

- total assets
- net assets employed (total assets less current liabilities)
- including or excluding intangible assets in either case.

For the purpose of these profitability measures, we shall assume that:

- profit means profit before interest and tax
- capital employed means total assets less current liabilities (which is the same figure as the aggregate of shareholders' funds and creditors falling due within one year).

This is a valid basis because the profit can be directly related to the capital employed in generating it. We now consider four commonly used profitability ratios:

- gross profit ratio
- net profit ratio
- asset utilisation ratio
- return on capital employed.

In the examples that follow, the figures relate to Stokkit Limited and are to be found in the accounts we have used previously.

GROSS PROFIT RATIO

Formula:

$$\frac{\text{Gross Profit} \times 100}{\text{Sales}} = \text{Gross profit \%}$$

Stokkit Year 5:

$$\frac{876 \times 100}{2,100} = 41.7\,\%$$

Stokkit Year 6:

$$\frac{1,017 \times 100}{2,898} = 35.1\%$$

This deterioration in Stokkit's gross profit ratio could be due to several individual or combined factors. One explanation could be that buying-in prices have gone up during Year 6, and that these have been absorbed by Stokkit rather than passed on to customers in selling prices.

Another is that Stokkit sells a very wide range of goods, with a correspondingly large difference in profit margins and that, in Year 6, its sales mix altered so that it sold proportionally less of the goods that carry higher profit margins.

NET PROFIT RATIO

Formula:

$$\frac{\text{Net profit before interest and tax} \times 100}{\text{Sales}} = \text{Net profit \%}$$

Stokkit Year 5:

$$\frac{263 \times 100}{2,100} = 12.5\%$$

Stokkit Year 6:

$$\frac{301 \times 100}{2,898} = 10.4\%$$

The fall from 12.5 per cent in Year 5 to 10.4 per cent in Year 6 reflects the deterioration in gross profit between the two years and changes in the level of expenses. We would be able to pin-point specific expenses by applying vertical analysis to the detailed profit and loss accounts used for internal management purposes for both Year 5 and 6, always assuming that they are available.

Stokkit Limited
Profit and loss accounts (for internal use only)
for the years ended 31 December

	Year 5		Year 6	
	£000	%	£000	%
Turnover	2,100	100.0	2,898	100.0
Cost of sales	1,224	58.3	1,881	_____
Gross profit	876	41.7	1,017	
Rent received	_____	_____	16	_____
	876	41.7	1,033	
	---------	---------	---------	-------
Less				
Wages and salaries	318	15.2	406	
Power, heat and light	76	3.6	79	
Postage and telephones	43	2.0	47	
Vehicle running expenses	39	1.9	44	
Audit and accountancy fees	11	0.5	11	
Stationery	26	1.2	29	
Debenture interest		excluded		excluded
Business rates	46	2.2	53	
Depreciation	50	2.4	58	
Sundry expenses	4	0.2	5	_____
	613	29.2	732	_____
Net profit before interest and tax	263	12.5	301	_____

ACCOUNT 4.1: Stokkit's internal profit and loss account, Year 6.

ACTIVITY 4

Account 4.1 shows the internal profit and loss account figures used by Stokkit in Year 6, and the corresponding figures for Year 5, which have been assumed. ('Internal' implies that these are not in the appropriate form for statutory purposes.)

Perform a vertical analysis, by working out the Year 6 figures as percentages of turnover (£2,898,000), and insert the results in the blank slots in the right-hand column.

Compare the ratios you have calculated for Year 6 with those for Year 5. What comments would you make in the light of the questions that we said shareholders and analysts might ask (see activity 2 above)?

SAT:
allow 15 mins

Communicating ✔

Managing tasks and solving problems ✔

Applying numeracy ✔

Commentary...

Your figures should show that net profit before interest and tax as a percentage of turnover has deteriorated from 12.5 per cent in Year 5 to 10.4 per cent in Year 6 (a fall of 2.1 per cent), that this is due to the previously noted reduction of 6.6 per cent in gross profit, and that this in turn has been substantially offset by a reduction of 4.0 per cent in total non-trading expenses. This does not suggest weak management, because indirect costs have actually been reduced. However, there is a problem of some kind with cost of sales (up from 58.3 per cent to 64.9 per cent) or total sales themselves.

ASSET UTILISATION RATIO

Formula:

$$\frac{\text{Sales}}{\text{Capital employed}} = \text{Net assets employed ratio}$$

Stokkit Year 5:

$$\frac{2,100}{1,243} = 1.7$$

Stokkit Year 6:

$$\frac{2,898}{1,498} = 1.9$$

The calculations show that Stokkit utilised its net assets more effectively in Year 6 than in Year 5. An alternative way of expressing the results of the calculation is to say that the net assets employed generated sales 1.9 times and 1.7 times greater than their own value or that each £1 of net assets produced £1.90 and £1.70 worth of sales, respectively, showing the improvement in utilisation between the two years.

RETURN ON CAPITAL EMPLOYED (RoCE)

Formula:

$$\frac{\text{Net profit before interest and tax} \times 100}{\text{Capital employed}} \quad = \quad \text{RoCE } \%$$

Stokkit Year 5

$$\frac{263 \times 100}{1{,}243} \quad = \quad 21.1\%$$

Stokkit Year 6

$$\frac{301 \times 100}{1{,}498} \quad = \quad 20.1\%$$

This ratio indicates overall profitability. In Stokkit's case it has dropped from 21.1 per cent to 20.1 per cent between two years. Although Stokkit has improved its assets utilisation from 1.7 to 1.9, this advantage has been completely eradicated by the fall from 12.5 per cent to 10.4 per cent in the net profit before interest and tax ratio.

RECALL: allow 10 mins

Write down the formulae for calculating:

- **gross profit ratio**

- **net profit ratio**

- **asset utilisation ratio**

- **return on capital employed (RoCE).**

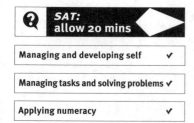

SAT:
allow 20 mins

Managing and developing self	✓
Managing tasks and solving problems	✓
Applying numeracy	✓

ACTIVITY 5

Turn again to the Annual Report and Accounts that you used in session 3.

Calculate the four profitability ratios which you have learned in this session (if the report provides figures for two consecutive years, make the calculations for both of them).

If two sets of figures are available, compare them and suggest possible reasons for differences between the two years' sets of calculations. If only the current year's figures are given, consider how the ratios compare with other examples that we have considered in this module.

Solvency and liquidity

A business is solvent if its assets are sufficient to meet external liabilities, i.e. those financial obligations to parties other than shareholders. It is therefore a simple matter to compare a company's external liabilities with the amount of assets out of which they can be met. By calculating total fixed and current assets less total (long-term and short-term) external liabilities, we can see if a business has a surplus or deficit.

A surplus shows that the business is solvent, while a deficit shows that it is insolvent – a situation that may arise if the company has sustained a series of substantial losses. In account 4.2, we apply this test to the figures for Stokkit for Years 5 and 6, obtained from Session 3.

	Year 5 £000	Year 6 £000
Assets		
fixed	926	1,021
current	839	1,062
total	1,765	2,083
External Liabilities		
Creditors		
due in less than 1 year	522	585
due in more than 1 year	200	300
total	722	885
Surplus/(deficit)	1,043	1,198

ACCOUNT 4.2: Assessing Stokkit's solvency.

You can see that Stokkit is solvent, as evidenced by the surplus figures for both years. These figures are identical with the total of shareholders' funds. Long-term solvency can be estimated by projecting the asset and external liability figures ahead on a year by year basis for, say, fifteen years.

Liquidity, in the context of financial analysis, means the availability of cash and near-cash items for settling short-term liabilities. There are two recognised ratios which indicate liquidity:

- current ratio

- liquidity ratio.

CURRENT RATIO

Formula:

$$\frac{\text{Current assets}}{\text{Current liabilities}} = \text{Current ratio}$$

The result is expressed as a ratio, such as 2:1 or 2.6:1 (this is expressed as 'two-to-one', or 'two-point-six-to-one'). In effect, the figure for current liabilities is used as a base of 1, with current assets being expressed as a proportion of it.

The calculation for Stokkit in Year 5, using account 3.7, is:

$$\frac{839}{522} = 1.6$$

This would be expressed as 1.6:1

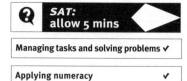

SAT:
allow 5 mins

Managing tasks and solving problems ✔

Applying numeracy   ✔

ACTIVITY 6

Use the Stokkit balance sheet for Year 6 (account 3.7 in Session 3) to work out its current ratio.

Commentary...

Stokkit in Year 6 has current assets of £1.062 million and current liabilities of £0.585 million. The ratio is therefore:

$$\frac{1,062}{585} = 1.8 \text{ (or 1.8:1)}$$

The figures show that the cover for current liabilities has improved slightly in Year 6 but the calculation must be viewed with caution, because the figures used are those at the end of the financial year, and these will not necessarily reflect a typical picture of the company through the year as a whole.

The individual items that make up current assets and current liabilities can fluctuate drastically on a day-to-day basis. Any changes affecting either the numerator (the top figure) or the denominator (the bottom one), or both, will be reflected in the current ratio. No norm can be given for this ratio but as a matter of logic it should never be lower than 1:1. On the other hand too high a ratio is not healthy either, indicating that the company may not be making profitable use of its working capital. Probably the best criterion is to judge it against other businesses in the same sector.

ACTIVITY 7

Current assets, which form part of the current ratio, include cash in the bank, stocks and debtors. A high current ratio means that one or more of these must be undesirably high. Give three reasons why a high current ratio may indicate inefficiency in the business.

Commentary...

Reasons include the following:

- If it is caused by having too much cash at the bank, could that cash be working harder elsewhere?

- If it is caused by stocks of goods being too high, this may point to sluggish sales, and/or to increased indirect costs in the future (more space needed to stock the goods, more deterioration).

- If the cause is a high debtors figure, this suggests that the company's customers are slow-paying and that the credit department is inefficient.

A really efficient business may well operate with a fairly low current ratio, reflecting slick stock operations, effective cash flow forecasting and efficient credit control.

LIQUIDITY RATIO

Also known as the acid test ratio and the quick assets ratio, this is a refined version of the current ratio, which recognises that not all current assets can be converted into cash at short notice to meet creditors' claims. Stock, for example, has to be sold before conversion into cash and, even then, there can be a sizeable time lag if, as is usual, it is sold on credit. For this reason, stock is excluded from the numerator which then contains only the so-called quick assets:

- debtors

- bills of exchange receivable

- marketable securities

- cash

- bank current account and deposit account balances.

Formula:

$$\frac{\text{Quick assets}}{\text{Current liabilities}} = \text{Liquidity ratio}$$

Like the current ratio, this calculation is expressed as a ratio of 1, so the liquidity ratio for Stokkit in Year 5 is:

$$\frac{(286 + 41)}{522} = 0.6 \text{ (i.e. 0.6:1)}$$

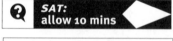

SAT:
allow 10 mins

| Managing tasks and solving problems | ✔ |
| Applying numeracy | ✔ |

ACTIVITY 8

Now calculate the current ratio for Stokkit in Year 6, using the figures in the balance sheet (account 3.4 in Session 3).

What conclusions can you draw from this result?

Commentary...

As with the current ratio, there has been a marginal improvement during Year 6 but again, the figures are those at the financial year end and do not reflect the day-to-day situation.

Stokkit Year 6:

$$\frac{(370 + 53)}{585} = 0.7$$

On the face of it, with a ratio of 07:1, Stokkit looks to be in some trouble. If the ratio is correct it does not have sufficient cash funds to pay its creditors, though this situation would only arise if all the creditors required full payment instantly. Fortunately for Stokkit, this is unlikely to occur; though if creditors believed that Stokkit was at risk of failure it could happen. Also, among its creditors are the items taxation and dividends. The former is not due to be paid until nine months after the year end for which the ratio has been calculated and the latter about five months after that same year-end. In fact, many businesses can and do survive on a liquidity ratio of less than 1:1. This is particularly evident in retailing, where goods are bought on credit but sold to customers for cash.

RECALL:
allow 10 mins

1. What is the distinction between solvency and liquidity?

2. What are the formulae for calculating:

   (a) current ratio

   (b) liquidity ratio

3. What does a rising asset utilisation ratio indicate?

4. What does a falling current ratio indicate?

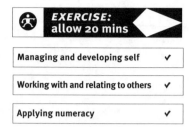

Managing and developing self	✓
Working with and relating to others	✓
Applying numeracy	✓

ACTIVITY 9

Move into groups of three or four. You will once more need one of the Annual Reports and Accounts that you have used before, and a calculator.

Imagine that you are an analyst working for the bankers of the business concerned. The company has approached you for a substantial loan, and you want to assess the risk involved.

1. Study the Profit and Loss account and Balance Sheet and note down any relevant facts.

2. Calculate any ratios that will help you judge profitability, management efficiency, solvency and liquidity.

Note down your main findings in the box below.

Commentary...

You should have been able to find enough information to calculate all the ratios that we have examined in this session so far. It is a legal requirement for all companies to publish corresponding figures for the previous year so you should work out ratios for both years and compare them. However, a comparison of two years' figures can be misleading. Some companies voluntarily publish figures for the last 5, or even 10, years and with this extra information it is far easier to draw realistic conclusions.

RoCE, gross profit ratio and the current ratio can be of significance in themselves, even when there is no direct comparison to be made. The asset utilisation ratio can be used as a general measure of management efficiency, as can any of the profitability ratios when a comparison is available.

Capital gearing

Gearing is the relationship, usually expressed as a percentage, between externally provided long-term funds and the total funds by which a company is financed. It is sometimes known by an alternative label, leverage. There are no hard and fast rules, but a gearing in excess of about 40 per cent would be regarded as high and below 40 per cent would be regarded as low.

The theory is that a certain amount of external finance from fixed interest borrowings is beneficial for a company, so long as the funds can earn a return greater than the rate of interest which has to be paid on them. There comes a point in every company at which this advantage is neutralised.

Too high a gearing brings various problems in its wake:

- the higher the borrowings, the greater will be the amount of interest needed to service them and the profit available for distribution to shareholders will be correspondingly less

- at a later stage, when the loans mature, a greater amount of money will be needed to repay them.

CALCULATING GEARING

We encounter the same sort of difficulty at this point as we did earlier when we were measuring profitability – the problem of definition. The term 'borrowings' embraces those funds that bear a fixed interest rate. As you would expect, this includes all long-term borrowings, including pure loans, debentures and convertible loan stock (a type of debenture which can be switched into ordinary share capital), but it also includes preference share capital on the grounds that the dividend payable on it is a fixed, pre-determined, amount. Short-term borrowings – bank overdrafts and loans – are not included in the gearing calculation.

Formula:

$$\frac{\text{Long- term borrowings plus preference share capital} \times 100}{\text{Shareholder's funds plus long term borrowings}} = \text{Gearing \%}$$

Using acount 3.7, Session 3, Stokkit Year 5:

$$\frac{200 \times 100}{1,243} = 16.1\,\%$$

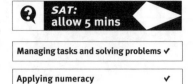

Managing tasks and solving problems ✔

Applying numeracy ✔

ACTIVITY 10

Work out Stokkit's gearing percentage for Year 6, using the figures available in the published accounts referred to previously (account 3.7, Session 3).

Suggest an explanation for any change in gearing that you identify.

Commentary...

Stokkit's gearing increased during Year 6, because of the issue of a further £100,000 9 per cent debentures, but it is still low. The calculation is:

$$\frac{300 \times 100}{1,498} = 20.0\,\%$$

EFFECTS OF GEARING ON DISTRIBUTABLE PROFITS

Gearing can have a significant effect on the amount of profits available for distribution to shareholders. This can be illustrated by comparing the effects within two companies, one with a low gearing, the other with a high gearing, under conditions of changing profit levels.

	Aye Ltd	Gearing	Bee Ltd	Gearing
	£000	%	£000	%
Creditors: amounts falling due in more than one year				
8% debentures	500	10	3,000	60
Share capital and reserves				
Ordinary share capital (£1 shares)	3,000		1,000	
Reserves	1,500		1,000	
Shareholders' funds	4,500	90	2,000	40
Total finance	5,000	100	5,000	100

ACCOUNT 4.3: Capital structure of Aye Ltd and Bee Ltd.

Account 4.3 shows the capital structure of two of Stokkit's customers, Aye Ltd and Bee Ltd. It is apparent that both companies have an identical amount of total finance but that Aye Ltd is a low geared company (10 per cent) and Bee Ltd a high geared company (60 per cent).

We can calculate the percentage of distributable profit in relation to ordinary share capital at two different profit levels: £600,000 in the first instance, before interest and tax; and £1,200,000 in the second. Account 4.4 shows the outcome: work through the figures carefully.

	Aye Ltd		Bee Ltd	
	£000	£000	£000	£000
Profit before interest and tax	600	1,200	600	1,200
less				
8% debenture interest	40	40	240	240
Profit before tax	560	1,160	360	960
less				
Corporation tax (25%)	140	290	90	240
Profit after tax	420	870	270	720
Return on ordinary share capital %	$\frac{420\times100}{3,000}$	$\frac{870\times100}{3,000}$	$\frac{270\times100}{1,000}$	$\frac{720\times100}{1,000}$
	14%	29%	27%	72%

ACCOUNT 4.4: Calculating the return on ordinary share capital at Aye Ltd and Bee Ltd.

In Aye Ltd, with 10 per cent gearing, the return to shareholders has approximately doubled in line with the doubling of the profit before interest and tax. By contrast, under the same circumstances, the return in Bee Ltd has increased almost three times. The converse is also true: when profits are falling Aye Ltd's return would be halved if profits before interest and tax were halved; while Bee Ltd's return would be only about one-third of what it was previously.

The conclusion that can be drawn is that the return on equity in a high-geared company is more volatile than in a low-geared company. With low gearing, return on equity moves more or less in line with profits before interest and tax.

INTEREST COVER

Closely associated with gearing is the calculation of interest cover. The higher the gearing the greater will be the amount of cash committed to the payment of fixed interest. It is important that a company earns sufficient profits to absorb the fixed interest charges. The interest cover calculation indicates the extent to which a company is able to achieve this.

Formula:

$$\frac{\text{Profit before interest and tax}}{\text{Fixed interest}} = \text{Interest cover}$$

In Year 5, Stokkit must pay fixed interest on its £200,000 9 per cent debentures. This amounts to £18,000 in a full year. In table 4.1, we can see that Stokkit's net profit before tax is £245,000 in Year 5. So, its net profit before tax and interest is £263,000. So the fixed interest cover for Stokkit in Year 5 is:

$$\frac{263}{18} = 14.6$$

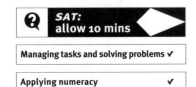

SAT:
allow 10 mins

Managing tasks and solving problems ✔

Applying numeracy   ✔

ACTIVITY 11

Work out Stokkit's fixed interest cover for Year 6, using the profit and loss account and balance sheets as sources of information (accounts 3.3 and 3.4) and comment on any change you find.

Commentary...

Stokkit Year 6:

$$\frac{301}{27} = 11.1$$

Stokkit's interest cover is reduced because, by Year 6, more debentures have been issued, but it is still more than adequate.

If, however, we look at Aye Ltd and Bee Ltd from the previous example, we get 15 times (600,000/40,000) and 2.5 times (600,000/240,000), respectively, which illustrates the 'strain' that high gearing can impose on the performance requirements of a business.

RECALL:
allow 10 mins

Make brief notes explaining:

(a) capital gearing

(b) interest cover.

Write down the formulae used to calculate:

(a) gearing

(b) interest cover.

SAT:
allow 15 mins

Managing tasks and solving problems ✔

ACTIVITY 12

If you are planning to invest in a particular public company you might find that you could buy either ordinary shares or debentures or some of each.

Write 100 words summarising the extent to which you might be influenced in your choice by the capital structure of the company and why this would be so. Summarise your key points below.

Commentary...

You should be interested in whether the company is high-geared or low-geared. This would affect the potential returns on the ordinary shares: high gearing increases the volatility of the returns, while low gearing lends itself to more predictable returns. Calculating the interest cover would indicate the ability of the company to meet its fixed interest commitments and the likely effect of changes in profit levels on the amount of distributable profit available. You would then have to decide what would be an acceptable level of risk and whether you would be likely to receive a higher return from the shares.

Investment ratios

We have already identified investment analysts, advisers, and actual and potential investors as being some of the users of published accounting information. They all have access to the three major accounting statements contained in the Annual Report and Accounts. From these they can calculate the ratios for profitability, solvency, liquidity and gearing.

Several other ratios are of interest to these particular users. The main ones are:

- earnings per share (EPS)

- dividend cover

- dividend yield

- price earnings ratio (P/E).

EARNINGS PER SHARE (EPS)

Earnings means profit attributable to ordinary shares, i.e. profit available after tax and after preference dividends.

Formula:

$$\frac{\text{Earnings} \times 100}{\text{Number of ordinary shares}} = \text{Earnings per share (in pence)}$$

Stokkit Year 5:

$$\frac{205 \times 100}{800} = 25.6 \text{ pence per share}$$

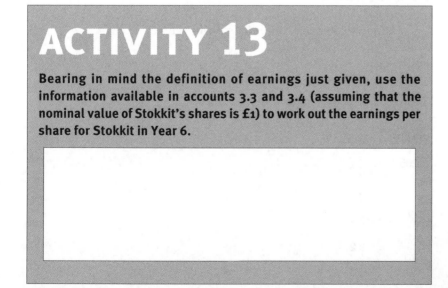

ACTIVITY 13

Bearing in mind the definition of earnings just given, use the information available in accounts 3.3 and 3.4 (assuming that the nominal value of Stokkit's shares is £1) to work out the earnings per share for Stokkit in Year 6.

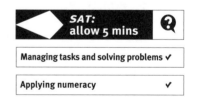

SAT: allow 5 mins

Managing tasks and solving problems ✔

Applying numeracy   ✔

Commentary...

Stokkit increases its earnings per share in Year 6. The calculation for Year 6 is:

$$\frac{225 \times 100}{800} = 28.1 \text{ pence per share}$$

There are two Financial Reporting Standard requirements in relation to earnings per share (EPS) of which you should be aware:

1. All companies must include the earnings per share figure as a note to the published profit and loss account.

2. EPS is always expressed in pence, and never in pounds sterling.

The real importance of EPS is that it is a component of the price earnings ratio, which we consider below.

DIVIDEND COVER

This ratio indicates the company's profit retention policy.

Formula:

$$\frac{\text{Profit after tax attributable to ordinary shares}}{\text{Ordinary share dividend (paid and proposed)}} = \text{Dividend cover}$$

Stokkit Year 5:

$$\frac{205}{55} = 3.7$$

Stokkit Year 6

$$\frac{225}{70} = 3.2$$

In Year 6, cover has fallen compared with the previous year, but is still adequate. A dividend cover of 3.2 is the same as saying that about one-third of the available profit has been set aside for distribution as dividend and two-thirds has been retained. This is a higher proportion than in Year 5, when only about a quarter of available profit was distributed as shares.

DIVIDEND YIELD

The dividend yield expresses the share dividend, not in relation to the nominal value of a share, but to its market price.

Formula:

$$\frac{\text{Dividend per share} \times 100}{\text{Market price for share}} = \text{Dividend yield \%}$$

It is not possible to calculate this figure for Stokkit Ltd because, as a private limited company, Stokkit is prohibited from selling its shares to the public, and therefore no 'open market price' exists.

Look instead at Pefgo Flooring plc, a large company which does a small amount of business with Stokkit. It has an ordinary share capital of 20,000,000 ordinary shares of a nominal value of 100 pence per share, currently listed on the Stock Exchange at 224 pence per share. Pefgo has declared a dividend of £1,800,000, which is equivalent to 9 pence per share (i.e. £1,800,000/20,000,000).

On the basis of the nominal value, the return on the ordinary shares would be:

$$\frac{\text{Dividend per share} \times 100}{\text{Nominal value per share}} = \text{Return per share \%}$$

In Pefgo's case, that is:

$$\frac{9 \times 100}{100 \text{ pence}} = 9.0 \%$$

However, the yield, being related to what it would cost to buy shares on the Stock Exchange, would be calculated by the yield formula as shown:

$$\frac{9 \times 100}{224} = 4.0 \%$$

This represents the return on the outlay needed to acquire the shares at the current price. The dividend is 9 pence per share, but the shares cost 224 pence each to buy.

PRICE EARNINGS RATIO (P/E)

The price earnings ratio is a multiple of earnings that reflects the expectations of the stock market. Viewed from a different perspective, it is the number of years required to recover the market price of the investment out of earnings. The higher the figure, the greater the confidence of the stock market. In relation to an individual company, whether the price earnings ratio is good or bad is a question of comparison with the corresponding ratios of other companies in the same sector.

Formula:

$$\frac{\text{Market price per share}}{\text{Earnings per share}} = \text{Price earnings ratio}$$

Again, there can be no price earnings ratio for Stokkit because there is no market price. Suppose, however, that the earnings per share figure for Pefgo is 26 pence and the market price 224 pence per share, the price earnings ratio would be:

$$\frac{224}{26} = 8.6$$

PUBLISHED FINANCIAL INFORMATION

Certain newspapers, principally the Financial Times, the Daily Telegraph and The Times, publish Stock Exchange data on a daily basis. Figure 4.2 shows how the financial information on Pefgo would be presented.

Year XX		Company	Price		Yield	P/E
High	Low		(P)	+/-	%	
301	192	Pefgo	224	+7	11	9

FIGURE 4.2: Financial information on Pefgo published in the business press.

The figures are rounded to the nearest whole number. The columns have the following meanings:

High/Low

These are, respectively the highest and lowest prices of Pefgo shares (in pence) in the year.

Price (p)

This gives the current middle market price at the close of the previous day's trading (in pence).

+/-

This shows the increase (+) or decrease (-) of the current price compared with the previous day's opening price (which must have been 217 pence).

Yield per cent

This is the dividend yield on a pre-tax basis (which is equivalent to the 9 per cent we calculated under dividend yield on a post-tax basis)

P/E

This is the price earnings ratio that we have calculated.

Shares have two prices at any one time, the offer price at which they can be bought and the bid price at which they can be sold. The average of the two prices is called the middle market price. Once a week, the financial newspapers disclose what is called market capitalisation. This is simply the value of the shares at the then middle market price at close of business on the last trading day of the previous week. If, in the case of Pefgo, this was 230 pence per share, market capitalisation would be £46,000,000 (20,000,000 shares at 230 pence per share).

RECALL:
allow 10 mins

Write down the formulae for calculating the following and explain what each is intended to show:

1. **earnings per share**

2. **dividend cover**

3. **dividend yield**

4. **price earnings ratio.**

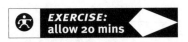

EXERCISE:
allow 20 mins

Working with and relating to others ✔

Managing tasks and solving problems ✔

ACTIVITY 14

In a group with two or three others, look at the financial columns of one of the newspapers cited earlier. You will find that listed shares are grouped by category – business services, chemicals, electricals, etc. Pick out the companies that are well known to you by name and discuss the extent to which the dividend yield and price earnings ratios of these companies are similar, or dissimilar, to others in the same category. Discuss reasons for the differences and note your key findings here.

Control of working capital

Working capital (or net current assets) is the term we apply to the excess of current assets over current liabilities.

All businesses need a certain amount of working capital to enable them to carry out their day-to-day operations. The actual amount needed will vary according to the nature of the business and the scale of operations. In a merchandising company like Stokkit, working capital will consist of:

- a stock of goods in sufficient quantity and range to meet customers' requirements

- debtor balances

- actual cash and bank account balances

less

- the amount of credit allowed by suppliers of goods for resale.

The amount of working capital needs to be controlled. If it is too little, the business can miss out on selling opportunities. For example, if stock is low then customers, unable to obtain the range and/or quantities of goods they require, may find alternative sources of supply.

There are also dangers in having too much working capital.

○ Excessive stocks are costly to store and are at risk from damage, deterioration and pilferage.

○ If debts are not collected by the end of the agreed period of credit, the risk that they may become bad debts increases.

○ Cash balance and bank current account balances in excess of requirements are a waste as they are not profitably employed.

Working capital is an important element in the analysis of financial information. There is a link with liquidity because individual items within working capital are components of the formulae for calculating the current ratio and liquidity ratio that we examined earlier. It is also a component of capital employed, of profitability, and of the asset utilisation ratio.

Some of the individual items within working capital can be measured as a preliminary to control, by a series of ratios:

○ stock turnover ratio

○ debtors' collection period

○ creditors' payment period

○ operating cash cycle.

STOCK TURNOVER RATIO

Formula:

$$\frac{\text{Trading stock} \times 365}{\text{Cost of sales}} = \text{Number of days' supply in stock}$$

The figures that follow are taken from one of Stokkit's unpublished balance sheets (accounts 3.1, 3.4 and 4.1).

Stokkit Year 5:

$$\frac{477 \times 365}{1,224} = 142.2 \text{ days}$$

Stokkit Year 6:

$$\frac{592 \times 365}{1,881} = 114.29 \text{ days}$$

In the above calculations, stock has been taken to mean closing stock. Although Stokkit's closing stock at the end of Year 6 has increased by £115,000 from the Year 5 figure of £477,000 it represents a smaller number of days' sales at cost because of the increased volume of sales in Year 6.

Alternative bases for stocks are average stocks, i.e. opening stock plus closing stock divided by two, or weighted average stock. If there are marked seasonal fluctuations in the volume and value of stock held, the use of closing stock or simple average stock may not give a meaningful figure. In that case, it would be appropriate to use weighted average stock, arrived at by adding up the totals of closing stock at the end of each month, and dividing the resultant aggregate by twelve.

In Section 2, Managing Information, we return to the subject of calculating the stock turnover ratio.

DEBTORS' COLLECTION PERIOD

Formula:

$$\frac{\text{Trade debtors} \times 365}{\text{Credit sales}} = \text{Period of credit taken by customers}$$

Using accounts 3.4 and 3.7, Stokkit Year 5:

$$\frac{286 \times 365}{2,100} = 49.7 \text{ days}$$

Again, the debtors' figure could be closing debtors or simple average or weighted average debtors.

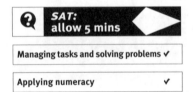

SAT:
allow 5 mins

Managing tasks and solving problems ✔

Applying numeracy ✔

ACTIVITY 15

Using figures from accounts 3.4 and 3.7 (Stokkit's profit and loss account and balance sheet), work out the debtors' collection period for Year 6, and comment on what the change in figures signifies.

Commentary...

The calculation is:

$$\frac{370 \times 365}{2,898} \quad = \quad 46.6 \text{ days}$$

In Year 6, debtors took slightly over six weeks to pay their accounts from the date they were invoiced, a small improvement on the Year 5 situation.

CREDITORS' PAYMENT PERIOD

Formula:

$$\frac{\text{Trade creditors} \times 365}{\text{Credit purchases}} \quad = \quad \text{Period of credit taken}$$

Stokkit Year 5:

$$\frac{380 \times 365}{1,391} \quad = \quad 99.7 \text{ days}$$

The comments we made above about the use of closing or simple average, or of weighted average figures, apply to creditors also.

ACTIVITY 16

Using figures from Stokkit's balance sheet and internal profit and loss account (use the accounts from Session 3), work out the creditors' payment period for Year 6, and comment on what the change signifies.

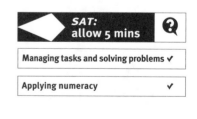

Commentary...

Stokkit's Year 6 creditors' payment ratio is:

$$\frac{401 \times 365}{1,996} = 73.3 \text{ days}$$

This is a significant increase in the speed of settling creditors' invoices – to just over two months from over three months.

From a financial standpoint, it would normally be in Stokkit's interest to extend credit to as long a period as the creditor will allow. However, it is bad policy to exceed agreed (or customary) credit terms, as this could damage relations with the creditor and call Stokkit's financial position into question.

THE OPERATING CASH CYCLE

When we first considered working capital, we noted that it moved in a cycle. The length of the cycle will vary from business to business but we can measure it by using the ratios we have already calculated:

Stock turnover days + debtors' collection days - creditors' payment days
= operating cash cycle

Using Stokkit's figures again, we can calculate the length of the operating cash cycle in account 4.5.

	Year 6 days	Year 5 days
Stock turnover	114.9	142.2
Debtors collection	46.6	49.7
	161.5	191.9
less		
Creditors payment	73.3	99.7
Operating cash cycle	88.2	92.2

ACCOUNT 4.5: Calculating Stokkit's operating cash cycle.

Net cash tied up in stock and debtors in Year 6 has decreased by four days, indicating a shortening of the cycle, which is generally considered to be a healthy sign. A reduction in the operating cash cycle contributes to an improvement in productivity and liquidity. The longer the cycle, the more working capital is required.

All the above figures have been calculated on the basis of closing figures for stock, debtors and creditors. Different results might have been obtained if simple average or weighted averages had been used instead.

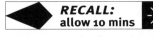

RECALL:
allow 10 mins

Write down the formulae for calculating the following indicators and explain what each is meant to show:

1. stock turnover ratio

2. debtors' collection period

3. creditors' payment period

4. operating cash cycle.

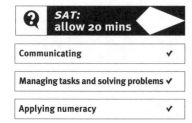

Communicating ✓

Managing tasks and solving problems ✓

Applying numeracy ✓

ACTIVITY 17

You are employed by the owner of a small cash and carry business which obtains its supplies from Stokkit. The owner has told you that, in the hope of increasing his sales, he is going to allow his customers eight weeks in which to settle their accounts instead of six weeks as at present. This means he will also have to increase his stocks to meet the expected increase in demand.

Advise your employer what the implications of his proposals are for working capital and the cash operating cycle.

Commentary...

Lengthening the debtor payment period will lengthen the cash cycle and require a greater amount of working capital.

Increasing the volume of stock held will have the same effect. This will be even more marked if the volume of extra stock is greater than the extra sales expected, though the increase in working capital required will be smaller than would otherwise be the case if the stocks are financed by creditors.

Overall, however, the result is likely to be a higher working capital and operating cash cycle requirement.

summary

The financial statements published by a company – the profit and loss account, balance sheet and cash flow statement – are used by a variety of interested parties, each having a different motive. They include shareholders, employees, creditors and financial analysts.

- ▶ Financial analysis is about measuring and evaluating profitability, liquidity and solvency, including ratio, horizontal, base period and vertical analyses.

- ▶ There is a difficulty in analysing profitability, in that there are various ways of interpreting both profit and the assets against which it is measured to establish profitability. The key ratios are gross and net profit, asset utilisation and return on capital employed.

- ▶ Liquidity is the degree to which a business has cash or near cash available to settle its short-term liabilities. A business is solvent if its assets are more than adequate to meet its external short-term and long-term liabilities. The assessment of liquidity is carried out using the current ratio and liquidity ratio.

- ▶ Gearing is the ratio of fixed interest and fixed dividend funds to the total finance of a company, for this purpose defined as shareholders' funds plus fixed interest borrowings.

- ▶ There are several ratios of specific interest to investors, apart from those relating to profitability, solvency, liquidity and gearing. These are centred on earnings, dividends and market prices of shares.

- ▶ Adequate working capital is essential for the daily operations of every business and consists of the net resources which each business uses to generate revenue and to pay accounts outstanding.

- ▶ Too high or too low an amount of working capital can have an adverse effect on the profit and profitability of a business. It is, therefore, important that it be closely monitored and controlled. Four ratios enable this to be done: stock turnover ratio, debtors' collection period, creditors' payment period, and operating cash cycle.

Analysis of costs

ASCERTAINING COSTS

DIRECT AND INDIRECT COSTS

FUNCTIONAL ANALYSIS OF COSTS

BEHAVIOURAL ANALYSIS OF COSTS

ABSORPTION COSTING AND MARGINAL COSTING

MARGINAL COST APPLICATIONS

BREAK-EVEN ANALYSIS

Objectives

After participating in this session, you should be able to:

▶ understand the need to ascertain and analyse costs

▶ explain the elements of cost and the nature of direct and indirect costs

▶ analyse actual costs into their elements and into prime costs and overheads

▶ understand the functional analysis and behavioural analysis of costs, and apply these to actual costs

▶ describe the meaning and nature of absorption costing and marginal costing

▶ apply marginal cost principles to actual situations

▶ explain break-even analysis and ascertain break-even point by graph-plotting and calculation.

In working through this session, you will practise the following BTEC common skills:

Managing and developing self	✔
Working with and relating to others	✔
Communicating	✔
Managing tasks and solving problems	✔
Applying numeracy	✔
Applying technology	
Applying design and creativity	

Ascertaining Costs

One of the aims of any business is to operate at a profit. In session 3 you learned that profit results when revenue is greater than expense (the cost of generating that revenue). To achieve this objective, the managers need to plan and control the operations and to establish selling prices for each product and service. As a profit will result only if sales exceed costs, it follows that it is essential to ascertain the cost of making each individual product, or of supplying each service as accurately as possible.

This gives rise to number of problems, one of which is that, although individual selling prices are known, the corresponding costs can only be estimated. This is because it is sometimes a matter of judgment whether, or to what extent, a particular item constitutes a cost. It is even more difficult to attribute some costs to particular products and services with absolute accuracy. A reasonably acceptable compromise has to be reached by which costs such as these are attributed to products and services on a fair, logical and methodical basis.

The first step in this process is to analyse costs into classifications of various sorts, so that the cost of individual products and services can be ascertained by the synthesis (i.e. building up) of the relevant analysed figures.

The cost of a product will depend on:

- the quantity and value of the raw materials from which it is made

- the cost of the time spent by operatives working on it

- the cost of the operations and processes which transform it into the finished product.

This ascertainment of total cost depends upon the careful analysis of costs at the outset.

COST ANALYSIS

Cost analysis begins with the coding of source documents. Every transaction entered into by a business, whether with an outside agency, such as a supplier, or internally (for example, the payment of wages), gives rise to some form of documentation – an invoice, a voucher, a schedule or a day book entry, for instance. When each source document is number-coded, both cost analysis and financial accounting analysis (the kind we looked at in session 3) can be carried out. We are concerned solely now with cost analysis as a means of aiding a business in planning, controlling and decision making.

ELEMENTS OF COST

Cost analysis recognises three elements, which we will look at in turn:

- labour cost

- materials cost

- 'other' costs.

Labour cost means the cost of remunerating employees. In its most obvious form, this means the cost of wages and salaries and National Insurance (NI). Also included are allowances for working in adverse conditions, productivity and performance bonuses, and similar payments. To constitute a labour cost, the item must:

1. be payable to employees, and

2. relate to work done or services performed.

Hence payments to outsiders (non-employees) for services performed for the business are classed as an 'other' cost and not as a labour cost.

Materials cost includes the cost of raw materials used in the course of production and throughout the business. Apart from the materials that obviously form part of the finished product, the cost of computer stationery and other office requisites, of oils and greases for lubricating machinery and vehicles, and of cleaning materials are all classed as materials costs.

As a rough guide, if a commodity is capable of being stored prior to use, its cost is a material cost. If, on the other hand, it is used at the point of supply, it is an other cost. Thus coal would be treated as a materials cost, but gas and electricity charges would be classed as an other cost because they are obtained from the mains supplies as needed and because they also result from the provision of a service.

Other costs comprises all costs not classed as either labour or materials costs, e.g.:

- postal and telephone charges

- travelling and subsistence expenses

- repairs and maintenance costs

- insurance premiums

- vehicle and other licences

- legal and other outside fees

- payments to non-employees for work done or services rendered, e.g.

  payments to sub-contractors

  payments of professional fees to, say, a firm of solicitors for legal advice or for property conveyancing

- local business rates

- fixed asset depreciation

- plant hire costs

- rent of premises

- gas, electricity and water supply and services.

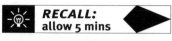

RECALL:
allow 5 mins

Define the three 'elements of cost' used in cost analysis.

ACTIVITY 1

Briefly explain what the financial consequences might be if a manufacturer fixed the selling prices of products without knowing their costs.

Classify each of the following costs as either labour, materials or 'other' costs, and briefly explain your choice in each case:

(a) electricity account paid

(b) salary of chief accountant

(c) reimbursement of employees' travelling expenses

(d) fee paid to marketing director

(e) fees paid to external auditors

(f) diesel fuel for delivery vehicles.

Commentary...

If selling prices are fixed without knowing costs, they may be too high or too low. If too high, the business would lose trade to cheaper competitors and to alternative sources of supply. If too low, the business would be trading at a loss, which if left unchecked could result in the business having to go into receivership or liquidation.

Your classification of costs should be as follows:

(a) other cost – it is both a non-storable commodity and a service

(b) labour cost – part of employee remuneration

(c) other cost – although paid to employees it is for expenses incurred in connection with work and not payment for work done or for services rendered

(d) labour cost – part of employee remuneration

(e) other cost – remuneration paid to non-employees

(f) materials cost – cost of a material used which is not inextricably linked to a service.

Direct and indirect costs

The three elements of cost can each be analysed further according to whether they are:

- direct costs

- indirect costs.

Direct costs comprise those labour, material and other costs which can be attributed directly to a product or service. Thus, the cost of raw materials which form the finished product is a direct materials cost, and the wages cost of the operatives who provide the service or whose work converts the raw materials into finished product is a direct labour cost. Direct other costs are less commonly encountered but would arise if a consultant or a specialised machine or piece of equipment is hired for a specific order or contract (rather than for general use within the business). Collectively, direct costs are called prime cost.

Indirect costs are the remaining labour, materials and other costs. They enable production to take place but are not directly part of it.

Examples of an indirect labour cost include the wages of:

- supervisors

- clerical staff

- computer help-desk staff

- the managing director.

In addition, indirect labour costs include almost all other wage costs of the individuals who plan, monitor and otherwise contribute to the production operations and processes but are not directly involved in producing.

Indirect materials costs include: lubricating oils and greases, which are essential for production but do not form part of the finished product; computer software, which constitutes the control systems for production; and general administration. Most other costs are indirect other costs; these usually form the greater proportion of total costs, and the more automated the business the greater is the proportion of other costs to total costs.

Collectively, indirect costs are called overhead costs, or simply overheads.

Total cost is the aggregate of prime cost and overhead costs.

FIGURE 5.1: The elements of total cost.

RECALL:
allow 10 mins

Briefly define the following terms and give three examples in each category:

(a) direct costs

(b) indirect costs.

EXERCISE:
allow 40 mins

Working with and relating to others ✓

Managing tasks and solving problems ✓

ACTIVITY 2

Move into groups of three or four to carry out this task.

Ball Brothers manufacture traditional garden furniture, incurring the costs set out below. Classify them into labour, materials or other costs, stating in each case whether they are direct or indirect costs. Give brief reasons for your choices.

(a) Depreciation of production machinery

(b) Timber for making wooden picnic tables

(c) Wages of security staff

(d) Wages of joinery craftsmen

(e) Cleaning detergents

(f) Business rates on premises

(g) Salaries of the wages office staff

Now consider the following transactions which were recorded in Stokkit's books for Year 6. Classify them into prime cost and overhead cost.

(a) Depreciation of office buildings, £1,000

(b) Foreman's salary, £12,000

(c) Repairs to fork-lift truck, £540

(d) Depreciation of delivery vehicles, £24,000

(e) Cost of goods sold, £77,500

(f) Diesel fuel used by delivery vehicles, £19,100

(g) Electricity consumed, £54,000

Session five: Analysis of costs

DIRECT AND INDIRECT COSTS

Commentary...

Ball Brothers' costs should be classified as:

(a) indirect other cost – not directly attributable to a particular product and not involving labour cost or materials cost

(b) direct materials cost – a material forming part of the finished product

(c) indirect labour cost – remuneration paid to non-production employees

(d) direct labour cost – remuneration paid to production employees

(e) indirect materials cost – materials used in the course of production but not forming part of the product

(f) indirect other cost – reason as for (a) above

(g) indirect labour cost – reason as for (c) above.

All Stokkit's listed transactions are overhead costs with the exception of (e), which is a prime cost.

Managing finance and information:165

Functional analysis of costs

We have discussed how costs can be analysed into elements, and then into prime costs and overheads. A further level of analysis is to collect and analyse costs on the basis of the function with which they are associated. Four functions are recognised for this purpose:

- production

- marketing

- distribution

- administration.

We now examine each one in turn from the viewpoint of a manufacturing business. The same principles can however be applied to any type of business.

Production costs

All costs incurred from the receipt of the order (or from the initiation of production operations, if manufacturing is carried out in expectation of orders) to the point at which the finished product is transferred to finished goods stock, are classified as production costs. By definition, therefore, all direct labour, materials and other costs (i.e. all prime costs), must be production costs.

In addition to prime costs, there are a various production overhead costs. All costs associated with the factory and workshops would fall into this category, including those for:

- factory building repairs

- plant and machinery maintenance and overhaul

- factory business rates

- power used by machinery

- wages of chargehands and other supervisory staff

- wages of factory cleaners

- cleaning materials

- depreciation of the factory and workshop buildings, plant and machinery.

Marketing costs

Sometimes known as selling costs, marketing costs are entirely overhead costs. They can arise both before any production takes place and after it has been completed. Pre-production costs include the costs of securing orders. In many businesses this will mean the costs of commissioning and placing advertisements in newspapers and trade magazines, salaries, bonuses and commissions paid to the sales staff, and their car running costs, and production and circulation costs of sales brochures and price lists.

Marketing costs do not necessarily stop when an order is placed. In many businesses, the sales force also carries out after-sales services, visiting customers to check on their satisfaction and that the products supplied are satisfactory in every respect.

Some businesses exhibit their products in the expectation of generating sales, in which case the showroom costs would be a marketing cost, as would the running costs of a mobile exhibition and the costs of attending a trade fair.

Distribution costs

Like marketing costs, distribution costs are also entirely overhead costs. The start point here is the receipt from the factory of the completed products and the end point is their despatch to customers. Distribution costs comprise the costs of the finished-goods warehouse and of the transport delivery vehicle fleet. Complications arise when not only finished goods but also raw materials and consumable stores are housed in the same warehouse building. The distribution element has to be attributed to distribution cost by a process of allocation and apportionment which we deal with shortly. Similarly, the costs of running vehicles can affect more than one functional classification and also have to be attributed.

- ● Warehousing distribution costs include the wages and salaries of storekeepers and their staffs, heating and lighting costs, insurance costs based on the value of the stockholding, depreciation of lifting equipment and of fixtures, repair costs and costs of packing.

- ● Transport distribution costs include the wages of drivers and drivers' mates, petrol, oil and diesel costs, depreciation of vehicles, repair and maintenance costs of the vehicles and of garaging, and road fund licences.

For cost analysis purposes, some businesses combine the two headings of marketing and distribution costs.

Administration costs

The production, marketing and distribution functions are all served by the central administration. This function bears the overhead costs of the purchasing department, sales ledger department, wages office, general accounts department, data processing team and the secretariat (including secretaries, word processor operators, personal assistants), and various managers. Overhead costs include wages and salaries of these staffs, costs of stationery, postage, telephones as well as those costs such as depreciation and repairs noted under the other headings.

The correct analysis is important because costs under each function are dealt with differently when arriving at product costs, as we see below.

RECALL:
allow 5 mins

Give three examples each of:

1. **production costs**

2. **marketing costs**

3. **distribution costs**

4. **administration costs.**

Behavioural analysis of costs

The quality of many business decisions is linked to the quality of the predictions of the costs involved. This in turn is based on the knowledge of how costs behave at various levels of activity and under particular conditions. In fact, costs behave in one of three ways, being:

- fixed

- variable

- semi-variable.

FIXED COSTS

These are overhead costs which tend not to be affected by changes in the level of output or turnover. They are also period costs, i.e. they are associated with the lapse of time, not with the activity which takes place during it. In other words, even if no activity is taking place at all, fixed costs are still incurred (they are sometimes referred to as 'shutdown costs', because they are incurred even when the production process is shut down). Examples include:

- rents

- business rates

- fixed wage and salary costs

- various contractual payments.

Fixed costs in this context are fixed over a wide range of activity, but not fixed absolutely. Suppose, for instance, that the maximum business that a telesales business can conduct at its premises is 300,000 phone calls per annum. To meet an increasing demand, the directors decide to increase the capacity to an annual output of 400,000 units. This can only be achieved if the business moves to larger (and more expensive) premises. There will be a one-off increase in fixed costs (due to higher rent and business rates and additional plant and equipment, and supervisory wages and salaries).

When this happens, fixed costs exhibit a stepped effect, as shown in figure 5.2 where the costs rise abruptly when the level of activity reaches a particular level. In the case of the telesales company, the step occurs when the level of activity passes 300,000, and the move to larger premises gives rise to higher fixed costs.

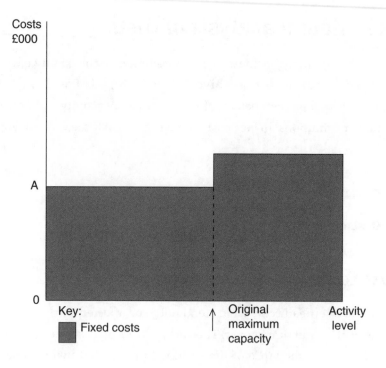

FIGURE 5.2: Fixed costs – the stepped effect.

At point A in the diagram, fixed costs are incurred even when no activity is taking place. They remain at a constant amount until the maximum capacity barrier is reached. Beyond this they increase and then continue on a plateau as before.

VARIABLE COSTS

Some costs tend to vary with the level of activity and are therefore known as variable costs. This is the case with prime costs – direct labour, direct materials and direct other costs – and some overheads. When drawn on a graph, the variable cost line starts at zero activity and cost, and forms an angle with the horizontal axis.

At zero activity, the variable cost is nil, but it increases as activity increases. Here, we have shown the variable cost as a straight line from its point of origin at zero, but in reality it would curve, with the slope reducing as activity level increased reflecting economies of scale. (Unit costs tend to fall as the scale of production rises because at higher activity levels, the greater amounts of raw materials needed may qualify for bulk discounts; there might also be more efficient use of direct labour on longer production runs.)

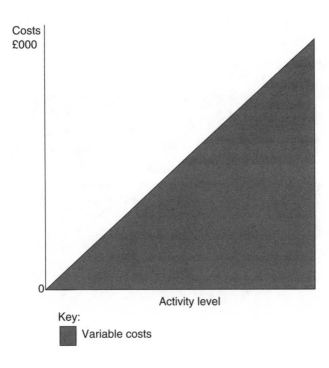

FIGURE 5.3: Variable costs.

SEMI-VARIABLE COSTS

The distinction between fixed costs and variable costs is not always clear cut. Some overhead costs exhibit the attributes of both, being partly fixed and partly variable. When drawn on a graph semi-variable costs are shown as originating at a point above zero, to reflect the fixed element, and rising at an angle to the horizontal axis:

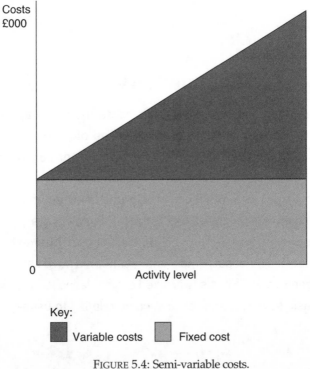

FIGURE 5.4: Semi-variable costs.

Like fixed costs, semi-variable costs step upwards when they encounter a maximum capacity barrier; like variable costs they may curve with economies of scale.

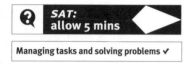

Managing tasks and solving problems ✔

ACTIVITY 3

Telephone bills are a familiar example of a semi-variable cost: they contain a fixed element (line and equipment rental), and a variable element (call charges).

Give three more examples of semi-variable costs.

Commentary...

Other examples of semi-variable costs include gas and electricity accounts, which are a composite of fixed standing charges and the variable cost of gas and power consumed. Vehicle running expenses are also semi-variable: the fixed element is insurance premiums, road fund licences and time-based maintenance costs; the variable elements are petrol, oil, diesel fuel and repairs. Public transport businesses experience similar costs. Hotels and restaurants have capacity-related semi-variable costs (with fixed costs relating to provision of the basic facilities, and variable costs relating to usage).

BEHAVIOURAL ANALYSIS AND COST ASCERTAINMENT

To determine the cost of a job or a product or a service, total costs must be:

1. identified as labour, materials or other costs

2. classified into direct or indirect costs

3. analysed into functional headings

4. identified by behaviour, as being either variable, semi-variable or fixed.

Prime cost (i.e. the sum of all direct costs) is analysed as production costs, as are some of the overheads. The remainder of the overheads are analysed under the headings of marketing, distribution and administration, as shown in figure 5.5.

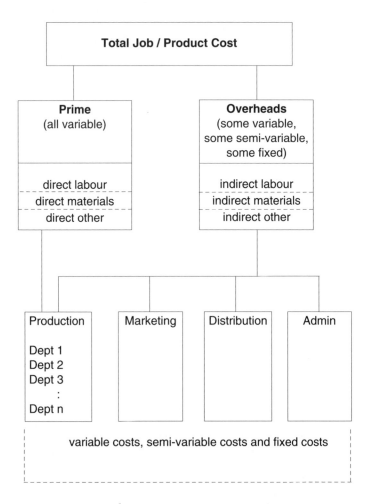

FIGURE 5.5 The allocation of costs between functions.

Production overheads are allocated to individual departments in which production takes place. Within production departments, the overheads are further allotted to cost centres by a process of allocation and apportionment.

A cost centre can be a location, an activity or an item of equipment for which costs can be ascertained and related to cost units. Cost centre costs are then attributed to jobs, products and services, which are said to absorb them.

The end result of this analysis – the total cost of a job – is the aggregate of production cost (i.e. prime cost plus production overheads) and appropriately attributed amounts of marketing, distribution and administration overheads. Different jobs will have different mixes of these elements.

RECALL:
allow 10 mins

Write brief definitions of the following:

1. **fixed cost**

2. **variable cost**

3. **semi-variable cost**

4. **stepped cost.**

ACTIVITY 4

SAT:
allow 10 mins

Managing tasks and solving problems ✔

Classify the following overhead costs incurred by Ball Brothers, who supply traditional garden furniture to Stokkit as fixed, variable or semi-variable costs:

(a) depreciation of production machinery

(b) wages of security staff

(c) sales staff's basic salaries

(d) sales staff's commissions

(e) packing materials

(f) stationery and printing

(g) business rates

(h) water rates

(i) delivery vehicle costs.

Commentary...

Costs (a), (b), (c) and (g) are fixed. Costs (d) and (e) are variable, and costs (f), (h) and (i) are semi-variable.

Absorption costing and marginal costing

Absorption costing (or total absorption costing) is the normal system used for profit measurement and reporting. According to this method of costing, the production cost of a product includes prime cost plus all fixed, variable and semi-variable production overheads (the 'indirect other costs' referred to earlier).

For example, a TV production company that produces 40 hours of programmes in a year can establish its prime costs quite easily:

- labour costs, such as film crews' and actors' wages

- material costs, such as videotape

- direct other costs, such as scriptwriters' fees, rent of studios, etc.

However, in order to produce these revenue-earning programmes the company also incurs numerous indirect (overhead) costs, including such fixed costs as office rental, depreciation on equipment and the salaries of managerial, sales and administrative staff. It also incurs substantial costs in developing programme ideas that never reach fruition.

To know what to charge for its programme output in order to pay all these costs and make a profit, all the overhead costs must be added to the direct product cost. The products (the 40 hours of programme output) are therefore said to absorb the overhead costs. Thus the direct cost of an hour of programme may be £30,000, but it must also absorb a further £20,000 as its share of total overhead costs. The total cost of an hour of programme is therefore £50,000:

Production cost = Prime cost + all production overheads

MARGINAL COSTING

Marginal costing offers a different way of looking at costs, and is used in situations where a short-term choice has to be made as to which of two or more possible courses of action is the most beneficial in financial terms:

- Should we hire, or buy, a piece of equipment?

- Is it more profitable to price a product at £5 and sell more, or price it at £10 and sell fewer?

- Should we abandon a low-profit product and concentrate resources on those that are more profitable?

● We do not have resources to produce everything we would like to produce, so what should we concentrate on in order to maximise profit?

All these situations – of which we give examples shortly – are about changes in activity within an existing framework. Whatever the decision, the business will go on incurring its fixed overhead costs (the ones that absorption costing methods load onto product costs) just as before.

Fixed overhead costs are irrelevant to the financial analysis of short-term decisions involving changes in activity. Marginal costing therefore focuses on those costs that do change with level of activity (i.e. the variable costs) and ignores fixed costs. Thus:

Marginal cost = Prime cost + variable overhead

Note that here variable overhead includes the variable portion of semi-variable overheads such as electricity.

The key concept in marginal costing is contribution. In brief, contribution is what is left over after all the variable (marginal) costs have been subtracted from revenue. A positive contribution goes towards meeting fixed costs; any surplus after that is profit. In the short term, decision-making strategy is to maximise contribution; in the long term, it is to cover all fixed costs and to be left with a surplus representing profit.

		£			
(S)	Sales revenue	X			
	less				
	Marginal costs				
	Direct costs	X			
	Variable overheads	X			
	(including variable portion				
	of semi-variable overheads)	—			
(V)	Total	X			
(C)	Contribution (S) minus (V)	X	or	(X)	
	less				
(F)	Fixed costs (including fixed	X			
	portion of semi-variable				
	overheads)	—			
(P)	Profit/(loss) (C) minus (F)	X	or	(X)	

ACCOUNT 5.1: Format for marginal costing.

Some decision-making situations involve the avoidance of costs rather than the generation of revenue. In those instances, the positive contribution arises from the negative, i.e. saved costs. An example is given later.

For marginal cost purposes, only those costs and revenues relevant to a particular decision are used:

- Differential costs and revenues are those associated with the decisions that give rise to future cash flows. If they are positive, they can also be described as incremental. By definition, fixed costs which would be incurred irrespective of any decision cannot be regarded as differential.

- Opportunity costs and revenues are the cost of forgoing the most favourable alternative, in situations where there are two or more alternative courses of action. In other words, we ask: 'What will we lose by ignoring this opportunity, i.e. by not doing this?'

For example, suppose that a business has a piece of machinery that currently produces a positive contribution of £16,000 over its life. One alternative is to retain it and continue receiving this contribution. The other alternatives are:

- to hire it to another manufacturer (this would generate net revenue of £12,000)

- to sell it (this would net £8,000).

The opportunity costs here depend on what decision is taken. In each case, it is the higher of the alternatives not chosen:

- opportunity cost of selling the plant: £16,000

- opportunity cost of continuing to use it: £12,000

- opportunity cost of hiring it out: £16,000.

Marginal cost applications

Marginal costing would not be used for financial reporting purposes, because it does not set out to ascertain the true total cost of a product or service. However, it is useful in making various kinds of short-term decisions involving changes in activity. We now look at examples of four situations mentioned earlier.

HIRE OR BUY?

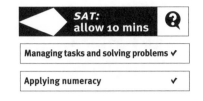

ACTIVITY 5

A common situation involving differential costs is a 'hire or buy?' decision.

Suppose that Stokkit needs extra lifting equipment for a limited period. It could either hire a fork lift truck for 90 days at £70 per day or buy one outright for £25,000. This could be resold for £17,000 when no longer required. In both instances, the running costs will be £18 per day for 90 days.

Work out the financial effects of each decision using the grid below, filling in the figures in the blank slots. Say which decision produces the smaller cash outflow.

	Hire £	Buy £
Marginal costs		
Hire charges [90 x 70]		Nil
Running costs [90 x 18]	———	———
Net acquisition cost [25,000 – 17,000]	Nil	8,000
Differential/incremental costs		

Commentary...

	Hire £	Buy £
Marginal costs		
Hire charges [90 x 70]	6,300	Nil
Running costs [90 x 18]	1,620	1,620
	7,920	1,620
Net acquisition cost [25,000 - 17,000]	Nil	8,000
Differential/incremental costs	7,920	9,620

These workings show that hiring would produce the smaller net cash outflow: £1,700 less than buying.

PRODUCT PRICING

Pricing policy is very important because of its effect on demand and on profit. Marginal costing is used to show the effects of various alternative price/demand situations.

For example, one of Stokkit's suppliers is a manufacturer of fibreglass garden ponds at a variable cost of £12 each and with fixed costs totalling £110,000 per annum. Demand for the ponds is price sensitive and market research (see table 5.1) has predicted the demand at three different selling prices. The business manufactures only the quantity that it can sell.

Selling price £ per unit	Estimated sales No. of units
16	25,000
20	20,000
23	16,000

TABLE 5.1: Estimated demand for garden ponds at different selling prices.

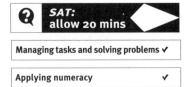

Managing tasks and solving problems ✔

Applying numeracy ✔

ACTIVITY 6

Compare the outcomes of the three pricing policies by filling in the gaps in the grid below. Summarise your conclusions, explaining which of the pricing policies would produce a positive contribution, whether the contribution will cover fixed costs, and which policy you would recommend be selected.

Comparison of pricing effects

Sales:units	25,000	20,000	16,000
price	£16	£20	£23
	£000	£000	£000
Sales (units x price)	400	400	368
less			
Marginal costs (units x £12)	300	____	____
Contribution	100		176
less			
Fixed costs	110	110	110
Profit/(loss)	(10)	____	____

Commentary...

Comparison of pricing effects

Sales:units	25,000	20,000	16,000
price	£16	£20	£23

	£000	£000	£000
Sales (units x price)	400	400	368
less			
Marginal costs (units x £12)	300	240	192
Contribution	100	160	176
less			
Fixed costs	110	110	110
Profit/(loss)	(10)	50	66

All three price levels would produce a positive contribution, but a price of £16 would be insufficient to cover fixed costs. Pricing at £23 per unit produces the highest contribution and profit and would therefore be selected.

In fact, further information is needed because of the issue of capacity: if the ponds were priced at £23 each and only 16,000 could be sold at that price, the unused capacity could perhaps be used to produce other fibreglass items, say, ornamental shrub holders. The extra contribution from the manufacture of these might be sufficient to produce an even larger overall profit.

SEGMENT CLOSURE

Most businesses ascertain the costs and revenues of each of their departments. An examination of the figures often reveals that one or more departments is apparently making less profit than other departments or is making a loss. The question then arises whether this department should be closed and the resources thus released to be used for more profitable activities.

One of Stokkit's customers is a retail shop whose cost statement (prepared on a fixed cost absorption basis) for the most recent period is shown in account 5.2.

	Departments				
	A	B	C	D	Total
	£000	£000	£000	£000	£000
Sales	20	26	18	15	79
less costs					
Marginal	13	17	13	10	53
Fixed	4	10	2	2	18
Total	17	27	15	12	71
Profit/(loss)	3	(1)	3	3	8

ACCOUNT 5.2: Cost statement.

At first sight it looks as though if department B is closed down, its £1,000 loss could be avoided and total profit across all departments would rise to £9,000.

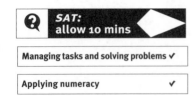

SAT:
allow 10 mins

Managing tasks and solving problems ✔

Applying numeracy   ✔

ACTIVITY 7

Look carefully at the figures below, which show the information contained in account 5.2 re-scheduled in a marginal cost format, so that the contribution made by each department becomes apparent.

	Departments				
	A	B	C	D	Total
	£000	£000	£000	£000	£000
Sales	20	26	18	15	79
less					
Marginal costs	13	17	13	10	53
Contribution	7	9	5	5	26
less					
Fixed costs					18
Profit/(loss)					8

What interpretation would you now place on the performance of department B? What would be the overall effect if it is closed?

Commentary...

Department B, which is under threat of closure, in fact produces the highest contribution. This would be lost if the department is closed.

Closing Department B would not reduced fixed costs: these would simply have to be re-attributed to the three remaining departments, reducing their apparent profitability considerably. Instead of total profit increasing to £9,000 if department B is closed, there would be an overall loss of £1,000. This is arrived at as follows:

		£000	£000
<u>Contribution</u>			
Department:	A	7	
	C	5	
	D	<u>5</u>	
			17
<u>less fixed costs</u>			<u>18</u>
<u>Profit/(loss)</u>			<u>(1)</u>

It can also be explained like this:

	£000
Original profit	8
less	
Loss of contribution from Department B	9
Profit/(loss)	(1)

This demonstrates the value of using marginal costing to assess the contribution that a particular operation or product makes to overall fixed costs and, ultimately, to profit.

SCARCE RESOURCES

Situations can arise where a business receives more orders for its products or services than it can meet with the resources at its disposal. Various resources – precious metals, machine capacity, skilled labour, working space – might be in short supply. These are termed constraints or limiting factors. Under these conditions, the business needs to decide where to allocate the resources in order to maximise contribution.

Such a problem faces Jarrett Ceramics, one of Stokkit's small suppliers, which produces three standard lines of hand-painted pottery: dinner services, tea services and decorative ware. The data relating to Jarrett's costs are shown in account 5.3.

	Dinner services per set	Tea services per set	Decorative ware per set
Labour hours	6	4	3
	£	£	£
Selling price	65	45	40
Marginal cost	41	25	19
	No. of sets	No. of sets	No. of sets
Stokkit's order	300	270	400

ACCOUNT 5.3: Jarrett Ceramics – costs and constraints.

The limiting factor is direct labour hours, because of the highly skilled nature of the work. A maximum of 3,504 direct labour hours is available. Account 5.4 shows the total direct labour hours required in order to complete all the orders.

	No. of sets ordered	No. of direct labour hours per set	total hours
Dinner services	300	6	1,800
Tea services	270	4	1,080
Decorative ware	400	3	1,200
Total			4,080

ACCOUNT 5.4: Jarrett's direct labour requirement.

Clearly, there are insufficient direct labour hours to meet the demand, so what is the optimum (i.e. most profitable) product mix in the circumstances? As a preliminary step, consider the financial figures in account 5.5.

	Dinner services per set	Tea services per set	Decorative ware per set
	£	£	£
Selling price	65	45	40
less			
Marginal cost	41	25	19
Contribution	24	20	21
Ranking	1st	3rd	2nd

ACCOUNT 5.5: Assessing the contribution of different products.

It would seem best to concentrate production on dinner services and decorative ware, based on the amount of their respective contributions. However, when resources are scarce we need to express the contribution in terms of the scarce resource, in this case in terms of the 'contribution per direct labour hour' (see account 5.6). This has resulted in a complete change of priorities.

	Dinner services per set	Tea services per set	Decorative ware per set
Contribution	£24	£20	£21
Direct labour hours	6	4	3
Contribution per direct labour hour	£4	£5	£7
Ranking	3rd	2nd	1st

ACCOUNT 5.6: Assessing the contribution per direct labour hour.

MARGINAL COST APPLICATIONS

SAT:
allow 15 mins

Managing tasks and solving problems ✓

Applying numeracy   ✓

ACTIVITY 8

Now work out the optimum production plan for Jarrett Ceramics, based on its maximum potential of 3,504 labour hours, and fill in the details in the grid below.

Calculate the total labour hours needed for decorative ware and tea services.

Calculate how many labour hours are available for dinner services, and how many dinner services can be completed.

What orders will be unfulfilled?

Ranking	No. of orders accepted	Direct labour hours per order	total
1st Decorative ware	400	3	
2nd Tea services	270	4	
3rd Dinner services		6	
Total			3,504

Commentary...

The original order for 300 dinner services has had to be restricted to 204 because, after completing the other items in order of priority, only 1,224 direct labour hours are available, which is sufficient only for production of 204 sets. The table therefore appears as follows:

Ranking	No. of orders accepted	Direct labour hours per order	total
1st Decorative ware	400	3	1,200
2nd Tea services	270	4	1,080
3rd Dinner services	204	6	1,224
Total			3,504

We can now summarise the distinction between marginal and absorption costing.

In absorption costing, fixed costs are taken into account and are treated as part of the cost of the activities under consideration, even though they are mainly associated with lapse of time rather than level of activity. That is, they will occur anyway, regardless of the outcome of the decision being made, and so are secondary to the decision.

Marginal costing ignores them by concentrating on (a) variable costs, and (b) the potential contribution that the project in question can make towards fixed costs and profit.

NON-FINANCIAL CONSIDERATIONS

Marginal costing indicates what decisions should be made on purely financial grounds, but there are broader issues, including non-financial ones, which management would take into account in short-term decision making.

Sometimes a loss-making (or lower-contribution) decision is made in order to secure a specific objective, such as a foothold in a particular market, or to attract a new customer. On the other hand, a seemingly optimum decision may have to be abandoned for various reasons, including:

- insufficient finance – perhaps the cash required for the project is not available

- effects on demand for linked products

- continuity of supplies – a short-term opportunity to buy raw materials cheaply may mean jeopardising a relationship with a long-standing supplier

- effect on staff relations – unforeseen demands for overtime or effort from staff may damage staff relations

- attitude of customers

- adverse publicity.

Break-even analysis

Break-even is an easily understood concept: up to a certain level of activity a business will make a loss, and above that level it will make a profit.

This is because even if a business is not generating any revenue it has still to meet fixed costs, and will be making a loss. There comes a point, however, where revenue is sufficient to meet all the fixed costs and also all the variable costs attributable to that level of activity. At this point of equilibrium, the business is making neither a profit nor a loss. This is the break-even point:

- below it, the business is operating at a loss
- above it, the business makes a profit.

It is of great importance to a business to know at what level of activity the break-even point occurs. There are two ways of establishing break-even point, one involves producing a chart, the other requires calculations.

BREAK-EVEN CHARTS

The construction of break-even charts depends upon the analysis of costs according to their behaviour, i.e. whether they are fixed, semi-variable or variable costs. The charts are graphs, in which the vertical axis represents cost and sales values, and the horizontal axis represents level of activity.

When we were considering behavioural analysis of costs above, we illustrated separate graphs on which fixed costs and variable costs are plotted. A break-even chart represents an amalgamation of the two, on which a sales line is superimposed. The sales line starts from a point of origin at zero value and activity, and rises at an acute angle to the horizontal axis. It is shown as a straight line, but in reality it could be a concave curve, reflecting the fact that higher levels of sales have been achieved by substantial discounts.

Break-even point is where the sales revenue line intersects the total cost line. Figure 5.6 shows a typical break-even chart.

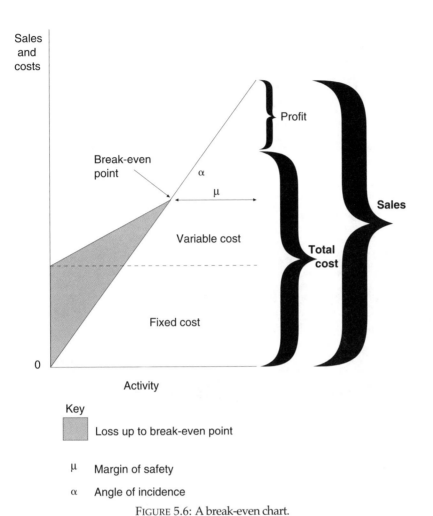

FIGURE 5.6: A break-even chart.

Two of the features, angle of incidence and margin of safety, require further explanation.

Angle of incidence is the angle between the sales revenue and total costs lines. A wide angle indicates that, after break-even has been achieved, profit is being made at a more rapid rate and that, conversely, relatively rapid loss will be made if activity falls below break-even point.

Margin of safety is the amount of activity between break-even point and the level of activity actually being achieved. The margin indicates the degree of vulnerability of the business to changes in activity levels. This is illustrated in the break-even charts for the two businesses shown in figure 5.7. Company A has relatively high fixed costs while those of company B are relatively low, and these circumstances are reflected in their margins of safety and angles of incidence:

BREAK-EVEN ANALYSIS

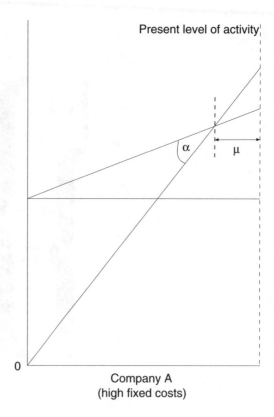

Company A
(high fixed costs)

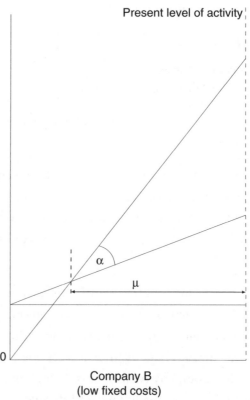

Company B
(low fixed costs)

Key:
α Angle of incidence

μ Margin of safety

FIGURE 5.7: The angles of incidence and margins of safety
in two different companies.

ACTIVITY 9

Look carefully at figure 5.7 and consider the position of companies A and B. What comments can you make on their respective situations?

Commentary...

Company A, with a narrow margin of safety and a wide angle of incidence, is very vulnerable to changes in demand, a relatively small reduction in which could plunge the company into loss. Company B has a wide margin of safety but a narrower angle of incidence and could withstand a 50 per cent reduction in demand and still remain in a profit-making situation.

BREAK-EVEN CALCULATIONS

Break-even point can be calculated in both quantity and value terms.

Formulae:

$$\text{Break-even quantity} = \frac{\text{Total fixed costs}}{\text{Contribution per unit}}$$

$$\text{Break-even value} = \frac{\text{Total fixed costs}}{\text{Profit/volume ratio}}$$

The profit/volume ratio (P/V ratio) is also known more accurately as the contribution/sales (C/S) ratio.

$$\text{P/V ratio (C/S)} = \frac{\text{Contribution per unit}}{\text{Selling price per unit}}$$

$$\text{\%margin of safety} = \frac{(\text{Actual activity minus break-even activity}) \times 100}{\text{Actual activity}}$$

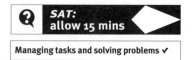

SAT: allow 15 mins
Managing tasks and solving problems ✔
Applying numeracy ✔

ACTIVITY 10

One of Stokkit's suppliers has an annual output of 60,000 units which it sells for £12 each. Variable costs are £7 per unit and fixed costs are £200,000.

Work out:

- the break-even quantity

- the P/V ratio

- the break-even value

- the current margin of safety.

Check the break-even results you have reached by multiplying the break-even quantity by the selling price: this should give you the break-even value.

Commentary...

- Break-even quantity equals 200,000/(12 - 7) i.e. 40,000 units.

- P/V ratio is (12 - 7)/12 = 5/12.

- Break-even value equals 200,000/(5/12) i.e. £480,000

The break-even value can be proved because it is equal to the break-even quantity multiplied by the selling price: 40,000 units at £12 per unit gives £480,000.

Margin of safety is [(60,000 - 40,000)/60,000] x 100, i.e. $33^1/_3$ per cent.

USING BREAK-EVEN ANALYSIS

Break-even charts are useful because they give a diagrammatical view of a situation and can be easily understood. It is a relatively easy task to see the effects of changes in the various factors – increase / decrease in fixed costs, variable costs and sales – by superimposing them.

Break-even charts and calculations are good pointers but must be viewed with caution. This is because of the problem of identifying fixed costs and of the impossibility of arriving at meaningful figures for multi-product businesses, where the various lines have different selling prices and contributions, and any attribution of fixed costs is on an arbitrary basis.

ACTIVITY 11

Describe the two methods of arriving at a break-even point.

Explain why break-even analysis is of limited value in a business like Stokkit.

Explain the significance of the margin of safety.

One of Stokkit's suppliers has an annual output of 20,000 soft toys which it sells at £2 each. Fixed costs are £10,000 and variable costs are £1 per toy.

(a) Prepare a break-even chart on these facts.

(b) Check your results by calculation.

(c) Also calculate:

- the break-even quantity

ASSIGNMENT: allow 45 mins

Managing and developing self	✔
Communicating	✔
Managing tasks and solving problems	✔
Applying numeracy	✔

- the break-even value

- the P/V ratio

- the actual profit being made at this level.

Write your answers on a separate sheet of paper. Summarise your findings in the box below.

summary

▶ The first step in cost analysis is to classify costs into labour, materials and 'other' costs, and separate further into direct and indirect costs. Direct costs are directly linked with the cost of the product or service. Indirect costs contribute to the product or service without actually forming an integral part of it.

▶ Second, the elements of each cost are analysed by function into production, marketing (selling), distribution and administration costs.

▶ Third, comes 'behavioural' analysis into fixed, variable or semi-variable categories: this is a key to short-term decision making.

▶ Finally, jobs and products absorb the overheads of the cost centres through which they pass. The manner in which the overheads are attributed depends on whether they are fixed, variable or semi-variable.

▶ Absorption costing is used for financial reporting purposes and takes both fixed and variable costs into consideration.

▶ Marginal costing is used for short-term decision making and is concerned with variable revenues and costs; marginal (i.e. additional) amounts of these result from particular decisions.

▶ Contribution is the difference between the revenue and the variable cost arising from a particular decision. A positive contribution goes towards meeting fixed costs and providing a profit.

▶ Break-even analysis involves calculating the level of activity at which a business's sales exactly equal its fixed and variable costs. Up to that point the business makes a loss, after it, a profit. Break-even point can be depicted on a graph or calculated mathematically. It is of less value in multi-product businesses because of the problems of fixed cost attribution.

Budgetary control

THE NATURE AND PURPOSE OF BUDGETING

APPLICATION OF BUDGETARY CONTROL

FLEXIBLE BUDGETS

CASH BUDGETS

Objectives

After participating in this session, you should be able to:

- ▶ understand the meaning and purpose of budgetary control

- ▶ construct a simple master budget

- ▶ compare actual and budgeted results, and interpret variances

- ▶ explain the principles of flexible budgeting, and its advantages and disadvantages

- ▶ construct and analyse a flexible budget

- ▶ understand and apply the principles of cash budgeting.

In working through this session, you will practise the following BTEC common skills:

Managing and developing self	✔
Working with and relating to others	✔
Communicating	✔
Managing tasks and solving problems	✔
Applying numeracy	✔
Applying technology	
Applying design and creativity	

The nature and purpose of budgeting

Business operations, and the revenue and expenses associated with them, can only be effectively controlled:

- if those operations are planned in advance, and

- if actual operations are regularly compared with the planned ones.

This means more than a retrospective comparison of actual results with those of the past periods. This may be interesting, and it may highlight areas where things have gone right or gone wrong, so that in future the business can avoid past mistakes or build on past successes. However, such comparisons are virtually useless for control purposes.

Detection of mistakes and successes as they are emerging is far more beneficial to a business: it can then both avoid further mistakes and capitalise on the successes. Mistakes and successes can only be identified early if there is a detection mechanism. This is what the system known as budgetary control provides.

The budgetary control process involves:

1. setting up budgets, i.e. planned targets of revenue, expenses, assets and liabilities relating to the activities concerned

2. measuring actual results against the budgets on a continuous basis

3. identifying and analysing divergences from budgets, and modifying both actual operations and subsequent budgets.

This process forms a cycle, as figure 6.1 shows.

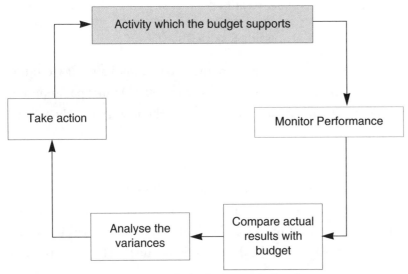

FIGURE 6.1: The budgetary control cycle.

The establishment of budgets is a time-consuming process that involves management at all levels. This is essential because subsequently, individual managers are held accountable for the divergences of actual results from the budgets that they have prepared and for which they are responsible.

The budget period, usually, but not necessarily, spans the financial year of the business, but many components of it are phased into quarters, months or weeks. Generally speaking, the larger and more complex the business, the further ahead it budgets. It is quite common for medium and large sized businesses to produce year-by-year budgets on a rolling basis for 15 years ahead. During the current budget period, the budgets for each of the remaining 14 years are updated and revised and a fifteenth is added.

BUDGET PREPARATION PRINCIPLES

The establishment of business objectives is the ultimate starting point for budget preparation. In a company, these overall objectives are set by the board of directors and, together with the principal budget factor, represent the main constraint within which the budget must be formulated.

The principal budget factor determines the starting point for the budget process itself, in relation to which the budget objectives are set. Depending on the nature of the business, the principal budget factor may be:

- market demand for sales

- production capacity ceiling

- availability of specialist, skilled staff.

The budget objectives must be realistic and achievable. It would be pointless to prepare a budget on sales of 200,000 units per annum if the maximum annual output capacity of the factory is only 160,000 units.

Where output capacity and availability of suitable staff are not constraints, the principal budget factor will be sales. In the case of a company in the manufacturing sector, the first budget to be prepared would therefore be the sales budget. The second would be the production budget and the third would be the finished goods stock budget.

Stokkit's position is different: as a wholesaling company, sales will still be its principal budget factor, and it too would first prepare a sales budget. This, however, will be followed not by a production budget but by a purchase-for-resale budget and a stock-for-resale budget.

Other budgets would be prepared for individual items of expense or 'cost centres'. Capital expenditure would also need to be budgeted to take account of such matters as the acquisition of new vehicles, plant and equipment or extension of the premises. Additionally, budgets would be prepared for:

- stocks of consumable stores

- debtors

- creditors

- cash.

The cash budget is particularly important and we cover it in more detail later on.

Each of these budgets requires input from most branches of management, the precise number depending on the size of the organisation. Information is gathered from all levels in the organisation and gradually channelled towards the production of these key budgets to create a master budget.

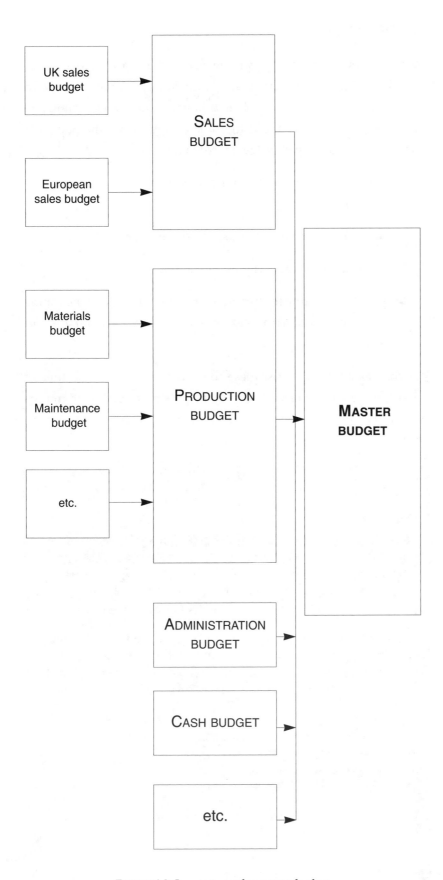

FIGURE 6.2: Inputs towards a master budget.

THE MASTER BUDGET

When the first drafts of the key budgets have been prepared, they are assembled to form a master budget. This takes the form of a budgeted profit and loss account, a budgeted balance sheet and a budgeted cash flow statement. A profit figure is derived from the budgeted sales and the total of the budgeted expenses.

At this stage, the budgeted profit has to be assessed to see whether it is adequate to:

- provide a reasonable dividend to shareholders

- counteract erosion of capital due to inflation

- set aside a residue to strengthen the company's working capital (through retentions) and as a basis for future development and expansion.

The company must prioritise these objectives. If any that the company regards as important cannot be met, then the other budgeted figures have to be revised in such a way that the desired results can be obtained.

SAT:
allow 15 mins

Managing tasks and solving problems ✔

ACTIVITY 1

Pefgo Flooring plc is preparing its annual budgets, which include provision for major improvements to production facilities. These call for capital spending but, in due course, will reduce unit costs and increase capacity. This effect starts to appear in the third quarter, but the full benefit will not be seen until the following year.

Meanwhile, the disruption caused by installation work will reduce output and increase wage costs, reducing in turn both total sales and gross profit in quarter 1, 2 and 3. This means that the company's financial objectives for the year cannot be achieved.

One option is to modify the objectives, but senior management is extremely reluctant to do this, since it may alienate shareholders. What other steps could Pefgo take to restore its gross profitability in the period in question?

Commentary...

The problem is a short-term one, so short-term solutions involving the reduction or postponement of various costs are appropriate. There are many possibilities, including delaying non-essential repairs, abandoning an advertising campaign, negotiating lower prices with suppliers, leaving vacant staff posts unfilled, and so on.

After adjustments have been made, the final draft is adopted as the definitive master budget, which is presented as a set of budgeted financial statements. These are then broken down into functional budgets (personnel, purchasing, etc.) and into sub-budgets on the basis of the spheres of responsibility of individual managers. Because the managers concerned have been involved with formulating their respective sub-budgets from the outset, they can therefore be held accountable for achieving the budgeted performance.

PUTTING THE BUDGET TO WORK

The purpose of budget preparation is to create planned targets against which actual figures can be measured, so that divergences can be identified and corrective action can be taken to eradicate them. Functional budgets and sub-budgets are phased down to quarters or months or, in the case of cash budgets, to weeks. Actual figures can then be compared constantly with budgeted figures throughout the year, so that adverse trends can be detected early, and corrected.

Budgets can be prepared according to one of the following approaches:

- incremental, i.e. adjusted versions of previous budgeted or actual figures

- zero-based, which means that they are prepared as if for the first time.

THE NATURE AND PURPOSE
OF BUDGETING

SAT:
allow 10 mins

Managing tasks and solving problems ✓

ACTIVITY 2

Zero-based budgeting is considered a more powerful approach to controlling the cost of activities, but the incremental approach is more popular with the people who have to prepare the budget.

Why should this be? Consider what is involved in each approach, and then say briefly what you think.

Commentary...

Zero-based budgeting is a much more searching examination of each activity:

- Does the activity actually make a significant contribution to overall objectives, or can it be reduced, or even ceased altogether?

- Are the means of carrying it out that were used in the past still the most economic, or should new ways of doing it be considered?

- Precisely what resources are needed to carry out this activity, and can their cost be reduced?

It is also much harder work. Incremental budgeting, by comparison, often consists of little more than adding a percentage 'uplift' to last year's actual results.

This tends to be inflationary in its impact, and it contrasts strongly with the 'kaizen' or continuous improvement approach to budgeting used in Japan, whereby active efforts to reduce costs are part of the budgeting process.

RECALL:
allow 10 mins

Briefly define:

1. **principal budget factor**

2. **master budget**

3. **functional budget.**

Application of budgetary control

Now that we have examined the principles of preparing budgets, we can apply them to the construction of a budget, and compare actual results with it.

We can construct a simple budget from a few facts. For this purpose we will assume that the master budget for the year has been prepared already and that the present task is to phase it to months. We will do so just for the first month, January in Year 7. (The same procedure would apply to the other eleven months.)

The budget data from which we will produce a phased master budget for January Year 7 is shown in account 6.1.

Budget data

Sales	10,000 units at £45 per unit	
Opening stock	20,000 units at £30 per unit	
Purchases	15,000 units at £31 per unit	
Closing stock	25,000 units (by derivation),	£755,000

		£000
Fixed assets:	opening balance	330
	additions in January Year 7	60
Debtors (trade):	opening balance	650
	receipts in January Year 7	400
Creditors (trade):	opening balance	500
	payments in January Year 7	415
(other):	opening balance	25
	payments in January Year 7	Nil

Bank: opening balance	70
various cash expenses in January Year 7	90
other receipts and payments as given for debtors, fixed assets and trade creditors	

	£000
Expenses in January Year 7	
wages and salaries	39
power, heat and light	14
repairs	20
depreciation of fixed assets	30
other cash expenses	17

ACCOUNT 6.1: Budget data.

From this data it is now possible to produce the phased version of the master budget for January Year 7 (account 6.2).

**Budgeted profit and loss account
for the month ended 31 January Year 7**

	£000	£000
Sales (10,000 x £45)		450
Opening stock (20,000 x £30)	600	
Purchases (15,000 x £31)	465	
	1,065	
Closing stock (25,000)	755	
Cost of sales (derived)		310
Gross profit (derived)		140
less		
Wages and salaries	39	
Power, heat and light	14	
Repairs	20	
Depreciation	30	
Other cash expenses	17	
		120
Profit/(loss) (derived)		20

Budgeted balance sheet
as at 31 January Year 7

	£000	£000
Fixed assets		
(330 + 60 additions – 30 depreciation)		360
Current assets		
Stock	755	
Debtors (650 + 450 sales – 400 receipts)	700	
	1,455	
Creditors due in less than one year		
Trade creditors	550	
(500 + 465 purchases – 415 payments)		
Other creditors	25	
Bank overdraft (Workings 1)	95	
	670	
Net current assets		785
Total assets less current liabilities		1,145
Shareholders' funds (derived)		1,145

Workings 1

	£000	
Bank account		
Opening balance	70	
Receipts from debtors	400	
	470	
Payments to creditors	415	
Fixed asset purchases	60	
Other cash expenses paid	90	
	565	
Closing balance (derived)	(95)	overdraft

(Outline) Budgeted cash flow statement
for the month ended 31 January Year 7

	£000
Net cash (outflow) from operating activities (Workings 2)	(105)
Net cash (outflow) from investing activities	(60)
Decrease in cash and cash equivalents	(165)

This net decrease is the same as the difference between the opening cash balance at the bank and the overdraft at the end of the period (70 – (95)).

Workings 2

	£000
Operating profit	20
Depreciation of fixed assets	30
Increase in: debtors (700 – 650)	(50)
stock (755 – 600)	(155)
creditors (550 – 500)	50
Net cash (outflow) from operating activities	(105)

ACCOUNT 6.2: Budgeted profit and loss account, balance sheet
and cash flow statement.

APPLICATION OF

BUDGETARY CONTROL

MAKING THE COMPARISON WITH ACTUAL PERFORMANCE

At the end of January, the actual figures will be compared with the budgeted figures and the variances (differences) between the two sets of figures will be derived (i.e. identified) and then analysed. We describe the variances as:

- favourable (F), if they are better than budgeted

- adverse (A) if they are worse than budgeted.

Thus higher actual sales and lower actual costs would both produce a favourable variance; while lower sales and higher costs would result in an adverse variance. The budgeted/actual comparisons which now follow are restricted to the profit and loss account only although in practice they can be applied to the balance sheet and cash flow statement. Actual figures have been assumed.

Profit and loss account
for the month ended 31 January Year 7

	Budget		Actual		Variances		
	£000	£000	£000	£000	£000	£000	
Sales		450		460		10	(F)
Opening stock	600		631				
Purchases	465		493				
	1,065		1,124				
Closing stock	755		792				
Cost of sales		310		332		22	
Gross profit		140		128		12	
less							
Wages and salaries	39		41		2		
Power, heat and light	14		13		1		
Repairs	20		27		7		
Depreciation	30		30		-		
Other cash expenses	17		18		1		
		120		129		9	
Profit/(loss)		20		(1)		21	

ACCOUNT 6.3: Making comparisons of budgets against actual costs.

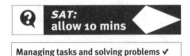

SAT:
allow 10 mins

Managing tasks and solving problems ✔

ACTIVITY 3

Look carefully at the two 'variance' columns in account 6.3 (the two right-most columns). Write F (for favourable) or A (for adverse) against each of these numbers, according to your judgement. We have already identified the first one: the sales variance of 10 is favourable, because sales are above budget, and this would be a good thing.

Commentary...

The only other favourable variance is cost of power, heat and light and, in any case, this variance is too small to be significant. All the other variances are adverse. There is no variance for depreciation because this is a 'book' figure set in advance.

A small monthly loss, instead of a budgeted profit of £20,000, is a serious matter, and clearly the variances will need to be examined and analysed to see what action needs to be taken.

ACTIVITY 4

In groups of three or four, discuss the implications of account 6.3. Management will want to investigate and analyse the main variances.

1. What are the main sources of the overall adverse variance?

2. Where do you think the explanation may lie, and what points do you think merit further investigation?

Summarise your main points in the box below.

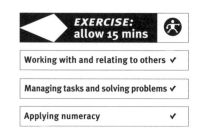

**EXERCISE:
allow 15 mins**

Working with and relating to others	✓
Managing tasks and solving problems	✓
Applying numeracy	✓

Commentary...

The investigation of the variances will try to answer the question: 'Why, even when sales are above budget, has the company made an actual loss for the period, compared with a budgeted profit?' Investigation is likely to focus on:

- the sales variance, which, though favourable, would be further analysed to establish how much of the variance was attributable to increased volume of sales and how much to increased price

- the expenses, which would be analysed to assess whether the increased cost of wages and salaries might be due to pay awards and/or overtime payments not included in the budget

- the adverse variance on repairs, which could be due to an overspend and/or major repairs out of phase with the budget

- the cost of sales, which has produced the highest adverse variance.

The variance in the cost of sales is probably due to price increases on goods bought for resale. It would seem that these have not been passed on to the customers in selling prices, and consequently gross profit has been adversely affected. Higher prices might have reduced sales somewhat, but would have maintained gross profit.

It is not usual to investigate all variances, but only those regarded as significant.

In some cases – activity 4, for example – this analysis of the variance between budgets and outcomes is fairly straightforward, but this is not always so. Stokkit, for instance, sells a large range of dissimilar goods, and this creates certain difficulties:

- Stokkit's sales budget is an aggregation of various quantities of different lines, all at different prices, and actual sales will be a similar aggregation of actual items.

- An added problem is that the sales mix, i.e the proportion of each line to total sales, will be different in the budget from the actual.

- Differences due to price, volume and mix will have to be identified separately for each sales line.

Flexible budgets

We have examined how actual results are compared with budgets and how the resultant differences, i.e. variances, are identified and analysed.

One difficulty with this approach is that the level of actual activity rarely, if ever, coincides with the budgeted level. The variances between the two sets of figures are then partly due to differences in the activity level, and partly due to underspending or overspending. From a control viewpoint, a manager cannot be held responsible if the department is required to work at an activity level different from that which had been budgeted, but the same manager is responsible for the amount of spending at that actual level.

An example should help to explain this issue. Moore & Law is a manufacturer which supplies Stokkit. Moore & Law's maximum output is 30,000 units each month, but normal output is in the region of 20,000 units and the budget has been prepared on this basis.

	Period 5			
	Budget	Actual	Variances	
Sales (units)	20,000	24,000	4,000	[F]
	£000	£000	£000	
Sales	500	576	____	__
less				
Costs:				
Direct labour	80	72		
Direct materials	160	216		
Production overheads	150	176		
Selling and distribution overheads	20	23		
Administration overheads	15	14	____	__
Total costs	425	501	____	__
Profit/(loss)	75	75	____	__

ACCOUNT 6.4: Moore & Law – Period 5 budget analysis.

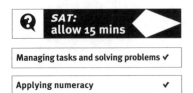

SAT:
allow 15 mins

Managing tasks and solving problems ✔

Applying numeracy ✔

ACTIVITY 5

Look carefully at the data given in account 6.4.

1. Work out the variances and enter them in the blank slots.

2. Indicate whether each variance is favourable (F) or adverse (A).

3. Comment generally on the scale and source of the variances.

Commentary...

The variances are: sales, 76 (F); direct labour, 8 (F); direct materials, 56 (A); production overheads, 26 (A); selling and distribution overheads, 3 (A); administration overheads, 1 (F); total costs, 76 (A). There is no variance for the profit/loss figure.

It would be misleading to take these variances at their face value because we know that the costs associated with the extra sales are partly responsible. For example, we would expect direct materials cost to be higher by reason of the additional amount of materials needed for the extra 4,000 units sold.

One solution to this problem is to prepare budgets at different levels of activity and to flex them to coincide with the actual level of activity. Any variances between the actual results and the flexed budget can then be regarded as controllable by, and therefore the responsibility of, the departmental manager.

PREPARING A FLEXIBLE BUDGET

Budgets are prepared for appropriate levels of activity, based on the manner in which costs behave, i.e. whether they are fixed, variable or semi-variable. Using the facts of the earlier example, Moore & Law might produce a 'flexed' budget for three levels of activity – maximum, normal and minimum output/sales levels – as shown in account 6.5.

Flexed budget – Period 5			
	Minimum	Normal	Maximum
Sales (units)	10,000	20,000	30,000
	£000	£000	£000
Sales	250	500	750
less			
Costs			
Direct labour	40	80	120
Direct materials	80	160	240
Production overheads	90	150	210
Selling and distribution overheads	20	20	20
Administration overheads	15	15	15
Total costs	245	425	605
Profit/(loss)	5	75	145

ACCOUNT 6.5: Moore & Law – Period 5 flexed budget analysis.

The actual sales for Period 5 were, as in the previous example, 24,000 units. The budget is therefore flexed to coincide with this level. Before this can be done we have to identify the variable costs, which will change with the volume of sales, and the fixed costs which will not.

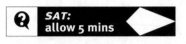

SAT:
allow 5 mins

Managing tasks and solving problems ✔

Applying numeracy ✔

ACTIVITY 6

Applying what you know about the behaviour of fixed costs at different levels of activity, identify the fixed costs in this flexible budget (account 6.5) and list them in the box below.

Commentary...

An examination of the flexed budget reveals that selling and distribution overheads and administration overheads are the same figures at all three sales levels. This clearly indicates that they are fixed.

The other items produce different figures at all three sales levels, which indicates that they must be either variable or semi-variable. We can make a positive identification by calculating costs per unit:

Formula:

$$\frac{\text{Total cost at this level of activity}}{\text{Quantity produced}} = \text{Per unit cost}$$

The activity below shows how the per-unit cost can be calculated for each cost at each level of activity.

ACTIVITY 7

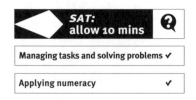

Managing tasks and solving problems ✔

Applying numeracy   ✔

Look again at the figures in the table below which are based on account 6.5.

Flexed budget   -   Period 5

Sales (units)	10,000		20,000		30,000	
	Total £000	Per unit £	Total £000	Per unit £	Total £000	Per unit £
Direct labour	40	4	80	4	120	
Direct materials	80	8	160	8	240	
Production overheads	90	9	150	7.5	210	

Calculate the per-unit cost for each of the three items when the volume of sales is 30,000. Comment on what your results show about the behaviour of each of these costs.

Commentary...

The per-unit cost for direct labour is (120,000/30,000 =) 4; for direct material it is (240,000/30,000 =) 8; for production overheads it is (210,000/30,000 =) 7.

As expected, direct labour cost and direct materials cost are both variable costs; the cost per unit has remained constant at each sales level. Production overheads are not a fixed cost, in the normal sense, because the amount changes at each sales level; but since the unit cost has also changed, this indicates that production overheads are also not a variable cost.

Production overhead can, therefore, only be a semi-variable cost. The problem now is to identify constituent elements of the production overhead, so that we can budget for production levels that fall between these very convenient, round amounts that we have included on the flexed budget. This can be done by further analysis. We know that any difference in cost at the three different levels must be attributable to the variable element.

	Volume 000 units	Cost £000	Variable cost Per unit £
Production overheads			
	10	90	
	+10	+60	6
	20	150	
	+10	+60	6
	30	210	

ACCOUNT 6.6: Calculating the variable cost element of the production overhead.

In account 6.6, activity increases under the first column, the semi-variable costs in the second column are added, and this produces the per-unit variable cost in the third column. We have now identified the variable cost element of production overheads as £6 per unit, thereby enabling the flexed budget for production overheads to be re-written in an expanded form (account 6.7).

	Flexed budget - Period 5		
Sales (units)	10,000	20,000	30,000
	Total	Total	Total
Production overheads	£000	£000	£000
variable (£6)	60	120	180
fixed	30	30	30
total	90	150	210

ACCOUNT 6.7: Moore & Law – Period 5 flexed budget for production overheads.

Using this information in conjunction with the facts we previously discovered about per-unit costs, we can now prepare a flexed budget for the actual sales volume of 24,000 units, and derive variances of actual results from it. Work through the figures in account 6.8 carefully, line-by-line.

	Period 5							
	Flexed budget		Actual		Variances			
Sales (units)	24,000		24,000		---			
	Per unit £	total £000	Per unit £	total £000	Per unit £		total £000	
Sales	25	600	24	576	1	(A)	24	(A)
less								
Variable costs								
Direct labour	4	96	3	72	1	(F)	24	(F)
Direct materials	8	192	9	216	1	(A)	24	(A)
Production overheads	6	144	6	144	–	—	–	—
	18	432	18	432	–	—	–	—
Contribution	7	168	6	144	1	(A)	24	(A)
less								
Fixed overheads								
Production		30		32			2	(A)
Selling and distribution		20		23			3	(A)
Administration		15		14			1	(F)
		65		69			4	(A)
Profit/(loss)		103		75			28	(A)

ACCOUNT 6.8: Comparing actual costs with flexed budgets.

ACTIVITY 8

Look carefully at the variances produced by this flexed budget for Moore & Law in Period 5, and compare it to the results produced by the fixed budget (account 6.4) for the same period.

Explain how the results differ from those produced in the fixed budget, in the light of the additional costing information.

SAT: allow 15 mins

Managing tasks and solving problems ✔

Applying numeracy ✔

Commentary...

This comparison with the flexed budget discloses an entirely different situation from the earlier comparison with the fixed budget, and is far more informative and useful.

We can now see that there is an adverse sales variance of £24,000, whereas originally there was a favourable variance of £76,000. The original favourable variance on direct labour of £8,000 has increased to £24,000. Even more drastically, the adverse variance of £56,000 on direct materials has been reduced to £24,000. Production overheads now have a £2,000 adverse variance; the original £26,000 adverse variance was mainly due to variable overhead on which there is now no difference. Overall there was no variance originally but on a flexed basis it is £28,000 adverse.

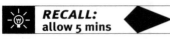

RECALL:
allow 5 mins

Distinguish between:

1. **fixed and flexible budgets**

2. **fixed and variable costs.**

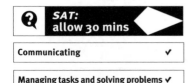

SAT:
allow 30 mins

Communicating	✔
Managing tasks and solving problems	✔

ACTIVITY 9

The business for which you work employs a system of budgetary control based on fixed budgets, but the budgeting process is under review.

Write a short report outlining the arguments for and against introducing a system of flexible budgeting, for discussion at a forthcoming management meeting. Summarise your key points below.

Commentary...

Arguments against change include:

- preparation of flexible budgets would require a much greater input of time and effort

- use of a fixed budget based on normal level of activity, highlights effects of actual activity above or below this level

- separate calculations can be used to calculate differences due to changes in levels of activity.

Arguments for change include:

- with the elimination of volume changes, all the variances relate to factors which are controllable by the budget holder, such as underspending, overspending, re-scheduling and so on, making managers more accountable

- it easier to compile if a marginal cost system is used for decision making because the various figures will have been analysed on a behavioural basis.

Cash budgets

Cash, and what we described as 'near cash' (cash equivalents), are very important in the management of finance:

- A classified statement of cash inflows and outflows is a mandatory annual requirement in the Annual Report and Accounts of companies.

- Cash and bank balances are components of solvency and liquidity calculations, and are central to the control of working capital.

In fact, cash budgeting is regarded as so important that it warrants closer examination.

RECALL:
allow 10 mins

Define the following terms:

1. cash equivalent ('near-cash')

2. solvency

3. liquidity.

ACTIVITY 10

The balances of cash and bank account disclosed by the balance sheet relate only to the balance sheet date. Similarly, the cash and 'cash equivalents' movements schedule in the cash flow statement are only a summary of transactions during the period.

These are significant drawbacks, greatly reducing the value of these mandatory statements for management purposes. Why?

Commentary...

In neither case do they shed any light on the cash position at intermediate points throughout the period. The fact that a business may have adequate cash resources at the start and end of the year, and an overall cash surplus for the year, fails to tell us anything about whether, and at what point during the year, there has been a cash shortage.

A cash budget helps to prevent this situation arising by planning the cash requirements at regular intervals throughout each year. In practical terms, this may mean monthly, but sometimes they are prepared weekly.

The cash budget has to reflect the cash implications of all the other budgets that either produce or require cash, including budgets for:

- sales

- debtors

- purchases for resale

- creditors

CASH BUDGETS

- cash expenses
- fixed assets.

A monthly cash budget is prepared as follows:

1. Budgeted receipts and payments are detailed so that the cash surplus or deficit for the month can be derived.

2. The surplus or deficit is adjusted by the balance brought forward from the previous month, to produce the closing balance for the current month.

3. This closing balance then becomes the opening balance for the next month.

Weekly, or even daily, cash budgets are prepared on precisely the same lines.

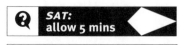

SAT:
allow 5 mins

Managing tasks and solving problems ✔

ACTIVITY 11

At any one time, a business should have separate monthly cash budgets available for at least twelve months ahead.

If any month shows a negative closing balance, the business has two options. What do you consider these would be?

Commentary...

One option is to arrange for an overdraft to cover the deficit (in practice, most businesses arrange a standing overdraft facility to cover precisely this eventuality). Alternatively (or in addition) the budgeted plans can be altered to eliminate the need for an overdraft.

CONSTRUCTING A CASH BUDGET

A cash budget must be compatible with all the other individual budgets. This being so, each budget involving revenue, expense, asset and liability items must be examined and the cash aspects scheduled on a cash budget statement. An outline for this is given in account 6.9.

	Jan £	Feb £	Mar £	Apr £	May £	June £	July £	Aug £	Sept £	Oct £	Nov £	Dec £
Receipts												
(itemised)	x	x	x	x	x	x	x	x	x	x	x	x
(A) :total	x	x	x	x	x	x	x	x	x	x	x	x
Payments												
(itemised)	x	x	x	x	x	x	x	x	x	x	x	x
(B) :total	x	x	x	x	x	x	x	x	x	x	x	x
(C) Surplus(A)-(B)	x	x	x	x	x	x	x	x	x	x	x	x
or Deficit (B)-(A) for month	(x)	(x)	(x)	(x)	(x)	(x)	(x)	(x)	(x)	(x)	(x)	(x)
(D) Opening balance	x	x	x	x	x	x	x	x	x	x	x	x
or (overdraft)	(x)	(x)	(x)	(x)	(x)	(x)	(x)	(x)	(x)	(x)	(x)	(x)
(E) Closing balance	x	x	x	x	x	x	x	x	x	x	x	x
or overdraft (C)+(D)	(x)	(x)	(x)	(x)	(x)	(x)	(x)	(x)	(x)	(x)	(x)	(x)

ACCOUNT 6.9: Model cash budget.

We can apply these principles to the budgeted activities of Fullerton's, one of Stokkit's customers. In preparing the monthly cash budget for the second half of the year, the following information contained in account 6.10 is available.

The data provided in account 6.10 has to be processed into a form suitable for inclusion in a cash budget.

Sales on credit

There is a time lag of two months' between the sale taking place and payment being received. May's sales (£40,000) will result in a July receipt. Sales made in November and December will not be received in cash until the following year.

Credit purchases

There is a time lag of one month between purchase and payment. June's purchases (£28,000) will be paid for in July, while those made in December will not be paid for until the following year.

Wages and salaries

The effect of a payment two weeks in arrears is that the July payment will consist of the last half of June's earnings (£8,000) plus the first half of July's earnings (£10,000), a total actual payment in July of £9,000 (i.e. £4,000 plus £5,000). Similar reasoning is applied to the earnings of the other months.

Fullerton's: Budget data

		£000
Cash sales:	July and August	2
(per month)	September and October	3
	November and December	1
Credit sales:	May	40
	June	42
	July	48
	August	38
	September	46
	October	44
	November	44
	December	48

Customers are required to pay the amounts they owe two months after the month in which the sale has taken place.

Sale of asset for cash:	August	2

Purchases on credit:	June	28
	July	30
	August	26
	September	28
	October	28
	November	30
	December	30

Suppliers are paid in the month after the month in which the purchase has taken place.

Wages and salaries earned:	June	8
	July	10
	August	10
	September	10
	October	12
	November	12
	December	10

Wages and salaries are paid fortnightly in arrears.

Other cash expenses:	July to September	7
(per month)	October to December	8
Corporation tax paid:	September	19
Vehicles bought for cash:	July	15
	November	16
Agreed overdraft limit		10
Opening bank balance		35

ACCOUNT 6.10: Fullerton's budget data.

We are now in a position to construct the cash budget.

Cash budget - July to December Year XX

	July £000	Aug £000	Sept £000	Oct £000	Nov £000	Dec £000
Receipts						
Cash sales	2	2	3	3	1	1
Debtors	40	42	48	38	46	44
Sale of assets	—	2	—	—	—	—
Total	42	46	51	41	47	45
Payments						
Creditors	28	30	26	28	28	30
Wages and salaries	9	10	10	11	12	11
Other cash expenses	7	7	7	8	8	8
Capital expenditure- vehicles	15				16	
Corporation tax	—	—	19	—	—	—
Total	59	47	62	47	64	49
Surplus/(deficit) on month	(17)	(1)	(11)	(6)	(17)	(4)
Opening balance (b/fwd)	35	18	17	6	----	(17)
Closing balance (c/fwd)	18	—	—	—	—	—

ACCOUNT 6.11: Constructing a cash budget.

ACTIVITY 12

Work through account 6.11 carefully line-by-line, tracing where the figures have come from.

Calculate the closing balances for the months August to December and enter them in the blank slots in account 6.11.

Write down your conclusions about the cash flow situation during the six-month period.

SAT:
allow 20 mins

Managing tasks and solving problems ✓

Applying numeracy ✓

CASH BUDGETS

Commentary...

The closing balance figures are: 17, 6, nil, (17), (21). It is apparent that there is a serious problem in November and December because the budget discloses an overdraft of £17,000 rising to £21,000 whereas there is an overdraft ceiling of £10,000.

The question arises as to how to deal with the situation. There are various alternative courses of action. It might be possible to negotiate a higher overdraft limit with the bank. Failing that, the business must alter its plans in one or more ways.

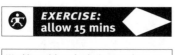

EXERCISE:
allow 15 mins

Working with and relating to others ✔

Managing tasks and solving problems ✔

Applying numeracy ✔

ACTIVITY 13

Work in groups to discuss this problem. Try to come up with tactics for improving cash flow so as to bring the overdraft back under control. Think about ways of both reducing outgoings and increasing revenue. What would be the impact of each suggestion? How practical would it be?

Note your main suggestions in the box below.

Commentary...

Receipts could perhaps be accelerated by reducing the period of credit allowed to customers from two months to one month. While this would theoretically solve the problem, if it were put into practice in July, it would almost certainly meet with resistance from the customers, who might then desert the company and buy from another source. Ideally, receipts might be increased by an increase in sales but this is not likely to be easy to achieve.

Delaying payments to creditors by an extra month would also solve the problem, but this is not likely to be a realistic option because the creditors would become apprehensive and would probably stop supplies.

Deferring the purchase of vehicles until the following year could be a workable solution. On the other hand, if it was essential to buy the vehicles, it would be advantageous to obtain them under a leasing or a hire purchase contract. (Refer back to session 2 to see how leasing assets, or buying them on hire purchase, could help the cash flow situation.)

Another option is that a reduction in purchases could be a strong possibility, as they seem high in relation to sales.

ACTIVITY 14

ASSIGNMENT: allow 45 mins
Managing and developing self ✔
Working with and relating to others ✔
Communicating ✔
Applying numeracy ✔

A group of friends has recently set up a company called Julludo Limited to develop, manufacture and retail games. There is a workshop, a small warehouse, a retail shop and an extensive retail mail-order business. Julludo also publishes a monthly subscription magazine for games enthusiasts. About a dozen people are directly employed in these various functions, and others are developing new games under contract.

Your task is to write a report recommending a budgeting system for Julludo. You should ensure that it answers the following questions:

1. How will the budgeting process be managed? Who will control it, and what do they do to ensure that all the information is produced on time?

2. For how many years ahead will budgets be prepared?

3. On what basis should they be prepared (e.g. incremental, zero-based, or other)?

4. Will a fixed budget or a flexible budget be more appropriate?

5. What periods should the budget be broken down into?

6. What subsidiary budgets will feed into the master budget?

7. How often should performance against budget be reviewed?

8. How will the various departmental managers be made accountable for their budgets?

You may find it useful to talk to someone with experience of drawing up budgets, but all the basic information that you need is contained within this session. Write your report on separate sheets of paper. Summarise your main findings below.

summary

▶ Budgetary control involves the planning and control of the financial aspects of the performance of a business.

▶ A master budget is prepared, supported by subsidiary functional and sub-budgets, against which actual results are compared and divergences identified leading to corrective action.

▶ The master budget comprises the profit and loss account, balance sheet and cash flow statement against which actual results are compared.

▶ Significant variances should be identified and analysed further so that decisions can be taken to rectify adverse trends.

▶ Use of a fixed budget for comparison of actual figures produces variances arising from spending.

▶ Substitution of flexible budgets eliminates the volume element leaving the spending variances within the control of, and remaining the responsibility of, the budget holder. They are therefore a more effective control mechanism.

▶ Cash is so important to the survival and progress of a business that it must be strictly monitored. This is done by means of a monthly or weekly cash budget in which details of budgeted receipts and payments are recorded and used to derive the balance of cash or overdraft at the end of each month.

Capital investment appraisal

CAPITAL EXPENDITURE

PAYBACK METHODS

ACCOUNTING RATE OF RETURN

NET PRESENT VALUE AND YIELD

INTEREST RATES, WEIGHTED AVERAGE COST OF CAPITAL

Objectives

After participating in this session, you should be able to:

 understand the characteristics of capital expenditure and its role in the budgeting process

 explain the nature and principles of payback, discounted payback, accounting rate of return, net present value, and yield, and their respective advantages and disadvantages

 undertake appraisals using these methods

 explain and apply the principles of discounting

 understand the considerations affecting the choice of an interest rate for capital expenditure purposes

 explain the principle behind weighted average cost of capital.

In working through this session, you will practise the following BTEC common skills:

Managing and developing self	✔
Working with and relating to others	✔
Communicating	✔
Managing tasks and solving problems	✔
Applying numeracy	✔
Applying technology	
Applying design and creativity	

Capital expenditure

All businesses are involved in transactions every working day that result in expenses. Examples of expenses, often referred to as revenue expenditure, are numerous and include:

- cost of goods sold in the period (cost of sales)

- wages and salaries paid for work done during the period

- power consumed during the period, and so on.

Revenue expenses are set against the revenue of the period to disclose a profit or a loss, and are financed by working capital.

Less frequently, but very importantly, businesses incur capital expenditure: expenditure incurred on acquiring or producing fixed assets, or on improving or extending them.

Fixed assets are those assets acquired by a business for retention beyond the current accounting period and not held for the purpose of resale. The service potential of a fixed asset endures for a number of accounting periods, whereas revenue expenditure is fully consumed in the period in which it is acquired. We have also seen that the cost of acquiring a fixed asset constitutes capital expenditure, but depreciation on it, which represents the part of the asset's life used up during the period, is an expense of the period.

Note that small items that meet the technical definition of fixed assets (because they have a life longer than the accounting period), are nevertheless treated as expenses for accounting purposes. This includes such items of equipment as filing boxes, pocket calculators, screwdrivers, etc. This is a matter of expediency, because the administrative cost of recording and tracking these items would be greater than their value.

Two defining characteristics of what we treat as capital expenditure are:

1. that it will involve a very significant outlay, and

2. that the benefits of the expenditure will last for a number of years.

ACTIVITY 1

Give three examples of capital expenditure projects that Stokkit might undertake.

Commentary...

Capital expenditure projects are usually associated either with the replacement and upgrading of existing assets, or the creation of new ones – i.e. expansion. A business like Stokkit might contemplate extending the warehouse, rebuilding part or all of the existing facilities, installing automated handling equipment, buying a new fleet of vehicles, refurbishing the offices or installing a computerised stock management system.

Unlike the decision-making situations looked at in session 5, decisions about capital expenditure are not short-term ones that can be made lightly or easily changed. They involve the commitment of substantial sums of money, and the financial outlays involved with capital expenditure would cripple many companies financially if such projects were to be abandoned in their early stages.

CAPITAL EXPENDITURE IN THE BUDGETING PROCESS

Capital expenditure is part of the budgetary control process. The production, selling, distribution and administration budgets will have been formulated on the assumption that adequate fixed asset resources exist to finance them. Where such sums are not available, they will have to be acquired, and this becomes an objective, which forms the basis of the capital expenditure budget.

When the need for fixed asset acquisitions has been identified, there will usually be several different versions of the scheme between which the business will have to choose. It can only select one of the alternatives, and once the capital expenditure commitment has been made it cannot change its mind without suffering heavy financial losses.

There are a number of techniques to help a business to discriminate on purely financial grounds between otherwise equally acceptable projects, and the business should decide on which technique is most appropriate in the circumstances.

THE FINANCING OF CAPITAL INVESTMENT

The implementation of a capital investment programme depends on the availability of an adequate amount of finance. Sources and types of finance are many and varied, as we saw in session 2, but not all of these sources and types are suitable for financing capital projects. For example, a bank overdraft, being repayable on demand or at short notice, could not be used to finance a project with, say, a five-to ten-year life.

The most usual types of finance for long-term projects are:

- retained profits
- share issues
- long-term borrowings
- leasing and hire purchase.

Retained profits are profits that have not been distributed as dividends or converted into share capital. They are an ideal source of capital expenditure finance, because they do not involve external providers or interest payments.

Share issues are a possibility when finance needs to be raised from outside the company. From the company's viewpoint, the most effective means would be to make a rights issue (see session 2), as this is cheaper than a public issue. Companies have the power to redeem and to purchase their own shares for cancellation, which is an important consideration if the project is expected to generate sufficient cash in later years to make the continued existence of the shares unnecessary.

Long-term borrowings usually take the form of a loan or a debenture issue. Both types of finance involve payment of interest, which will be included in the project costs for the purpose of the appraisal calculations. Companies will be aware that this type of finance affects their gearing.

Leasing and hire purchase are a common method of financing capital projects. The finance lease rentals are taken into account in the appraisal calculations. Hire purchase is relatively more costly than leasing and is usually for a maximum of three years.

 **RECALL:**
allow 10 mins

Briefly summarise the various method of financing capital projects, listing the advantages and disadvantages of each.

Payback methods

One method of appraising seemingly equally acceptable capital expenditure proposals is known as payback.

The method focuses on measuring the timing of net cash flows, by which we mean the net of the receipts generated by a project and of the payments attributable to it. Some projects do not produce receipts, as such, but cost savings which are treated as equivalent to receipts.

Imagine that you are trying to decide between two projects: both cost £400,000 initially, both have a life estimated at five years and during that time they both produce a net cash inflow (excess of receipts over payments) of £530,000. At first sight there appears to be nothing to choose between them. Payback, however, examines the pattern of the net cash flows and selects the project with the earlier payback, that is, the first project that generates a net cash inflow equal to its initial outflow (cost).

Year	Project A Inflow/(outflow) Current £000	A Cumul £000	B Inflow/(outflow) Current £000	B Cumul £000	C Inflow/(outflow) Current £000	C Cumul 3000
0 (Initial cost)	(400)	(400)	(400)	(400)	(400)	(400)
1	50	(350)	190	(210)	50	
2	60		160	(50)	60	
3	70		70		70	
4	160	(60)	60		200	
5	(net surplus)190	130	50		220	

ACCOUNT 7.1: Evaluating different capital expenditure proposals.

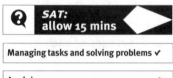

SAT: allow 15 mins

Managing tasks and solving problems ✓

Applying numeracy ✓

ACTIVITY 2

Suppose that a company is considering three capital expenditure projects. The details are shown in account 7.1.

Work through the figures in Account 7.1 carefully, and calculate the cumulative inflows (or outflows) that are blank.

Note the net surplus that is produced by each project. Ascertain the points at which the various projects reach payback. Using the payback as the criterion, decide which project would be selected. Comment on your decision.

Commentary...

The figures missing are: from project A, (290) and (220) respectively; from B, 20, 80 and 130; and from C, (350), (290), (220), (20) and 200.

From these figures, we can see that project C produces the biggest net surplus (of net cash inflows minus initial outlay) of £200,000 while those of projects A and B are identical at £130,000 each.

Using payback as the criterion, project B would be selected because it recovers its initial outlay and moves into surplus in Year 3, whereas projects A and C do not do so until Year 5. Although in total inflow terms there is nothing to choose between projects A and B, project B is regarded as superior on the basis of payback, because the reversal of the net cash inflow patterns means that the project pays for itself much sooner.

Payback is very simple to understand and apply but it has a number of drawbacks (apart from the general one that applies to all capital expenditure appraisal, i.e. the amount and timing of net cash flows are estimates).

1. Cash flows received after the payback period are ignored. On this basis project C was rejected even though it had an overall net cash inflow of £200,000, compared with only £130,000 for projects A and B.

2. Payback ignores the profitability of projects, concentrating solely on net cash flows.

Now consider projects E and F, both of which involve an initial outlay of £190,000 and last for five years. Project E produces a net surplus of £45,000 and pays back in Year 3, while project F produces a net surplus of £160,000 and pays back in Year 4.

	Project E		Project F	
Year	Inflow/(outflow)		Inflow/(outflow)	
	Current	Cumul	Current	Cumul
	£000	£000	£000	£000
0	(190)	(190)	(190)	(190)
1	40	(150)	50	(140)
2	110	(40)	60	(80)
3	70	30	60	(20)
4	10	40	90	70
5	5	45	90	160

ACCOUNT 7.2: Evaluating capital expenditure projects E and F.

It is clearly a drawback of the payback method of appraisal that project E would be selected in preference to F. Despite these disadvantages, payback is used not only because it is simple and easy to apply, but also because for many businesses, the early recouping of initial outlays is so important that it outweighs all other considerations. This might be the case if the project is being financed by a loan that must be repaid in, say, three years. The other factor in its favour is that the shorter the recouping period, the less are the associated risks.

A final criticism that can be levelled at the payback method is that it ignores the time value of money. This problem can be addressed by using a modified version of payback, known as discounted payback, which we now consider.

DISCOUNTED PAYBACK

This method still asks 'When does payback happen?' but it takes an additional factor into account – the so-called time value of money. It considers a further option: that instead of using the money to finance a capital expenditure project, the business could simply put it in the bank, or into a safe, predictable investment to produce a return which, for the sake of argument, we will assume to be in the form of interest.

In other words, given that the business could be earning, say, 8 per cent interest anyway, it asks 'What are the future inflows really worth as an alternative use of the money?' After all, if the business can earn 8 per cent with little or no risk, the proposed project must offer a return of at least 8 per cent! Otherwise why bother with it?

In the discount payback method, the future cash flows are discounted at a pre-determined interest rate (basically at the rate that could be earned elsewhere, with minimal risk), the effect of which is to strip out the presumed interest, leaving the principal element of the net cash inflow.

So, if a project provides an inflow of £100 in three years' time, the investor needs to calculate what that £100 is worth in terms of today's value, given that he or she could have been earning, say, 10 per cent interest on it for three years. In fact, as you see in a moment, if it is discounted at 10 per cent, the £100 turns out to be worth only £75.10 in present-value terms.

Discounted payback is a straightforward calculation based on this idea.

DISCOUNT FACTORS

The elimination of the presumed interest through discounting is relatively easy, thanks to the existence of published tables of discount factors (see Resource 1 at the end of this workbook). It is a simple matter to read off the factors for each year, for any given rate of interest, and to apply those factors to the net cash flows of the appropriate years to arrive at the principal elements of the net cash flows.

Look at Resource 1 now. Look across the columns until you find the discount factors for a rate of 10 per cent. You can see the following:

Year	10%
1	0.909
2	0.826
3	0.751
4	0.683
5	0.621

The figures show that we would have to invest £90.90 (£100 x 0.909) to produce £100 after one year at 10 per cent. Interest would be £9.09 (10% of £90.90) making a total of £99.99 (or £100 to the nearest £1) at the end of the year. Note that the year of the actual investment, Year 0, always has a factor of 1.000, irrespective of the interest rate.

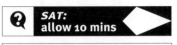

SAT:
allow 10 mins

Managing tasks and solving problems ✔

Applying numeracy ✔

ACTIVITY 3

How much would you need to invest now at a rate of 10 per cent to produce £100 in five years?

Using the discount tables, calculate how much you would need to invest at 9 per cent to produce £100 in the same five years?

Commentary...

1. To produce £100 after five years at 10 per cent interest would require an initial investment at the outset of £62.10 (£100 x 0.621).

2. To produce £100 after five years at 9 per cent interest would require an initial investment at the outset of £65.00.

APPLICATION OF DISCOUNTED PAYBACK

We are now in a position to recalculate payback periods on the basis of discounted figures. The formula below shows how the discounting is applied to produce present-value figures:

inflow / (outflow) × discount factor = present value

The discounted payback for project A is a net outflow of £25,000, as shown in account 7.3.

		Project A				
Year	Discount Inflow/(outflow)		Present value factor (10%)	Inflow/(outflow)		
	Current £000	Cumul £000		Current £000	Cumul £000	
0 Initial cost	(400)	(400)	1.000	(400)	(400)	
1	50	(350)	0.909	45	(355)	
2	60	(290)	0.826	50	(305)	
3	70	(220)	0.751	53	(252)	
4	160	(60)	0.683	109	(143)	
5	190	130	0.621	118	(25)	

ACCOUNT 7.3: Discounted payback for project A.

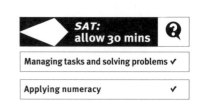

Managing tasks and solving problems ✔

Applying numeracy ✔

ACTIVITY 4

Now apply the same techniques to projects B and C, figures for which are shown below. Fill in the blanks to identify:

1. the discounted net present value of project B after 5 years.

2. the current and cumulative figures for Year 4 and Year 5 of project C (this calculation will be the same as for project A up to the end of Year 3.)

		Project B				
Year	Discount Inflow/(outflow)		factor (10%)	Present value Inflow/(outflow)		
	Current £000	Cumul £000		Current £000	Cumul £000	
0 Initial cost	(400)	(400)	1.000	(400)	(400)	
1	190	(210)	0.909			
2	160	(50)	0.826			
3	70	20	0.751			
4	60	80	0.683			
5	50	130	0.621			

		Project C				
Year	Discount Inflow/(outflow)		factor (10%)	Present value Inflow/(outflow)		
	Current £000	Cumul £000		Current £000	Cumul £000	
0 Initial cost	(400)	(400)	1.000	(400)	(400)	
1	50	(350)	0.909	45	(355)	
2	60	(290)	0.826	50	(305)	
3	70	(220)	0.751	53	(252)	
4	200	(20)	0.683			
5	220	200	0.621			

In what year do projects B and C pay back, according to discounted payback techniques?

Which project would be chosen for selection according to the discounted payback criterion?

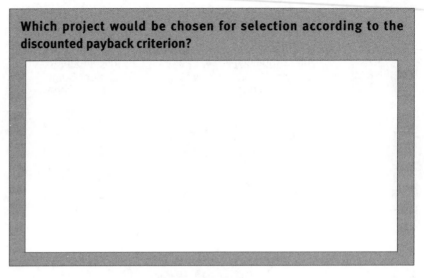

Commentary...

The figures you should have calculated for project B are as follows:

	Present value Inflow/(outflow)	
	Current £000	Cumul £000
0	(supplied)	
1	173	(227)
2	132	(95)
3	53	(42)
4	41	(1)
5	31	30

The figures for Year 4 and Year 5 in project C are:

	Present value Inflow/(outflow)	
	Current £000	Cumul £000
0	(supplied)	
1	(supplied)	
2	(supplied)	
3	(supplied)	
4	137	(115)
5	137	22

On a present-value basis, project A has failed to recoup its initial outlay at the end of Year 5 by an amount of £25,000. Project B has paid back in Year 5, although on a non-discounted basis this occurred in Year 3. Project C has also paid back in Year 5 on a discounted basis. Of the two projects that both pay back in Year 5, project B would be selected on purely financial grounds by reason of its greater net inflow.

In this case, B was the project of choice using both non-discounted and discounted versions of the payback method, but it is common for the two version to rank projects in quite different orders.

ACTIVITY 5

Prepare a short presentation outlining the respective advantages and disadvantages of using payback compared with discounted payback methods of capital investment appraisal.

SAT: allow 20 mins

Communicating ✔

Managing tasks and solving problems ✔

Commentary...

We have listed the advantages and disadvantages in the form of a table (table 7.1). If there is anything here that you are unsure about, consult your tutor.

	Payback	Discounted payback
Advantages		
Simple to understand	√	
Simple to operate	√	
Reduces risk due to passage of time	√	√
Disadvantages		
Based on estimates		
of amounts	√	√
of timing	√	√
of net cash flows		
Profitability is ignored	√	√
Ignores cash flows after payback	√	√
Ignores time value of money	√	

TABLE 7.1: Advantages and disadvantages of payback methods
of capital investment appraisal

Accounting rate of return

One of the criticisms of both payback and discounted payback is that they take no account of:

- net cash flows after payback

- profitability.

If a business's main criterion in selecting projects is profitability, then payback methods are not appropriate, and accounting rate of return (ARR), also known as the book rate of return, is used instead. This method expresses the average profits of a project as a percentage of the investment in the project. The result is compared with a predetermined criterion percentage (we see how this is determined later).

If a business uses 12 per cent as the criterion – i.e. as the cut-off for investment appraisal – then:

- projects with a profitability percentage below this criterion would be automatically rejected

- projects with a profitability percentage above it would remain acceptable, and from among these, the project with the better or best percentage would be selected.

There are different interpretations of what is meant by profit and by investment in the project.

- Profit is generally defined for this purpose as profit before interest and tax but after depreciation, which we call 'ARR profit'. Average profit is usually interpreted as simple average profits, although in some cases it can mean weighted average profits.

◉ Investment in the project can mean one of two alternatives, either initial investment or average investment. Average investment in this context is the sum of the initial investment and the figure of residual value, which is then divided by two.

We can express these two different views of accounting rate of return as formulae.

Rate of return on initial investment:

$$\frac{\text{(Average profit before interest and tax, after depreciation)} \times 100}{\text{Initial investment}}$$

Rate of return on average investment:

$$\frac{\text{(Average profit before interest and tax, after depreciation)} \times 100}{\text{(Initial investment plus residual value) / 2}}$$

We can re-analyse the same three projects that we used earlier (account 7.1) to illustrate payback, by adding further information. This is given in account 7.4.

	A	B	C
Estimated life	5 years	5 years	5 years
	£000	£000	£000
Initial cost	400	400	400
Residual value	100	50	80
Total depreciation	300	350	320
Average annual depreciation	60	70	64

ACCOUNT 7.4: Investment information on capital expenditure projects.

Now we can work out the average annual profits for each project.

Profits/(loss) (net cash flows minus depreciation)

Year	A		B	C	
	£000		£000	£000	
1	(10)	(50–60)		(14)	(50–64)
2	–	(60–60)		(4)	(60–64)
3	10	(70–60)		6	(70–64)
4	100	(160–60)		136	(200–64)
5	130	(190–60)		156	(220–64)
Total	230		—	280	
Average annual profits	46			56	

ACCOUNT 7.5: Calculating average annual profits.

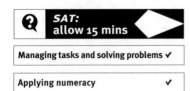

ACTIVITY 6

Work out the average annual profit for project B by calculating the values and filling in the blank slots in account 7.5.

Commentary...

You should have calculated the following figures for project B: Year 1, 120 (190-70); Year 2, 90 (160-70); Year 3, – (70-70); Year 4, (10) (60-70); Year 5, (20) (50-70). These amount to total profits of 180, which gives an average of 36. (Note that all these figures are in thousands.)

Now that we have the average profit for each project, we can substitute them from this schedule into the formulae.

First, we can calculate the rate of return on initial investment:

Project A $\quad \dfrac{46 \times 100}{400} \quad = \quad 11.5\%$

Project B $\quad \dfrac{36 \times 100}{400} \quad = \quad 9.0\%$

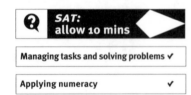

ACTIVITY 7

Work out the rate of return on initial investment for project C using the same formula as above and the data provided in account 7.5.

If the criterion rate is 12 per cent, which project would be recommended for selection – A, B or C?

Commentary...

The rate of return for project C is calculated as follows:

Project C $\quad \dfrac{56 \times 100}{400} \quad = \quad 14.0\%$

If the criterion for acceptance is 12 per cent, projects A and B would not be considered further, leaving project C to be selected.

Note that under both payback and discounted payback, project B would have been selected, and yet using ARR analysis, it is ranked the lowest of the three projects.

Now, we calculate the rate of return on average investment. Here are the calculations for projects B and C:

Project B $\quad \dfrac{36 \times 100}{(400 + 50) \,/\, 2} \quad = \quad 16\%$

Project C $\quad \dfrac{56 \times 100}{(400 + 80) \,/\, 2} \quad = \quad 23.3\%$

ACTIVITY 8

Calculate the rate of return on average investment for project A (using the formula above and the data from account 7.5).

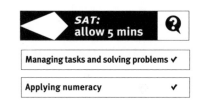

SAT:
allow 5 mins

Managing tasks and solving problems ✔

Applying numeracy ✔

Commentary...

The calculation for project A is:

$$\frac{46 \times 100}{(400 + 100) / 2} = 18.4\%$$

Project B, which would have been selected on the basis of both payback and discounted payback, is again the lowest ranked project. Project C, having the highest rate of return, would be selected unless the ARR cut-off rate is 24 per cent or higher, in which case all the projects would be rejected.

THE PROS AND CONS OF ACCOUNTING RATE OF RETURN

Accounting rate of return is easy to calculate and understand. It results in an easily comparable rate of return and takes all project profits/losses over the life of the project into account.

It does have disadvantages:

- We have seen that whenever a calculation calls for profit or investment to be defined, there is room for disagreement as to how it should be done.

- In common with other methods, it is reliant on estimated figures for the life of the project and for the profits and losses.

- All the years' profits/losses are accorded equal weighting although in actuality they may be skewed. This may be important if the business is depending on higher returns in particular years.

- The most serious criticism, however, in common with payback, is that it does not take the time value of money into account.

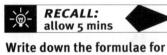

RECALL:
allow 5 mins

Write down the formulae for calculating accounting rate of return on the basis of:

- **initial investment**

- **average investment.**

ACTIVITY 9

SAT:
allow 10 mins

Managing tasks and solving problems ✓

Decide in each case whether payback or ARR will be the more appropriate appraisal method for the following businesses, all of which are evaluating a number of projects with the intention of selecting one. Give your reasons.

- Shepshed Catering will finance its selected project with a loan that must be repaid within four years.

- Hoprights Ltd has a 10-year objective of improving and maximising its return on capital employed.

- Newland Holdings Ltd has a risk-averse investment policy that requires total recouping of investment costs within three years.

Commentary...

If Shepshed's overriding concern is to pay back its loan at the end of the four years (or earlier) it should use payback to determine which, if any, of the projects it is assessing will pay back its investment outlay by that date.

Hoprights will use ARR: it will not be concerned about when projects pay back, but it will be concerned with the profitability of each, and will be anxious to ensure that its chosen project either meets or exceeds its current rate of return on capital employed.

Newland, like Shepshed, is primarily concerned about the project finance not being tied up for more than three years, and would use payback to determine which of its projects meet this criterion.

Net present value and yield

When considering discounted payback, we saw that the presumed interest element of each year's net cash flow is eliminated, so that the principal element is all that remained; it is this figure that is used to ascertain the point at which payback is completed. The elimination process is carried out using discount (present-value) factors given in Resource 1.

One of the criticisms of the two payback methods is that they only ask the question 'How long does it take the project to pay back?' and ignore net cash flows after payback point has been reached.

The net present value method avoids this criticism by:

- taking all net cash flows into account during the life of the project

- taking the time value of money fully into account, by using the discount factors.

THE PROCESS OF APPLYING NET PRESENT VALUE

Step 1

The discount factors (from Resource 1) are applied to the net cash flows of individual years. This reduces them to interest-exclusive figures which, being on the same basis as the interest-exclusive original outlay, are directly comparable with it.

Step 2

The individual present values are added together to give a total of the present values. If there is a surplus of these present values (discounted cash flows) over initial outlay it indicates that

(a) the project has a positive net present value (NPV), and

(b) that it will generate an income greater than its initial cost.

It is therefore acceptable. A negative figure (a deficit) would mean that the project cannot ever pay for itself and should be discarded.

Step 3

If a number of projects are involved, and two or more of them produce positive NPVs, the higher or highest would be selected on purely financial grounds.

Where, however, the initial outlays of the projects are different figures, the raw surplus figures have to be expressed as indices before the selection takes place. We explain this process later on.

APPLICATION OF NET PRESENT VALUE

We can now apply these principles to a practical problem. A company needs to choose between two items of plant, described as project X and project Y, on the basis of net present value. Account 7.6 shows the details.

	Project X	Project Y
Estimated life	6 years	6 years
Discount rate	9%	9%
	£000	£000
Initial cost	700	1,000
Estimate net cash inflows		
Year		
1	180	300
2	200	350
3	120	270
4	160	280
5	180	220
6	170	100
Total	1,010	1,520

ACCOUNT 7.6: Investment information on projects X and Y.

These figures can be processed by the application of discount factors appropriate to the 9 per cent rate.

SAT:
allow 10 mins

Managing tasks and solving problems ✓

Applying numeracy ✓

ACTIVITY 10

The net present value has been calculated for project X. Calculate the net present value of Project Y and enter the figures in the blank slots below.

		Project X			Project Y	
Year	Discount factor	Cash inflow/(outflow)	Present value		Cash inflow/(outflow)	Present value
	(9%)	£000	£000		£000	£000
0	1.000	(700)	(700)		(1,000)	(1,000)
1	0.917	180	165.1		300	
2	0.842	200	168.4		350	
3	0.772	120	92.6		270	
4	0.708	160	113.3		280	
5	0.650	180	117.0		220	
6	0.596	170	101.3		100	
Total		1,010	757.7		1,520	
less Initial cost (yr 0)			700.0			
Net present value (NPV)			57.7			

Can the company decide between the two projects on the basis of this information? Explain your answer.

Commentary...

The present values for project Y are: 275.1, 294.7, 208.4, 198.2, 143.0, and 59.6, totalling 1,179.0. When the initial cost is subtracted, the NPV that results is £179,000.

At first sight, it would seem that the company would opt for project Y because this project has the higher of the two net present values. In this instance, however, because the initial outlays are different, the raw figures of net present value are not comparable in their present form. Further calculations are necessary before a rational decision can be made.

INDICES

The solution to this problem lies in expressing the NPV for each project as a proportion of its initial cost. This is called the index. The project which has the higher or highest index number would be chosen.

Formula:

$$\frac{\text{Present value}}{\text{Initial cost}} = \text{Index number}$$

For project X this is:

$$\frac{757.7}{700.0} = 1.08$$

ACTIVITY 11

Work out the index for project Y. Now assess which project should be selected: X or Y?

SAT: allow 5 mins

Managing tasks and solving problems ✔

Applying numeracy ✔

Commentary...

The index for project Y is (1,179.0/1,000.0 =) 1.18. On this basis, project Y would be selected.

YIELD (INTERNAL RATE OF RETURN)

The calculations just carried out on the net cash flows of projects X and Y produce positive net present values. One of the implications of this positive figure is that it indicates that the rate of return, or yield, is greater than the discount rate (in this case, 9 per cent) used in the calculations. Conversely, a negative net present value would signify that the project fails to achieve a 9 per cent return.

In any given project, though, we do not know what the actual return of the project is, only that is either higher (in the case of a positive NPV) or lower (if it is negative) than the discount rate we have used.

The yield (or internal rate of return) method supplies the answer to this problem by providing the rate of return on the project in question. This solution can be obtained in one of two ways:

- by a combination of calculation and graph-plotting
- by calculation alone.

The initial calculations are common to both methods, and involve a certain amount of trial and error.

The common ground

We start by finding two discount rates, one of which will produce a positive net present value and the other a negative net present value. This is where the trial and error comes in. The best way is to select two discount rates about ten percentage points apart and calculate the NPVs that they produce. This is usually sufficient to produce one positive and one negative NPV, but if it is not, then a wider gap is needed.

Plotting the internal rate of return

When the positive and negative net present values have been established, they should be plotted on a graph on which the horizontal axis represents interest (discount) rates and the vertical axis represents NPV. Positive values are above zero and negative ones below it. The line joining the two plotted points intersects the horizontal axis at the yield percentage (i.e. the internal rate of return) of the project.

Suppose that a 7 per cent discount factor for a given project produces an NPV of 60. This is plotted at point A. A 17 per cent discount factor applied to the same project produces an NPV of (35), which is plotted at B. (Bear in mind that a higher discount rate means that a larger interest element is stripped out of the future inflows, and so reduces the net present value.)

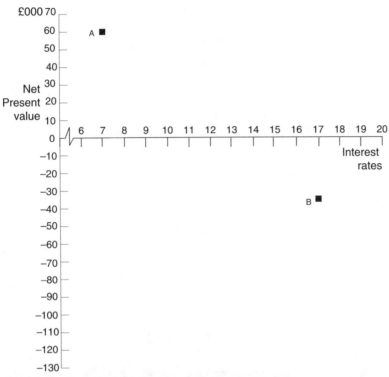

FIGURE 7.1: Plotting the internal rate of return.

ACTIVITY 12

Using figure 7.1, join the line between the two points and estimate the approximate yield of the project (shown by the point where the line intersects the horizontal axis).

Bearing in mind the drawback common to all methods of capital expenditure appraisal, explain briefly why this method of ascertaining the yield – by eye – is usually sufficiently accurate.

SAT:
allow 5 mins

Managing tasks and solving problems ✓

Applying numeracy ✓

Commentary...

The line drawn between these points suggests an internal rate of return of around 13 per cent.

The intersection of the line with the horizontal axis usually provides a sufficiently accurate yield for appraisal and selection purposes, because all cash inflows and outflows are necessarily estimates in the first place. It would be pointless to calculate yield to three decimal places.

Now we apply this technique to the data for project X. We have already calculated that a 9 per cent rate produces a positive NPV of £57,700 (see activity 11). Next we use a discount rate ten percentage points higher at 19 per cent, in the hope of obtaining a negative NPV.

EXERCISE: allow 15 mins

Working with and relating to others	✔
Managing tasks and solving problems	✔
Applying numeracy	✔

ACTIVITY 13

Work in a group with two or three others, so that you can compare your results.

Using the discount factors from Resource 1, calculate the NPV of project X at a 19 per cent discount rate.

Plot the data produced by the two discount rates on a graph and estimate the internal rate of return of Project X.

Commentary...

You should have produced the following NPV figures for project X using the 19 per cent discount rate.

<u>Project X</u>

Year	Discount factor (19%)	Cash inflow/(outflow) £000	Present value £000
0	1.000	(700)	(700)
1	0.840	180	151.2
2	0.706	200	141.2
3	0.593	120	71.2
4	0.499	160	79.8
5	0.419	180	75.4
6	0.352	170	59.8
Total		1,010	578.6
less Initial cost			700.0
Net present value			(121.4)

The line joining the two plots intersects the interest line at approximately 12 per cent (see figure 7.2), the yield percentage.

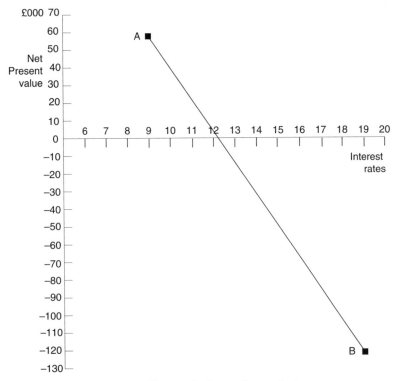

FIGURE 7.2: Plotting the internal rate of return.

Calculating the internal rate of return

It is possible to arrive at the yield without resorting to a graph, just by using calculation. The figures we have calculated already can be put into a formula:

$$A + \left(\frac{(B-A)}{1} \times \frac{a}{(a+b)} \right)$$

The symbols in the formula represent the following values:

A = positive net present value rate %

B = negative net present value rate %

a = positive net present value

b = negative net present value

ACTIVITY 14

Work with your group again for this activity.

Using information you already have, insert the appropriate values in the above formula and calculate the yield for project X.

Commentary...

Substituting project X's figures for the symbols gives:

$$\text{Internal rate of return} = 9 + \left(\frac{(19-9)}{1} \times \frac{57.7}{(57.7+121.4)} \right)$$

$$= 9 + \left(10 \times \frac{57.7}{179.1} \right)$$

$$= 9 + (10 \times 0.322)$$

$$= 9 + 3.22 = 12.2\%$$

The calculation produces a yield for project X of 12.2 per cent. This is a more accurate version of the result we obtained from the graph, and so confirms what we deduced earlier.

ACTIVITY 15

SAT: allow 20 mins

Managing and developing self	✔
Communicating	✔
Managing tasks and solving problems	✔
Applying numeracy	✔

Prepare a short presentation covering the following points:

- The ordinary payback and the net present value methods are both based on net cash flows. Explain why the net present value method, although the more complicated of the two methods to operate, is generally regarded as the better method.

- Explain the index calculation, and describe the circumstances in which you would undertake it.

- Describe two methods available for ascertaining the yield of a project.

Note your main points in the box below.

Commentary...

Your presentation should incorporate the following points.

- Payback concerns itself with net cash flows up to the payback point and ignores all subsequent cash flows, even though they may be significant. It also ignores the fact that money has a value over time. Net present value overcomes both these objections by accounting for net cash flows over the whole life of each project and by reducing net cash flows by an amount equivalent to a presumed rate of interest.

- The index calculation it is a way of assessing each project's NPV as a proportion of initial outlay. It is undertaken when the projects being appraised have different initial outlays, as a measure of profitability.

- The yield can either be ascertained by calculation and graph-plotting, or it can be ascertained by calculation alone.

Interest rates, weighted average cost of capital

In each of the appraisal illustrations up to this point, we have referred to, and used, interest rates and discount rates:

- The accounting rate of return (ARR) method involves calculating an average rate of return (on either the initial or the average investment) and comparing it with a pre-determined, target percentage figure.

- To calculate discounted payback, we use an interest rate,

expressed as a discount factor, to discount net cash flows back to a present value amount.

- In the net present value method, this same procedure is used to arrive at discounted cash flow and yield figures.

However, we have not yet seen how the interest rates, which serve as criteria for the various methods, are arrived at. This is our next step.

Weighted average cost of capital

A common way of calculating an interest rate that will serve as an appropriate criterion for appraisal is to establish the weighted average cost of capital. This recognises that the long-term finance of a business is derived from various sources, each of which has a specific cost, but that these costs can be manipulated so as to reflect an average cost against which proposed investments can be measured.

Long-term loans and debentures

These are raised and issued (respectively) at fixed rates of interest, so their cost is apparent, but even within the same company these rates differ according to a number of factors, including:

- the lender's perception of risk

- the duration of the loan or the life of the debentures

- prevailing interest rates at the date the loan was negotiated or the debentures issued

- the presence, or absence, of security by means of fixed or floating charges

- the forecast rate of inflation.

Share costs

The remuneration paid to shareholders is in the form of dividends, which are an appropriation of profit and not, as in the case of interest, a charge against profit. However, dividend yields are regarded as a cost of capital for this purpose, on the grounds that investors would be unwilling to acquire shares in the absence of financial rewards in the form of dividends. Dividend yields are therefore regarded, like interest yields, as a cost of capital.

However, it is difficult to establish what that cost actually is. In the case of preference shares, which carry a fixed rate of dividend, their yield is calculated from their market value but no such fixed rate exists for equity (ordinary) shares. This problem is overcome by settling on what would be regarded as an acceptable rate and possibly adding on an extra amount for anticipated growth.

APPLYING THE WEIGHTINGS

Once the costs of the various elements of capital have been established, the next steps are:

1. to decide upon the yield, i.e. the nominal rates of interest, and the dividends, expressed in relation to the market values of the securities and investments to which they are attached (see session 4 for more about yields)

2. to calculate what each type of capital constitutes as a proportion of the total capital (to provide its weighting)

3. to multiply the yield of each type of finance by its weighting, to produce their weighted yields which, when totalled, produce the weighted average cost of capital for that business.

For instance, account 7.7 represents the capital employed by Westwood Ltd, and from this information, we are able to calculate weighted average cost of capital.

Type	Amount	Proportion of total capital	Yield	Weighted yield
	£000	%	%	%
6% loans	200	4.4	5	0.22
7% debentures	1,300	28.9	8	2.31
9% preference shares	400		7	
equity shares	2,600	____	6	____
Total	4,500	100.0		____

ACCOUNT 7.7: Capital employed by Westwood.

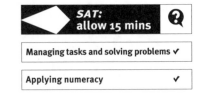

ACTIVITY 16

Using account 7.7, calculate the following figures and enter the results in the blank slots in the account:

- ○ the proportions of total capital that is represented by the two kinds of shares

- ○ their weighted yields

- ○ the total weighted average cost of capital for **Westwood**.

Commentary...

The proportions of preference share and equity share are 8.9 per cent and 57.8 per cent respectively. The weighted yields are 0.62 per cent and 3.47 per cent. Westwood's weighted average cost of capital is 6.62 per cent.

In this example, weighted average cost of capital would be 6.6 per cent or 7 per cent to the nearest whole number.

OTHER INTEREST RATES

There are several other interest rates which can be used for capital appraisal purposes. The company's return on capital employed is often used as a criterion for projects being assessed under the accounting rate of return method. The effect of undertaking an investment project with a rate of return below the return on capital employed would be to depress this latter figure.

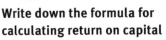

RECALL:
allow 5 mins

Write down the formula for calculating return on capital employed.

Under circumstances where a company has surplus funds available for investment, the criterion rate for capital investment appraisal purposes could be the rate of return which could be expected on an outside investment, i.e. regarding it as an opportunity cost.

The situation could arise where a business could only finance an investment project by borrowing, in which case the rate of interest payable on the borrowings may be used as the criterion rate for capital appraisal purposes.

Overview of capital investment appraisal methods

We have looked at various methods of evaluating capital projects, from the simple to the complex. There is no single universally acceptable method. Some, like payback, are simple to understand and to apply but ignore important aspects of the issue. In an attempt to reach an optimum decision, some businesses use a combination of methods, perhaps using net present value first, followed by payback.

Sometimes, however, choice of projects may be made on grounds other than simply financial ones. Cost-benefit analysis, for instance, attempts to analyse both the costs and the benefits of particular decisions and, in this respect, it is like capital investment appraisal. In practice, however, it ranges much wider, taking into account not only the tangible costs and benefits (those that can be quantified) but also the intangible ones, such as human, social, environmental costs and benefits.

These may have considerable impact on a decision, as we saw in session 5, when discussing non-financial considerations in marginal costing. Planning law, for example, allows the public to have a say on the operation, siting and design of new industrial and commercial developments, but even when the business is not obliged to do so by law, it increasingly makes sense to consider the wider impact of its plans.

In the past, it has been thought impossible to put a financial value on intangible costs and benefits but, in recent years, there have been experiments with ways of doing so, for example through approaches such as:

- social accounting

- accounting for the environment

- human asset accounting.

In the case of 'accounting for the environment', for example, an attempt might be made to put a value on matters relating to the 'greening of the environment' including the use of recyclable and biodegradable materials. This is an area where businesses would be well-advised to adopt a broader approach, since governments are increasingly using tax penalties and incentives to encourage the adoption of environment-friendly practices. Certainly, it would be short-sighted for any business to make strategic decisions based on financial analysis alone: a failure to take into account the wider impact on society and the environment will often result in political and operational difficulties and these, in turn, will ultimately damage the financial 'bottom line'.

summary

Capital investment appraisal is the name given to those techniques which enable a business to make a rational choice, from a purely financial viewpoint, between two or more otherwise equally acceptable capital projects. The projects themselves have to be matched with a compatible source of finance.

▶ The payback methods focuses on the interval of time between the outlay on a project and its recoupment. The project with the shorter or shortest (if more than two) payback period is selected. The methods is easy to understand and apply but has various disadvantages. The main one is that it ignores the time value of money as represented by the interest which can be earned from investing it.

▶ A more refined method, discounted payback, overcomes this objection by working on the present values of the net cash inflows.

▶ The accounting rate of return (ARR) method relates the average annual profit of the project to either the initial or average investment. This method has some flaws, the most serious being that, as with payback, it ignores the time value of money.

▶ The net present value (NPV) accounts for all the net cash flows and eliminates the interest which they are presumed to contain at the required rate. Net cash flows, after elimination of this interest, are compared with the original outlay, to give a net present value. The project with the highest net present value is accepted.

▶ Yield, the internal rate of return, can also be calculated by graph or formula. It shows the rate of return inherent in the net cash flows and can be measured for adequacy against a required rate.

▶ All the appraisal methods except payback require the use of an interest rate. The various possible rates include: the weighted average cost of capital rate, the return on capital employed rate, the borrowing rate and the investing rate. The choice of rate depends on its appropriateness in the circumstances.

Managing Information

Why organisations need information

THE INFORMATION AGE

INFORMATION AND DECISION MAKING

WHAT KIND OF INFORMATION IS USEFUL?

HARD AND SOFT INFORMATION

DIFFERENT FUNCTIONS, DIFFERENT NEEDS

Objectives

After participating in this session, you should be able to:

▶ **explain why organisations need information in order to function successfully**

▶ **state the principal categories of information which are relevant to organisations**

▶ **indicate what aspects of management are particularly dependent on information**

▶ **list the qualities that information must possess in order to be useful**

▶ **contrast the nature and uses of 'hard' and 'soft' information.**

In working through this session, you will practise the following BTEC common skills:

Managing and developing self	✔
Working with and relating to others	✔
Communicating	✔
Managing tasks and solving problems	✔
Applying numeracy	
Applying technology	
Applying design and creativity	

The information age

According to many commentators, our societies have passed through the age of steam, the age of steel and even the age of electricity. Today, while we still need and use all those things, we have entered the 'age of information'.

This is not primarily about the huge amounts of information which are available for 'personal interest' or entertainment. The Guinness Book of Records contains an extraordinary number of facts, and television, radio, newspapers and magazines keep up a constant flow of information on every conceivable topic. Leisure information, however, is essentially a sideline. The reason why we can call the late twentieth century the information age is because information has become an essential resource of every significant organisation, from national governments to commercial businesses. They need information just as much as they need human, material and financial resources. They cannot function without money, machines and people, but these resources are virtually useless unless they are deployed effectively. This means formulating the right strategic plans and making the right operational decisions, and while the right plans and decisions are, on rare occasions, made by inspired guess-work, any organisation that functions without adequate information is like a passenger train that sets off on a journey with the driver blindfolded. Sooner or later, there will be a crash.

This is particularly true in the commercial sphere. Imagine a skilled designer who is cast away on a desert island, with only his drawing board, pencil, calculator and plenty of paper for company. He lives for 20 years in perfect isolation, whiling away the time by perfecting the design for a new kind of motorbike. Rescued at last, he tries to interest manufacturers in his machine, but they only laugh at him. 'You've wasted your time', they tell him. 'It will cost too much to build, it doesn't meet the safety regulations, and the market won't like the style.'

Managing tasks and solving problems ✓

ACTIVITY 1

Using information available to him previously, our modern Robinson Crusoe is perfectly capable of designing an excellent motorbike; but after spending 20 years without any new information, he is incapable of designing one that would succeed. What information could help him create a successful design?

Commentary...

The new information that he lacks includes, crucially:

- information about changing safety and emissions regulations

- information about new materials used in construction (cheaper, lighter, stronger, easier to process)

- information about new manufacturing technologies and systems that imply different approaches to structural design

- information about the market for motorbikes:

  - what the other manufacturers are doing

  - what customers want to buy.

Major changes can occur in all of these areas within five years, let alone in 20.

> Other resources, money or physical equipment, for instance, do not confer any distinction. What does make a business distinct, and what is its peculiar resource is its ability to use knowledge of all kinds – from scientific and technical knowledge to social, economic and managerial knowledge. Indeed, business can be defined as a process that converts an outside resource, namely knowledge, into outside results, namely economic values.
>
> Drucker, P. F. (1964) Managing for Results, Harper & Row.

For commercial businesses, keeping up to date with a changing world is vital. Drucker refers to knowledge rather than information, but knowledge in this context simply means information that is specific to the business's needs. He goes on to say: 'Knowledge is the business.' In order to survive, and particularly to succeed, in an environment that is ever more competitive, a business will need information in a variety of categories, the principal ones being:

- information about its markets, i.e. statistical information about the outside world

- scientific and technical information about its products and how they are designed, produced, delivered and maintained

- financial information about its own costs, revenues, debts, cashflow, asset values, investment plans, etc.

- information about performance in terms of output, progress, productivity, efficiency, and the meeting of operational objectives.

It is easy to see how (and why) these types of information might be needed by a commercial business, but the principles are the same in all kinds of organisation.

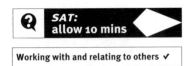

SAT:
allow 10 mins

Working with and relating to others ✔

Managing tasks and solving problems ✔

ACTIVITY 2

Here are some examples of the kinds of information that a razor-blade manufacturer would need.

- Information about markets:

    – number of males of shaving age in the market

    – percentage using 'wet shave'.

- Scientific/technical information:

    – metallurgical qualities of blades

    – information on high-speed packaging technology.

- **Financial information:**

  - weekly and monthly sales revenues across various market sectors.

- **Information about performance:**

  - output per head

  - machine down time.

With a small group of colleagues, fellow-students or friends, draw up a comprehensive list of the specific information that would be needed by a leisure centre run primarily as a service by a local authority. Present your conclusions under the four headings:

- information about markets

- scientific/technical information

- financial information

- information about performance.

Commentary...

The leisure centre's outputs are 'products' which may include swimming for fun, swimming for training, fitness training, squash, badminton, various team games, climbing and, of course, catering (snacks and drinks). To select the right product mix, and to promote particular products effectively, the centre's managers will want to know about their market:

- What is the catchment area?
- What sort of people live in it?
- How many are likely to want these products?
- What are they prepared to pay?
- Who else is offering them?

Scientific/technical information is less important than in manufacturing, but some staff would need to develop expert knowledge in matters of fitness, exercise, coaching and equipment, and the risks/benefits associated with them; and perhaps also nutritional/dietary information.

The relevant financial information will be much the same as for any organisation:

- revenues and costs overall and per product
- numbers of customers
- direct (labour and materials) and indirect (overhead) costs
- cashflow, annual profit and loss, and so on.

In terms of performance information, managers will want to know:

- utilisation levels of all facilities
- whether cleaning schedules were met
- what complaints were made
- what the response was to special promotions and events
- how staff training is progressing, environmental standards (heating levels, levels of bacteria in the pool, etc.)

and so on.

Information and decision making

Organisations exist to achieve certain goals. In commercial organisations these are ultimately to make profit and create capital growth for the shareholders; non-profit-making organisations have other kinds of goals, for example the goal of a cancer research charity may be 'to encourage and support research leading to the cure of cancer'. To achieve their goals, organisations must act in some way; to act, they must develop and deploy resources; to guide this deployment they must have plans. In simple terms, the process that bridges the gap between 'now', where the goals have not been achieved, and 'the future', when they have, is illustrated in figure 1.1.

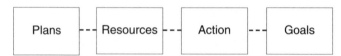

FIGURE 1.1: How organisations achieve their goals.

Assuming the organisation is clear about its goals, this obviously raises three questions:

1. What plans?

2. What resources?

3. What action?

Obviously they must be 'the right ones', but these must be selected from among an infinite variety of 'wrong ones', so there must be a decision-making process. To ensure that each decision is as right as possible, information is necessary.

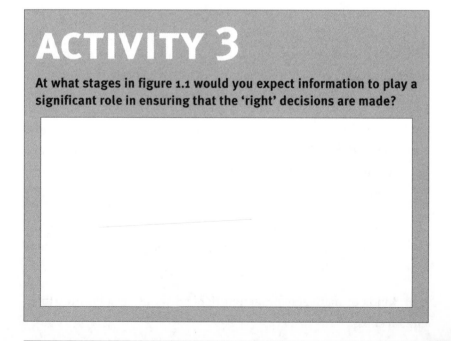

ACTIVITY 3

At what stages in figure 1.1 would you expect information to play a significant role in ensuring that the 'right' decisions are made?

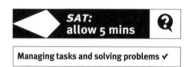

SAT:
allow 5 mins

Managing tasks and solving problems ✓

Commentary...

Decisions about the plans, decisions about the resources, and decisions about the actions all require information. There is also a case for saying that information is relevant to 'goals', as we will explain later.

In a perfect world, the optimum plan would lead smoothly to the desired goals, and the organisation's executives could go off to play golf; in practice, unfortunately, this could only happen in a 'closed system', where everything is controlled and outside influences are excluded. In reality, organisations pursue their goals in an open system, which is subject to many uncertainties and uncontrollable influences from outside:

- Plans tend to be imperfect, containing estimations, errors and misunderstandings and reflecting false assumptions about reality.

- The organisation's human resources (the most important resources, in the view of most experts) are not machines and do not necessarily behave as required or perform as predicted.

- The external environment within which the plan is implemented is not fixed, and may be reshaped by accidental events, economic fluctuations and the action of competitors.

A farm is an open system; a clock is a closed system. Apart from winding it up, a clock scarcely needs management at all. A farm, by contrast, needs constant, flexible and skilful attention.

The tendency for ordered plans to become increasingly chaotic over time has always been recognised. Hence, there is a need for structures of management and control that can counteract the tendency for delays to occur, costs to rise, quality to fall, concentration to waver, and so on. This managerial input takes one of two forms:

1. preventive action, whereby managers plan and organise operations effectively, provide leadership and motivation, communicate with their staff, train individuals and build teams; and

2. corrective action, whereby they monitor operations, identify where performance is deviating from the plan, and take action to restore the situation.

Both kinds of management action depend on information for their effectiveness.

We can now expand figure 1.1 to reflect these processes more accurately, showing where information is a crucial element.

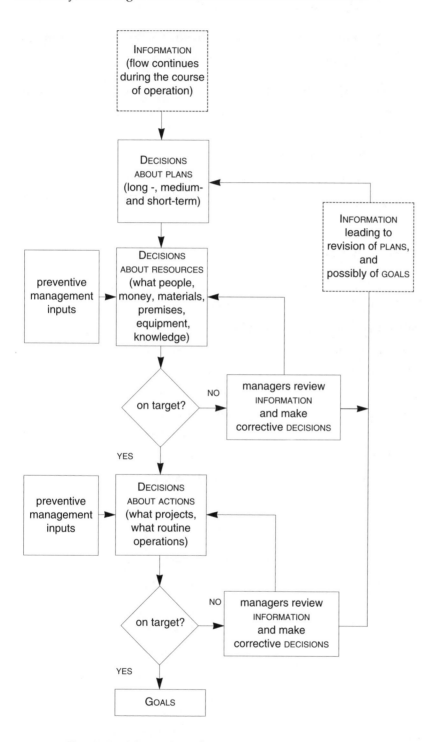

FIGURE 1.2: Management, decision making and information.

As figure 1.2 shows, information has two main roles in organisations:

1. to help to formulate plans at all levels of detail

2. to enable managers to take corrective action where operations are not proceeding according to plan.

As part of the latter role, information coming from within the organisation, together with the continuing flows from outside, may lead to the plans (and even sometimes the goals) being modified. Thus, if the goal is finding a cure for melanoma (skin cancer) but in time these are proved to be incurable, the goal may be changed to 'educating people in how to prevent the development of melanoma'.

LEVELS OF DECISION MAKING

Information is particularly crucial at any point where decisions are made, but decisions may be taken at many different levels of authority. One interpretation of this phenomenon is Anthony's classification (Anthony, R.N. 1965, Planning and Control Systems, Harvard University Press) of decisions in terms of 'management planning and control systems', with 'operational control' at the lowest level, 'tactical control' in the middle, and 'strategic planning' at the top. In practice, the concept of 'tactical control' used in the so-called 'Anthony's Triangle' is not very meaningful for most organisations. Perhaps a better way to think about decision-making levels is shown in table 1.1.

Level	Duration of impact	Decisions made by
Strategic	Long-term	Senior management / Board of Directors *often with participation of middle management*
Managerial	Short- to medium-term	Middle and lower (operational) management *often with participation of non-managerial experts, operational staff and, on occasions, senior executives*
Operational	Short-term	Operational staff *under powers delegated by operational management*

TABLE 1.1: Levels of decision making in organisations.

As table 1.1 shows, the division into levels is not always clear-cut, since other levels may participate in them, and higher levels may overrule decisions taken by those below them. Furthermore, there is a trend towards devolving decision making downwards, in the interests of developing individuals, speeding up the decision-making process, and encouraging organisational flexibility.

MANAGERIAL AND OPERATIONAL DECISIONS

The distinction between managerial and operational levels can be explained by a simple example.

Dolly has been told that she needs a further appointment with a specialist, but is not sure whether this should be the orthopaedic consultant or the neurosurgeon. Ken, who operates the appointments system, listens to her explanation, and decides to make the appointment with the neurosurgeon. This is an operational decision.

Ken believes this is probably correct and, if so, by booking Dolly the appointment now she will have it earlier. Ken makes a note to check with both departments; if his decision turns out to be incorrect, Dolly's appointment will be delayed a little, but Ken thinks this is unlikely. However, Ken went on sick leave before he could check the appointment and his decision turned out to be wrong. Dolly turned up for a pointless consultation, and the surgeon complained to the appointments manager. The latter reprimanded Ken informally, and issued an instruction that, in future, appointments must not to be made until the relevant details have been confirmed. This is a managerial decision.

INFORMATION FOR PROBLEM SOLVING

In most organisations, middle management, who are responsible for the efficient running of operations and projects, have to deal with a steady stream of problems. Indeed, problem solving is one of the main components of a typical manager's job, both in terms of the time it takes up and the value of reaching a successful outcome. Francis (Francis, D., 1991, Effective Problem Solving: a Structured Approach, Routledge) divides 'problems' into six categories:

1. mysteries

2. assignments

3. difficulties

4. opportunities

5. puzzles

6. dilemmas

each of which has different characteristics. A 'mystery', he states, is 'an unexplained deviation from what is expected', while a 'puzzle' is a situation where we know that a solution exists, but don't know what it is. For our purposes, the principal features of any problem are that:

- it is a situation where a decision is required, but is difficult to make for some reason

- the situation is non-routine and relatively unstructured (otherwise, procedures, guide-lines and precedents would be available to simplify the task).

Solving individual problems is a typical example of 'corrective' management action as shown in figure 1.2. However, it also takes place 'preventively', as managers anticipate actual and potential problems in order to prevent them from developing. Figure 1.3 shows where information is important to a problem-solving situation.

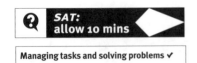

SAT:
allow 10 mins

Managing tasks and solving problems ✔

ACTIVITY 4

Look carefully at figure 1.3. What role will information play in each of the three stages – investigation, analysis and implementation – shown on the left of the diagram?

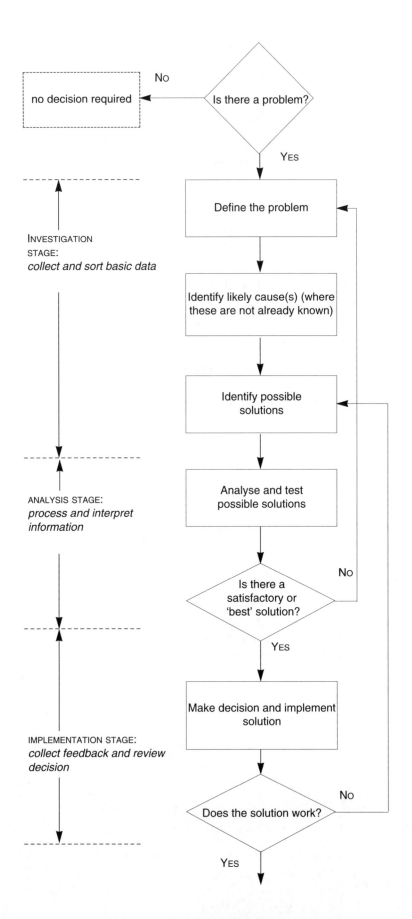

No

no decision required ◄—— Is there a problem?

YES

Define the problem

INVESTIGATION
STAGE:
collect and sort basic data

Identify likely cause(s) (where
these are not already known)

Identify possible
solutions

ANALYSIS STAGE:
*process and interpret
information*

Analyse and test
possible solutions

No

Is there a
satisfactory or
'best' solution?

YES

IMPLEMENTATION STAGE:
*collect feedback and review
decision*

Make decision and implement
solution

No

Does the solution work?

YES

FIGURE 1.3: A model of the problem-solving process.

Commentary...

In the investigation stage, data and information must be collected and sorted or classified prior to analysing it. This may involve collecting opinions and views as well as facts and figures. The information can be sorted for example by matching ideas about solutions to causes.

In the analysis stage, the basic information is analysed, tested (perhaps using spreadsheets, decision support systems, or other techniques which we will consider in session 3).

The role of information in the implementation stage may not be so obvious: however, the merit of a solution cannot be proved until it is put into effect. At this stage, therefore, information about the effectiveness of the solution should be collected and fed back so that the managers who made the decisions can review and, if necessary, alter them.

This approach is designed for the solution of the kind of problems that Francis calls mysteries and puzzles, but as he explains, 'problems' may also consists of 'assignments', 'difficulties' and 'dilemmas'. These may require 'solutions' to be found, but clearly they also involve choosing between known alternatives. Although this is generally thought of as decision making rather than problem solving, the basic approach can be much the same.

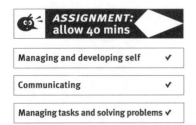

ASSIGNMENT:
allow 40 mins

Managing and developing self	✔
Communicating	✔
Managing tasks and solving problems	✔

ACTIVITY 5

Here is a non-routine problem that may face you personally before long – whether to take a further course of study when you have completed this one. To reach the optimum decision you will need to consider:

- how you intend your future career to develop

- what study courses and qualifications will be of most relevance to this development

- your study skills and aptitudes (an accountancy qualification may seem desirable, but if you are not sufficiently numerate it may be impractical)

- where and how the course(s) you want are 'delivered' (i.e. locally or elsewhere; full-time, part-time, as sandwich courses, on day-release from work, by self-study open learning, etc.)

> ○ the direct cost of the course and the 'opportunity cost'
> involved (see Section 1 Session 5: Analysis of costs).
>
> Work through the problem on the lines laid down in figure 1.3, and
> write a short report explaining what information you would bring to
> bear on the problem, and how this would be useful in reaching a
> decision.
>
> Use a separate sheet of paper to record your answer. Summarise your
> findings in the box below.

Information is primarily used in organisations for planning and operational management purposes, and especially for making decisions associated with them, so its applications are numerous and varied. In this workbook, we refer especially to the use of information in:

- ○ financial control/budgeting

- ○ performance management

- ○ production control

- ○ resource management

- ○ business and project planning/forecasting

- ○ technical development

- ○ marketing

- ○ monitoring and developing customer service

- ○ supporting executive decisions.

We shall see that applications are often interconnected. For example, information about marketing, customer service, operational performance, production standards, costs and prices all come together in business planning; hence there is a need for systems of information.

Having emphasised that organisations need information, and having illustrated where and how this is of most importance, we now consider what qualities information must possess if it is to be useful in such situations.

What kind of information is useful?

In the information age, it has become relatively easy to obtain large quantities of information, either by collecting it oneself, or by buying it from someone else. Two problems present themselves, however:

- A quantity problem: How can you handle enormous volumes of data so as to make sense of them? Unless the genuinely useful parts are carefully selected and sorted, information users may find themselves swamped with irrelevancies.

- A quality problem: How can you ensure that the information that emerges from this process is both correct and useful?

Thames Valley Police encountered both problems simultaneously during the 1970s. The police were aware that better 'intelligence' might help them link up different strands of information in order to identify potential and actual law breakers. For example, a police officer in one part of Oxford might hear unofficially that a certain Mr N was a burglar. A second officer in another part of the city might hear of someone called Mr N moving into a particular address. If the two officers could put this information together, it might suggest grounds for investigation; however, the opportunity for them to do so would probably never arise. But what if the two officers were to feed their separate bits of information into a computer database? The computer could then make the connections, and churn out a steady stream of 'leads' that would give the police a significant advantage in fighting crime.

Officers in the region were therefore told to collect any piece of data that might be of interest, and to feed it into the computer. Unfortunately, this resulted in a massive information processing problem: all kinds of gossip, errors and trivia flooded into the database, and the vast majority of outputs were too inaccurate, out-of-date and irrelevant to be of any use. The scheme was abandoned amid much embarrassment.

ACTIVITY 6

In order to meet the needs of modern businesses and other organisations, information must be relevant. List five other characteristics that information must have to ensure that it is useful.

Commentary...

Organisations need the right information in the right way at the right time. We can sum up the characteristics of useful information with the acronym RARTAC. It must be:

- relevant – it must focus on the subject(s) about which the organisation needs to know

- accurate – a small degree of error is usually acceptable, but too many errors make information useless, or even dangerous

- reliable – it should be collected from a reliable source by reliable methods

- timely – information that comes too late might as well not come at all

- accessible – if what we need to know is the sales figures for July, we do not want to have to wade through the entire company accounts for the last five years in order to find them

- comprehensible – the information should be presented clearly, simply and in an easily assimilated form.

In some circumstances there may be other requirements, such as confidentiality and security, but RARTAC sums up the criteria for useful information that always apply.

Hard and soft information

Most of the information that we are considering in this workbook is hard, i.e. it consists of facts and figures. Hard information has two important characteristics:

1. within pre-determined limits it is either correct or it is not

2. in principle, its handling, whether by computerised or manual methods, presents no major difficulties.

Where hard information consists of numbers, or of measurable elements such as 'boxes', 'months' or 'production units', it is often described as quantitative. Qualitative, or 'soft' information is of a different character. It generally does not take the form of hard facts and figures, but of opinions, views, attitudes and feelings. Such information may be expressed in loose and even ambiguous ways, and it is often impossible to categorise it as correct/incorrect in a clear-cut way.

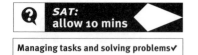

SAT:
allow 10 mins

Managing tasks and solving problems✔

ACTIVITY 7

Consider a commonplace question like: How did Arsenal do in their match against Liverpool? Below are three responses. Each response is perfectly valid, but which is qualitative and which is quantitative, and why?

Responses:

1. They lost 4–2.

2. I think they lost by a couple of goals.

3. They lost, but who cares – they put up a tremendous performance.

Commentary...

The first response is quantitative, 'hard' and factual in all respects. The second is also quantitative, even though the respondent is not sure of the actual score.

In the third response, 'They lost' is a hard fact, but the rest of the statement is qualitative. No quantitative information is provided.

Soft information may seem unattractive to some business managers, but it has its uses. The greatest bankers in sixteenth-century Europe were the Fugger family of Augsburg in Germany. Their business was in providing loans and credit facilities to governments and merchants on an international scale. Naturally, they were careful to record all the relevant 'hard' facts about how much was lent, when, to whom, on what terms, and so on. However, they were so interested in 'soft' information that they also set up a world-wide network of correspondents to keep them supplied with news, there being no television news programmes nor newspapers in those days. Their letters are fascinating catalogues of scandals, royal weddings, wars, bizarre incidents, rumours, religious disputes, celebrations and disasters.

The Fuggers wanted this information for good reasons. As bankers, they dealt with clients in far-flung places of which they had no personal knowledge. Yet their commercial success depended on making the right decisions about the degree of risk to their investments. Reports from their correspondents helped them form such judgements; they were also better able to forecast where the most profitable and least risky business opportunities were likely to be in the future.

Financial analysts and business development managers are doing very much the same thing today, though from a wider range of sources and using more reliable information.

HARD AND SOFT INFORMATION

SAT:
allow 10 mins

Managing tasks and solving problems ✔

ACTIVITY 8

Soft or qualitative information consists of attitudes, ideas and opinions, rather than hard facts and figures. What kind of soft information do you think might be considered useful by major industrial concerns like the UK electricity generators PowerGen and National Power? Give your reasons.

Commentary...

It is important to such organisations to know what their customers, their staff, the public, politicians, environmental campaigners and other 'opinion formers' think of them, because these opinions can have an indirect but real impact on their business performance:

- A poor image on environmental matters makes it more likely that the companies will be pressured into decisions that they would otherwise not have taken. (The decision to close large coal-fired power stations, and invest in cleaner gas-fired stations instead, was partly influenced by environmental concerns.)

- A fall in workforce morale may affect output and productivity, unless management action is taken to reverse it.

- A negative public perception of the generating companies

may create political pressures which may affect their ability to optimise prices.

In the long run, a positive 'image' is seen by most organisations as an important asset, and a negative one as a liability.

Most large organisations therefore collect certain kinds of soft information, by such means as:

- paying agencies to collect relevant newspaper reports

- commissioning public opinion surveys

- conducting employee attitude surveys.

ACTIVITY 9

EXERCISE: allow 30 mins

Managing tasks and solving problems ✔

Browse through the financial pages of the quality press. These pages aim, among other things, to provide information that may be relevant to investors when deciding what shares to sell and what to buy.

What examples of soft information can you identify that may have relevance to such decisions?

Commentary...

Looking at one day's papers, at random, we found:

- an article comparing and commenting on two recent reports that feature diametrically opposed views on the housing market

- an opinion column discussing the relationship between the inflation rate, the value of sterling, and political developments

- a profile of a leading businessman.

Other ways of gathering and using soft information include:

- 'brainstorming' sessions, the intention of which is to harness creativity and lateral thinking to raise large numbers of ideas and angles on a problem

- employee suggestions schemes

- marketing research (where information about people's attitudes to products, their prejudices, and subconscious preferences is collected and analysed)

- asking customers for feedback about product and service quality.

Many large organisations also use qualitative information in forecasting. Short-term forecasts can be made reasonably reliable by quantitative methods. However, reliability declines rapidly when forecasts are projected more than a few years into the future. After this point, human judgement – the ultimate qualitative factor – comes into its own. For example, in the Delphi system of forecasting, several recognised experts give their considered opinions on how the situation will develop, and these are then debated and refined until a common view is reached. It is particularly used for predicting demographic, political, market and technological change; see Jarrett, J. (1991) Business Forecasting Methods, 2nd edn, Basil Blackwell.

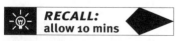

RECALL:
allow 10 mins

Briefly define:

- **hard information**

- **quantitative information**

- **soft or qualitative information.**

ADVANTAGES AND DISADVANTAGES OF SOFT INFORMATION

Soft information, being qualitative, can bring additional insights to an analysis, as the Arsenal versus Liverpool example showed. The fact that it was 'a tremendous performance' was more important than the score, and indeed a defeat of this quality may have brought the Arsenal players, team and supporters more benefit than a victory in a dull match would have done. Soft information, because of its human dimensions, can attract attention, develop ideas, highlight problems and reveal opportunities more effectively than pages of factual data.

On the other hand, soft information tends to be open-ended and unstructured, and this makes it:

- relatively difficult for the reader to assimilate and analyse

- awkward to process using computer technology.

For example, when Stokkit Ltd advertised for a new sales representative, it received over 200 letters and CVs from would-be applicants. Each one gave a slightly different selection of information, and presented it in a slightly different way (typically mixing soft and hard information together).

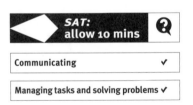

ACTIVITY 10

Stokkit's personnel officer thought it might take many days to sift through this mass of information. Think about this problem:

- Why is it likely to take so long?

- What can applicants do to help?

- What can Stokkit do, next time, to minimise the problem?

Prepare a short verbal briefing on the subject for your colleagues or fellow students, and summarise your key points below.

Commentary...

The recruiter is duty bound to treat all applicants fairly, and this means trying to extract and codify the relevant information in some way. If information is presented in a non-standard manner, this becomes a complex task.

Applicants can help by following a standard format in their letters of application and CVs. It is in their interests to do so, since recruiters tend to be less sympathetic to CVs that present them with extra difficulties; see Jackson, T. (1991) The Perfect CV, Pitkus Press.

Next time, Stokkit could encourage standardised responses, by specifying in the advertisement what the initial letter should contain, and by sending each applicant a standardised application form. This will simplify the task considerably; it will also enable Stokkit to put these details on a computer database if it feels this is appropriate.

Standardisation and codification are the keys to processing soft information. It is widely applied in the design of questionnaires and surveys. The favoured approach is to turn open-ended responses into closed ones. An open-ended question such as 'How do you feel about Western Electricity's pricing policy' generates a wide range of open-ended and even rambling responses. However, such a question can easily be restructured in a closed format. Figure 1.4 shows how it might appear on a questionnaire.

"How do you feel about Western Electricity's pricing policy?"

1. strongly against   ☐

2. against   ☐

3. neither for nor against   ☐

4. for   ☐

5. strongly for   ☐

FIGURE 1.4: Structuring open-ended questions to receive a standardised and easily codified response.

This technique channels the response into one of five options (a great improvement on an infinite number). Soft information has thus become much harder, and there is the additional advantage that it can be scored numerically and analysed by computer. More information about survey techniques and questionnaire design is contained in a companion volume to this workbook, Market Relations.

But, there is still the problem of how to deal with genuinely soft information, such as the letters of enquiry that mental health charity Anxia receives in large numbers (around 200 a week, mostly handwritten) from people suffering from anxiety disorders. Anxia would like to analyse these letters so as to establish:

- which of a dozen or so anxiety conditions are most prevalent

- what type of people are affected (age, sex, role in family, etc.)

Administrative staff automatically record writers' names, addresses and telephone numbers on a database, so that a reply can be generated. However, to extract the other information with reasonable reliability an experienced person has to read each letter with care, and to complete a coded analysis form. These forms are later input to the enquirer database.

HARD AND SOFT INFORMATION

Q SAT:
allow 10 mins

Managing tasks and solving problems ✓

ACTIVITY 11

Suggest ways of reducing the demand on the time of skilled personnel that this information-sorting task creates. (It is accepted that not all enquirers will provide clues to all the information categories in which Anxia is interested.)

Commentary...

As with the questionnaire example above, the key is to find some way of 'hardening up' the soft information. One possibility might be to identify a range of keywords, such as 'depression' or 'panic' and to scan the letters for such words, and record their incidence. This simplifies the task, but it will not eliminate all the difficulties (such as the need to resolve ambiguities) and some initial analysis and planning will be required.

It may be simpler to send inquirers a structured questionnaire (and pre-paid reply envelope) with their reply.

Anxia recognises that it is important not to lose sight of the overall meaning of such letters in the desire to extract and codify the facts that they contain.

Different functions, different needs

Organisations need information to fulfil their functions and meet their objectives. But when we say 'organisations' we are talking in very general terms. Large organisations contain a complex substructure of departments with different functions. Thus the functions of the accounts department are different to those of the marketing department, and their information needs differ accordingly.

SAT:
allow 10 mins

Managing tasks and solving problems ✓

ACTIVITY 12

Harley Hospital contains many departments, including those listed below. Indicate which types of information (from the list below) each department is likely to need if they are to function effectively.

Select from these types of information:

(a) hours worked by consultants

(b) blood and plasma stocks

(c) clinical test results

(d) nurses' duty rosters

(e) patient records

(f) spending on drugs

(g) number of in-patients

(h) staff sickness records

(i) personnel records

(j) appointments data

(k) inventories of equipment

(l) nutritional data

(m) stocks of addictive drugs

(n) whereabouts of specialists.

We have completed the first line to show you what is required.

Departments:	Information needed:
Surgery	a, c, d
Accident and emergency	
Accounts	
Hotel services	
Pharmacy	
Security	
Management	
Orthopaedic medicine	
Fertility clinic	

Commentary...

Note that some information will be needed by more than one department. For example, medical departments and management will both need nurses' duty rosters; management and security will both need inventories of equipment; security and pharmacy will both need to know what quantities of addictive drugs are stored, and where. In general, management and accounts will need the widest range of information, though sometimes it may be in summary form. Thus they will want to know the total cost of drugs purchased and dispensed, and the running value of stocks (because this represents cash tied up in the pharmacy), but they will not need to know precisely how many bottles of aspirin are on the shelves.

Given that such large amounts of information are available within modern organisations, it is important to ensure that people are not overloaded with information that they do not need, and yet the right information goes to the right people at the right time – on RARTAC lines.

RECALL:
allow 5 mins

RARTAC is the acronym we have used to sum up the characteristics that information needs to have in order to be useful. What does each letter in the acronym RARTAC stand for?

To underline the importance of the qualities summed up in RARTAC, consider the possible consequences in Harley Hospital if:

- a surgeon starts to operate on a patient with a rare blood group, but stocks of blood in that group are less than stated on the records

- the Pharmacy can only find 500 units of Benzedrine, but thinks it should have 1,000

- the kitchen does not know how many patients will need a cooked meal this evening

- the orthopaedic consultant does not know which patients are booked to see her today

- nobody is sure whether a little girl's test results have arrived

- the appointments database was only updated once a week.

What kind of confusion would reign?

So, organisations need information of various kinds, and the specific needs of various departments within them also differ. There is a further level of variation, in that the people within each department – from temporary clerks to departmental managers – also have different needs. These issues are of obvious significance in the design of information systems, and we will return to them in session 3.

In the sessions that follow, we also explain the nature of information in more detail, and give more extensive examples of how it is used in practice by both commercial and non-profit-making organisations. With the exception of Stokkit and Harley Hospital, which are fictional organisations, the case studies are for the most part based on real organisations. Their names have been disguised in the interests of confidentiality.

Before moving on, let us first correct one possible misapprehension: although the present era both needs and generates more information than any previous one, it is not the first to appreciate its value. Ever since settled societies arose over 10,000 years ago, rulers, priests, merchants, officials, generals and scientists have collected and used information of many different kinds. Information is something that civilised societies cannot live without.

summary

Information is an essential resource for modern business, alongside the human, financial and material resources. In a competitive environment, it is particularly important for organisations to have information that is up to date.

- ▶ Information is essential for managerial decision making, in setting goals, and in making plans and deploying resources in order to achieve results. Decisions are taken at three distinct levels (strategic, managerial and operational) and the information needs at each level are different.

- ▶ Effective problem solving also depends on accurate information at each stage in the process.

- ▶ Modern organisations have access to enormous quantities of information: managing such volumes and ensuring quality therefore become important issues.

- ▶ In terms of quality, information needs to be RARTAC: relevant, accurate, reliable, timely, accessible and comprehensible.

- ▶ Information may be hard (including figures, which are known as quantitative information) or 'soft' and qualitative. Hard information is more important, but soft information can also be valuable in assessing attitudes and opinions.

- ▶ The information needs of the various departments within an organisation are often different. Management and accounts functions need the widest range of information, but there are many specialised needs as well.

From data to information

WHAT DO WE MEAN BY DATA?

WHAT DO WE MEAN BY INFORMATION?

COMPUTERS AND INFORMATION MANAGEMENT

PROCESSING DATA INTO INFORMATION

INFORMATION TECHNOLOGY

METHODS OF DATA CAPTURE

INFORMATION OVERLOAD

Objectives

After participating in this session, you should be able to:

- distinguish between the terms 'data' and 'information' as they apply to information management

- explain the function of transaction processing systems (TPS)

- identify the specific features of computer systems that make them suitable for information processing

- give detailed examples of the processes by which data is turned into information

- explain the elements to be considered in a costs-benefits analysis of computerising the processing of information.

In working through this session, you will practise the following BTEC common skills:

Managing and developing self	✔
Working with and relating to others	✔
Communicating	
Managing tasks and solving problems	✔
Applying numeracy	✔
Applying technology	
Applying design and creativity	✔

What do we mean by data?

We must start by being clear about what we mean by information and data. In session 1 we used the two words interchangeably, but it is time to make a precise distinction between them.

> **¡?¡** Data are recorded facts and figures.

(Strictly speaking, the word data is plural; the singular is datum, meaning a single fact or figure. Datum on its own is seldom used outside scientific circles and, in practice, data is often treated as a singular word. Thus people often say: 'This data is faulty.' They should say: 'These data are faulty.')

A datum – a piece of data – could be almost anything. Here are some examples:

- 23 Dalkeith Terrace
- Incident timed at 10.33
- 12,655
- medium
- 0044 31 2 65566
- riboflavin 0.06 per cent
- £2.99
- Ambrose 6 for 41
- Rostrum Camera: Ken Morse.

One obvious point about isolated pieces of data like these is that they do not actually tell us much.

ACTIVITY 1

Take the first item on the list above: 23 Dalkeith Terrace. Obviously it is an address, but in what contexts might we come across it? List five or six specific contexts in which it might appear.

SAT:
allow 5 mins

Managing tasks and solving problems ✓

Commentary...

The address might be a property for sale in an estate agent's window, one of a list of houses scheduled for demolition, or part of a commercial address. If it is part of a private address it might be an extract from a telephone directory, part of a customer's details in an insurance company's database, an entry on the Council Tax register, a newsagent's delivery list, and so on. It might be part of the instructions to an ambulance or fire crew answering an emergency call – or even the title of a thriller.

A single datum tell us very little: it is only useful when it is put in context with other data, creating a data record, as for example shown in figure 2.1.

FIGURE 2.1: A data record: details of a property for sale.

Put together, these data make sense. Indeed, businesses and other organisations depend on the collection and recording of such data in an organised way for the efficient running of their day-to-day operations. K. P. Crisp and Partners need to collect details of houses from their clients, and need to record them in an organised way, so that they can be retrieved quickly when needed.

These data records are the raw material with which they work. The charity Anxia, to which we referred in session 1, works with data in a similar way. It receives many letters from people seeking help with mental health problems. The data in each letter are entered into a standardised record, which will form the basis of the charity's interaction with that particular client thereafter.

The data that Anxia records about each writer include:

- name: first name / surname / title

- address: number or name of house / street / town / postcode

- telephone number if given

- role: sufferer / carer / professional / other

- if carer, who is cared for: parent / child / spouse / other

- category of problem, if stated

- date letter received.

Each record is given a unique identifying code. It also contains spaces for information to be added later, such as the date of Anxia's response, and any further transactions. When records are grouped together and stored by a computer, this is known as a file.

Note that since these details are kept on a computer system, they are subject to the conditions laid down by the Data Protection Act (1984).

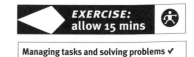

EXERCISE:
allow 15 mins

Managing tasks and solving problems ✔

ACTIVITY 2

The Data Protection Act (1984) affects almost every organisation that maintains computerised records of members of the public. Look up the provisions of the Act in your college library and note down the key points here. Ask your tutor or the librarian for guidance on finding the right texts if necessary.

Here is another example of data recording. Every time a customer makes a purchase at a Kellaways store, the electronic till records:

- stock codes of the item(s) sold

- price of the item(s) sold

- total value of the transaction

- method of payment

- amount of cash tendered, if any

- amount of change given, if any

- till reference number

- till operator's reference number

- date and time of transaction

- any errors made and corrected during the transaction.

These data, together with additional data registered at the till, such as details of customer returns, staff purchases (which are discounted) and cheques cashed by staff, are sent to the store's computer, where they are used to update a master file. The customer is given a till slip which contains some of the data, and if subsequently there is a query, the original record can, if necessary, be retrieved and consulted.

Both Anxia and Kellaways record data about the transactions which are their main source of activity and their main point of contact with their customers. Not surprisingly, the computerised systems through which they record them are called transaction processing systems (TPSs).

TPSs are a fundamental and essential feature of modern business information systems but, in themselves, they contain only data, not information. They 'process' data only in the sense that they collect and record it for later use in a systematic and standardised way; it remains data. Thus Anxia's system processes data records from letters written to it; Kellaways' records the transactions that take place at its tills, and Stokkit Ltd's records stock movements.

What do we mean by information?

TPSs only record data. However, they are usually designed so that the data can be processed to provide the information needed by managers.

RECALL:
allow 5 mins

In session 1, what were the three levels of decision making at which we said information was capable of being useful?

In an organisation like Kellaways, managers operate at four distinct levels, as figure 2.2 shows.

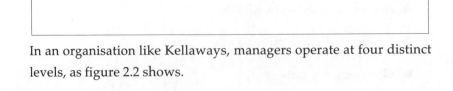

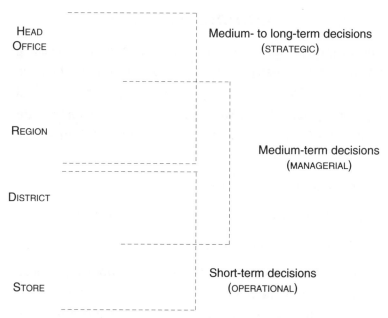

HEAD OFFICE	Medium- to long-term decisions (STRATEGIC)
REGION	
	Medium-term decisions (MANAGERIAL)
DISTRICT	
STORE	Short-term decisions (OPERATIONAL)

FIGURE 2.2: Kellaways: three levels of decision making distributed between four layers of management.

Store managers are in charge of essentially operational matters, under the supervision of district managers. District and regional managers share responsibility for broader aspects of short- to medium-term management, while Head Office also has the task of managing and guiding the business at a strategic level.

ACTIVITY 3

Given the data that Kellaways' tills collect and record, what questions do you think store managers might expect to be able to answer, using these data?

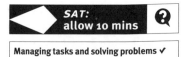

SAT:
allow 10 mins

Managing tasks and solving problems ✔

Commentary...

The till records can answer a very wide range of questions, among the most basic of which is 'How much money did we take today?' This is something that managers from store level right up to Head Office will be asking. Store managers are responsible for many things, but the highest priority is inevitably placed on the financial 'bottom line', which means:

(a) achieving sales targets

(b) minimising variable costs, above all staff costs

(c) minimising 'shrinkage' (mainly theft).

Managers want to know how their store is performing in these respects, and where they need to take corrective action. When the TPS data has been processed, it is capable of answering the many questions about operational performance:

- How many tills were open, and for how long?

- How productive (number and value of transactions) was each till in absolute terms?

- How productive was each operator?

- How many errors did each operator make in ratio to the number of transactions he or she handled?

- How much cash should be in each till at the end of the day?

- How many hours were worked in total by till operators?

- What hours of the day were busiest?

- What was the overall ratio of sales to hours worked by till operators?

The processing that turns TPS data into useful information is simple. Operator productivity, for instance, involves totalling the time during which each operator is 'logged on' to the system, and the number and value of transactions he or she completes during that period. The latter are then divided by the former, to produce useful information in the form of an index of productivity.

How managers use operational information

It should be fairly obvious how each of these pieces of information can be used in practice, but here are two examples worked out in detail.

1. Till throughput data

It costs money to operate a till, because the operator must be paid. If a store has six tills, it may be possible to close three of them for most of the day, opening an extra one or two during the hours that are shown to be busiest. However, not having enough tills open is risky, because if queues build up, customers may shop elsewhere. The position of tills may also be relevant; if the data show consistently low turnover at a particular till, then provided this is not due to the operator being slow, it may be better to reposition the till. This in turn may affect decisions about which tills are closed and when. Such 'fine-tuning' may well have a measurable impact on store performance, optimising sales while minimising costs.

2. Operator data

If the data show that a particular operator, irrespective of which till he or she is working at, processes fewer transactions, or transactions of lower average value, then there is a problem that needs investigation. This may lead to the individual being given more training or closer supervision, or being transferred to less results-sensitive work. Alternatively, this may turn out to be a security issue.

ACTIVITY 4

Turning from operational to strategic levels of management, what questions do you think Kellaways' transaction data can answer at the level of the business as a whole? Think about such issues as product mix, financial planning, cash flows and areas of profitability.

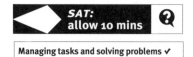

SAT:
allow 10 mins

Managing tasks and solving problems ✓

Commentary...

Data collected at the tills can be used to answer a wide range of questions which will help top management plan and guide the business appropriately. For example, product mix has to be monitored constantly to see whether the balance should be changed for optimum results. Relevant questions would include the following:

- What sales is a particular stock item achieving?
- What sales is this 'department' achieving?
- How are sales split between main product groups?

For financial planning and control purposes, the company needs to know the answers to the following questions:

- How much money is taken nationally each day?
- How much cash enters the company each day?
- What is the breakdown between methods of payment, e.g. cash, credit card, cheques, vouchers, etc.? (These release cash into the company at different speeds.)

All such information may have strategic significance, as do the answers to the following questions:

- What is the average value of each transaction?
- What are average sales per square metre of floor space or per cm of shelf space?

Since the central computers will have access to cost prices for all items, it is also possible to answer questions about:

- the gross profit per item, department and product group
- the average percentage gross profitability per item, department and product group
- the profit performance of small stores compared with large ones.

All such information can be subdivided to reveal results by region (useful to Head Office), by district (useful to regions) and by store (useful to district managers). It can be presented either as absolute values or as percentages (see section 1 session 6: Budgetary Control).

At all levels, information is a guide to action, and managers are looking for 'differences that make a difference', i.e. areas where they can (or must) change the existing situation in order to improve overall performance. At the operational level, a Kellaways store manager may retrain a till operator. At the managerial level, a district manager may instruct a store manager to reduce staffing costs to the district average. At the strategic level, central management may decide to allocate 50 per cent less space to products like toys and games, and give more to giftware; or to close small stores and open more large ones. On the broadest possible plane, the information reaching the Kellaways directors may persuade them to make a strategic move away from retailing and towards some other kind of business.

MAKING COMPARISONS

Much of the information derived from TPS data, fascinating though it may be, is not much use as it stands. It may inform us that this month Tom, a checkout operator, has taken £550 on average for every hour he has operated a till, but until that is put into context we have no way of knowing whether it is good, bad or indifferent. To interpret information, managers need something with which to compare it.

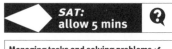

SAT:
allow 5 mins

Managing tasks and solving problems ✔

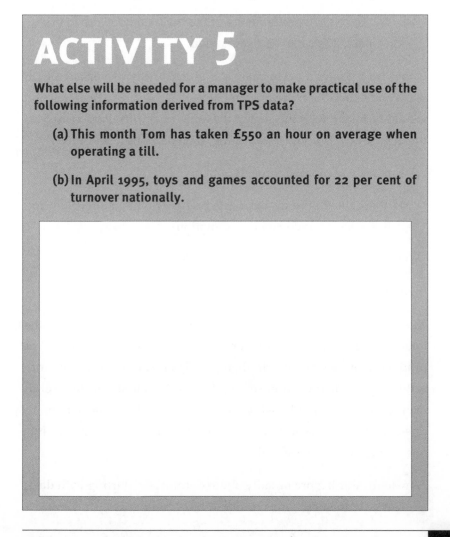

ACTIVITY 5

What else will be needed for a manager to make practical use of the following information derived from TPS data?

(a) This month Tom has taken £550 an hour on average when operating a till.

(b) In April 1995, toys and games accounted for 22 per cent of turnover nationally.

Commentary...

Tom's store manager will want to compare Tom's performance this month with:

- his performance in previous months

- the average performance of other till operators in the store

- the company, regional and district average.

Head Office will want to know:

- monthly sales (and relative share per cent) of toys and games over previous months and years

- sales and gross profit per square metre (since either of these may be moving in a different direction to total sales)

- the likely development of any trends that can be discerned (e.g. if toys and games's share of sales is declining, what sales can be forecast for two years' time?)

- the relative performance of the main competitors in this field, if this can be ascertained.

If toys and games's performance is significantly at variance with plans and expectations, management needs to decide whether action should be taken, with the goal of maximising profits. For example, if the department is under-performing, then perhaps it should be:

- marketed more vigorously

- overhauled in terms of product range, pricing policy, location in the stores and visual presentation

- given less space, or even

- abandoned.

Alternatively, if the product group is selling more in proportion to the total, selling more in absolute terms, selling more per square foot or producing more gross profit, then perhaps it should be given more selling space at the expense of other departments. Senior retail managers are constantly using such 'merchandising' information to fine-tune their stores in order to maximise turnover and profit: it is one of their key business skills.

Now let us think more broadly about definitions, starting with data, which we defined earlier as recorded facts and figures.

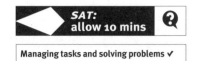

Managing tasks and solving problems ✓

ACTIVITY 6

Consider carefully the examples we have examined, and give a definition of:

1. a data record

2. information.

Commentary...

Data are facts and figures. Organisations like Kellaways and Stokkit Ltd record vast quantities of data on their computers via their transaction process systems. These are grouped together to form records, such as the stock record shown in figure 2.3. We can therefore define a record as items of related data.

When a computerised system stores a large number of similar records together, as is usual, this is known as a file.

A definition of information, which we use for the rest of this workbook: Information is knowledge derived from data.

We now refine this definition a little further. Businesses and other organisations are not interested in information for its own sake (unless they happen to trade in information, like market research firms or Reuters news agency). They require it for a practical purpose. Stokkit, for instance, holds records like the one shown in figure 2.3 on more than 20,000 stock lines because it needs to know, among other things:

- what product lines it stocks

- the quantities of each product line presently in stock

- the pack quantities

- their location in the warehouse

● the quantities of each line presently on order and their expected delivery dates

● the cost and sales value of each item and the totals within various categories.

Item code	0556
Dept code	109
Item name	Billie Doll (medium)
Supplier code	0044
Pack size (cm)	h 20 w 12 d 10
Pack qty	3
Weight (kg)	0.404
Reorderable	Y
Min order*	250
lead time† (days)	44
Notes	nil.

* This is the minimum quantity that can be ordered.

† This is the average time between placing an order and the goods arriving in stock.

FIGURE 2.3: Content of a computerised stock record at Stokkit.

SAT:
allow 10 mins

Managing tasks and solving problems ✔

ACTIVITY 7

In overall business terms, summarise the benefit that Stokkit obtains from recording all this data and processing it into information.

At the operational level, describe how Stokkit might use information it has gathered about stocks.

Commentary...

Overall, the data and information derived help Stokkit to achieve its business goals, which broadly speaking will be:

- to maximise the efficiency and cost-effectiveness of the warehousing and distribution operations

- to satisfy existing customers and win new ones

- to maximise the profits made by the business.

At the operational level, the collection of accurate and up-to-date data on stocks enables Stokkit:

- to maintain sufficient stocks to meet anticipated levels of demand

- if an order cannot be fulfilled immediately, to tell a customer when it can be done

- to plan and manage its warehouse operations efficiently

- to monitor performance and costs at frequent intervals so that action can be taken to improve them or to correct shortfalls.

In a large warehouse, data about the location, pack size, weight and even 'crushability' of each item will be a key element in the generation of 'picking lists'. The computer can calculate the optimum order in which the items in each consignment should be collected from their storage bins, so as to minimise the distance travelled, and hence the time taken. This may be varied to ensure that heavier items are packed low in the consignment, and crushable and lighter items higher.

At a higher level of management, performance indexes and ratios will be useful. These represent the way in which two factors, such as number of staff employed and units of work performed, vary in relation to one another. Relevant indices and ratios to Stokkit's storage/despatch operation include:

- stock items processed – per hour, per shift, etc.

- stock items 'picked' – per hour of labour time

- average number of despatch errors – total number of despatches.

Such calculations would require data about labour productivity and customer orders to be brought together with the stock control data, but this would already be taking place where the computer system issues picking lists.

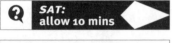

SAT:
allow 10 mins

Managing tasks and solving problems ✔

ACTIVITY 8

One useful performance ratio might be average distance travelled per item picked. Management might wish to test whether changes to the computer program might produce shorter distances, thus lowering the ratio. If the ratio itself was seen to be rising, an investigation might be launched to see whether this could be reversed. The ratio might even be higher on some days than others (on Fridays, perhaps). This too would merit investigation.

What other performance ratios might be useful in a distribution warehouse?

Commentary...

Relevant ratios might include:

- orders processed per shift

- average time to pick an item

- average time to pick an item per individual operator

- proportion of out-of-stocks to total items ordered

- proportion of customer orders despatched within 24 hours

- proportion of errors per total items despatched and per total orders despatched

○ proportion of breakages per total items picked.

Some of these ratios might be reported daily, others less frequently.

Given that our examples have shown how organisations put information to practical use, we can refine our definition of information.

Information is knowledge derived from data and used for a purpose.

Computers and information management

Small quantities of data are easy to interpret. If a Kellaways store only had five transactions a day, and Stokkit only received a dozen deliveries a week, there would be no justification for using elaborate computerised systems. A few minutes with a calculator would be sufficient to reveal what information there is to reveal.

Table 2.1 and figures 2.4 and 2.5 show what Smolensky Electricals' new sales director managed to achieve when she started to hand-produce management reports.

Sales: six months to July (Pounds Sterling)							
Item:	Feb	Mar	Apr	May	Jun	Jul	Total
12V motors	127	95	216	109	55	78	680
9V motors	60	88	12	135	101	47	443
110V motors	450	333	356	210	394	267	2010
ALL MOTORS	637	516	584	454	550	392	3133
12V transformers	144	168	95	230	151	269	1057
9V transformers	82	96	111	57	61	119	526
110V transformers	595	411	379	655	790	696	3526
ALL TRANSFORMERS	821	675	585	942	1002	1084	5109
TOTAL SALES	1458	1191	1169	1396	1552	1476	8242

TABLE 2.1 Smolensky Electricals: Sales chart – six months to July.

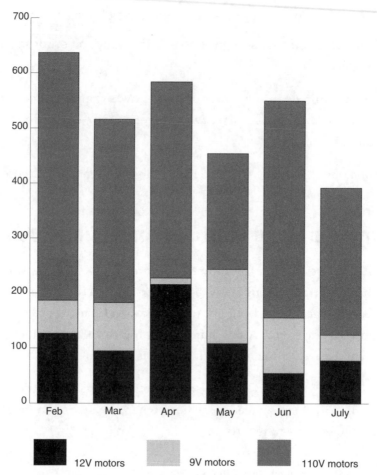

FIGURE 2.4: Smolensky Electricals: Sales to July: summary graph.

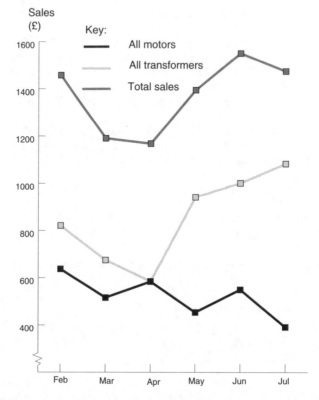

FIGURE 2.5: Smolensky Electricals: Sales to July: motors only.

ACTIVITY 9

What conclusions can you draw from the information contained in table 2.1 and figures 2.4 and 2.5?

Commentary...

The small amount of data given in table 2.2 allows few conclusions to be drawn. For example, the graph (figure 2.4) shows sales of motors declining and sales of transformers rising, over the six months, but total sales are at much the same level in July as they were in February. To reach any conclusions, we would need comparable data going back for two or three years; then we would be able to compare trends month by month and year by year, including any obvious seasonal patterns.

Conclusions drawn on the basis of small amounts of data can be very unreliable, particularly where data such as the sales figures for individual items vary considerably from month to month (e.g. 9V motors – lowest £12, highest £135).

If a similar analysis was performed on Anxia's 10,000 letters, Stokkit's 20,000 product lines or Kellaways' daily total of 250,000 transactions, the results would be much more meaningful and statistically reliable. This is the opportunity that collecting masses of data provides. However, the opportunity is also a problem, because collecting, recording and analysing the data manually would be an impossibly slow and expensive task.

The answer to this data handling problem lies in using the power of computers (together with other elements of modern information technology). This facilitates the collection and storage of masses of data, and allows it to be analysed as much and as often as necessary.

Processing data into information

Information is, by definition, derived from data and, as we have seen, this means processing the data in some way to derive meaningful information from it.

At its minimum, processing may consist only of adding up total quantities and values, and perhaps dividing them between periods. We now look first at a stock record system, which contains data, and then examine how these data are processed into information. This helps to explain why organisations may decide to move from a manual system to a computerised system.

Problems and opportunities with a stock record system

In the card-based stock record system originally operated by Stokkit, the individual processes are quite simple. Movements of stock in and out are written onto the card. At the end of every month, the stock is physically counted and the total on the card is corrected. The calculations involved are therefore addition, subtraction and counting.

Item name: Billie doll (medium)		Code number: 0556	Supplier: Stephensons	
Min reorder qty: 250		Min stock level:	200	
Date	Physical Chk	Qty in	Qty out	Balance
1 May 95	412			412
3 May 95			45	367
8 May 95			45	322
10 May 95			106	216
16 May 95			25	191
17 May 95		500	90	601
20 May 95			100	501
23 May 95			85	416
28 May 95			60	356
31 May 95			200	156
1 June 95	153			153

FIGURE 2.6: Old-style manual stock record card at Stokkit Ltd.

A card is kept for each stock item, which is stored in its own 'bin'. All other documentation (delivery notes, goods received notes, copies of invoices for reconciliation, ledgers, etc.) is kept in the stockroom office.

PROCESSING DATA

INTO INFORMATION

Managing tasks and solving problems ✓

Applying numeracy ✓

ACTIVITY 10

Consider carefully all the data on the card shown in figure 2.6. The system tells us:

(a) what quantities of stock are being held on any given day

(b) what quantities have moved in and out of the warehouse, and when

(c) what errors and/or losses have occurred

(d) when stocks need reordering.

How well do you think this system would work in practice, and what problems might arise from it?

Commentary...

First, such a system is labour-intensive, implying a relatively high cost, and also a relatively high incidence of human error. Nevertheless, it is quite capable of functioning, on two conditions:

1. It must be operated by experienced people who are thoroughly familiar with all its aspects.

2. The number of stock records must remain relatively small. If the total number of items rises above a few hundred, one individual can no longer keep track, and labour costs will also have to rise.

A detailed problem with the record card shown in figure 2.6 is that the reorder process is unlikely to prevent the item going out of stock. You can confirm this by comparing the minimum stock level (200), which triggers a reorder, the quantities actually dispatched in one month, the minimum reorder quantity and the order lead time. In practice, an experienced storekeeper will monitor actual stocks, and ensure that reorders are placed early.

There is a further problem connected with the reorder question: a manual system, which relies on human inspection of numerous data records, and which is periodically overridden in the interests of preventing out-of-stocks, is unlikely to result in the optimum stock levels.

WHY ACCURATE STOCK RECORDS ARE OF FINANCIAL SIGNIFICANCE

Businesses today try to reduce stockholding to the minimum that is consistent with ensuring the smooth flow of production and the timely despatch of customers' orders. Stock ties up money: it has to be paid for, and as long as it stays in stock, these outgoings cannot be recovered. Since money invested in stock is part of the business's working capital, this can have a serious effect on cash flow, and also on the overall return on capital employed. There are other considerations too:

- Stock held for too long may deteriorate.

- The longer stock is held, the greater the risk of it becoming obsolete. Who will pay £100 for Version 3.0 of a software package when Version 4.0 is available at £105?

- Some perishable goods have a strictly limited shelf-life, and once past their 'use-by' date they are a complete loss.

Except in small-scale operations, manual systems cannot provide enough information to manage stock levels efficiently, but a computerised system not only handles very large numbers of items, but can also:

- store the data reliably

- be updated instantly as stocks enter or leave the warehouse and/or bin

- combine the data records with other kinds of data (customer orders and a picking-route planning program) to automate other aspects of the operation

PROCESSING DATA

INTO INFORMATION

- make further calculations to provide extensive management information from the basic data recorded.

One practical example is calculating stockturn, a measure of the speed with which stock is 'turned over' and despatched to customers. (See Section 1, Session 4: Analysis and evaluation.) While manually calculating stockturn for one or two items is not a problem, analysing the whole range is a daunting task. Yet stockturn analysis can be extremely valuable for management, as table 2.2 shows.

Stock Turn	Jul	Aug	Sep	Oct	Nov	Dec	Jan	Feb	Mar	Apr	May	Jun	Average
Billie doll 1994–5	2.23	2.40	2.12	1.88	2.60	3.80	2.03	2.10	2.10	2.16	2.20	2.10	2.31
Billie doll 1993–4	2.41	2.50	2.55	2.20	2.90	4.02	2.31	2.35	2.38	2.48	2.44	2.46	2.58
Average all toys 1994–5	2.61	2.63	2.50	2.30	3.10	4.36	2.46	2.52	2.55	2.63	2.61	2.61	2.74
Average all products 1994–5	2.83	2.78	2.80	2.83	2.89	2.95	2.78	2.86	2.91	2.90	2.91	2.95	2.87

TABLE 2.2: Stockturn data: comparison of one product with its
product group and all products

SAT:
allow 10 mins

Managing tasks and solving problems ✔

ACTIVITY 11

The stockturn ratios in table 2.2 are based on quantities, not money values (as in Section 1, Session 4), but their implications are the same. What information does table 2.2 give us, and what management action does it suggest?

Commentary...

The stockturn figures show that the average stockturn for all products in the toys and games category was lower than that for 'all products', and that the stockturn for Billie dolls was lower than that for the toys and games group generally. Furthermore, figures for 1994–95 were lower than for 1993–94. This means that the performance of toys and games needs attention; the proportion of stocks to sales, and therefore the cash tied up in stocks, are higher than the average for all products. Within the group, the Billie doll was a worse-than-average performer. This points to action to tighten up stock management of the toys and games group, and of Billie dolls in particular.

You may also have noticed that toys and games shows a fall in stockturn in September and October, followed by a sharp rise peaking in December and falling again in January. This pattern (which it would be useful to show as a bar chart) clearly shows the seasonal effect of Christmas, which strongly affects the toy market. Stockturn falls as stocks are built up prior to Christmas, and rises in the peak selling months. This needs to be taken into account when deciding what action to take to improve stockturn within this group.

ASSESSING COSTS AND BENEFITS OF COMPUTERISATION

Computer processing of numerical and financial data can improve management control considerably. However, such a major (and expensive) change in operating practices is unlikely to be undertaken solely or even primarily to generate better management information. In Stokkit's case, the old system was replaced by computer stock control to improve operational efficiency and reduce costs. It may not be possible to justify the expense of computerisation where the only gain is in more and/or better management information.

ANXIA – THE PROPOSAL TO COMPUTERISE DONATIONS DATA

The charity Anxia receives numerous donations from individuals and organisations. It records the name of the donor, the amount and the date received in a handwritten ledger called the donations book. Accompanying letters, which contain more detail, are filed elsewhere. The value of donations is totalled each month, and is reported in the monthly management accounts. This analysis takes a few minutes with a calculator each month.

A business studies student came to Anxia for work experience. She suggested that if the donations data were computerised, this could reveal information that might be useful in planning the charity's activities and in maximising its income:

1. Monthly figures could be presented graphically in order to make trends more obvious. This would be time-consuming to do manually, but easy using a computer.

2. The average value of donations could also be analysed and graphed. Together, these pieces of information would show how the pattern of donations was changing. Since the National Lottery is thought to be reducing individual donations to charity, it may be important for the charity's managers to know this.

3. The current year's figures could be compared with those for previous years, and projected into the future as a forecast. If a rise in donations is predicted, then the directors could plan other spending projects; if a reduction, then spending might have to be curtailed, and/or action taken to try to increase the number and value of donations.

4. The donations could be analysed more realistically. At present they vary from as little as 50p to as much as £500. In these circumstances, average donation values might well be highly misleading. If there are 24 donations of 50p and one donation of £500, the total is £512, giving an average of £512/25 = £20.48, which gives a false picture of the pattern of donations. It would be more useful to analyse the donations in discrete groups, e.g with the following values:
   - up to £9.99
   - from £10.00 to £49.99
   - from £50.00 to £249.99
   - over £250.

5. Using this analysis, larger private donors and organisational donors could be identified separately. Given that they are disproportionately important for the charity they could perhaps be approached personally to make a longer-term commitment. On the other hand, the figures might suggest that something more could be done to encourage medium-level donors, to ask them to make out standing orders, for example.

The student proposed that a new database and analysis package should be established on computer, recording additional details as outlined above.

ACTIVITY 12

The student was asked to analyse the cost and resource implications of her proposal. What resources would be required to implement the proposal?

Anxia's directors have to balance the benefits in information terms against the resources required to implement the proposal. What conclusion do you think they would reach?

At what level – operational, managerial or strategic – would the additional donor information be useful?

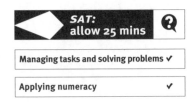

SAT:
allow 25 mins

Managing tasks and solving problems ✔

Applying numeracy   ✔

Commentary...

The resource implications are substantial. At present, completion of the handwritten ledger, filing the covering letters and adding up monthly totals makes only a small demand on resources. The human, physical and financial resources needed for computerisation are much more extensive.

Setting up the system involves:

- investigating suitable hardware and software, obtaining suppliers' estimates, etc.

- capital spending on hardware and software (with extra costs if the software needs to be customised)

- installing the software, testing the system and modifying it if necessary

- training one or more people to operate the system and enter data.

Subsequent operation will require:

- extra maintenance costs for the hardware

- permanent allocation of extra working space

- more labour hours, mainly for data entry.

The project will also absorb a good deal of management time.

The outcome will be much more management information, but will this repay the investment? Is it actually useful to have a full-scale analysis of donations every week or month? It will place extra demands on the directors' time, but will it in practice lead to any action? Some of the significant information, such as identifying large donors, can easily be found by looking at the donations book. The split between private and organisational donations can also be made simply by altering the way they are entered in the book.

All in all, the benefits do not appear to justify the costs. The chairman remarked that in his experience, the installation of new data analysis systems seldom went smoothly, and that the resource requirements were likely to be greater than stated.

He added that the additional information was of a strategic nature, because whatever the trends in donations, nothing could be done about them in the short term. There was therefore no point in calculating them more than once a year. He accepted that such an analysis would be useful from time to time, but suggested that this could be done manually if necessary. The proposal was rejected – with thanks.

Clearly, computers can be used to derive considerable amounts of information from all kinds of data, and potentially this information can be useful in planning and controlling an organisation's activities for optimum results. What the last example shows is that:

- changing from manual to computerised systems has implications for costs, resources and ways of working

- the value of the information generated should be considered against the costs associated with it

- information that in principle seems likely to be valuable may in practice not be acted upon

- creating additional information places additional demands on the time and energy of those who are supposed to use it.

We will return to some of these issues later. Next, we look at the technology that has made the explosion in information provision possible.

Information technology

Information technology (IT) has transformed many aspects of our lives in a dramatic manner. Few users of word processors can imagine how people wrote reports, contracts or a textbook when only mechanical technology (i.e. the typewriter) was available. Users of spreadsheets find it difficult to imagine how managers used to work out costings, sales forecasts or cash flow budgets before they were computerised.

The front line of IT is the computer, linked to various other devices such as printers and communications modems. To appreciate modern management information systems (MISs), you need to understand in general terms how computers and other IT devices work. If necessary, ask your tutor for guidance.

In a nutshell, computers can:

- store vast quantities of data very compactly

- process this data in many different ways, and do so very quickly

- copy the data store, or move all or part of the data to a remote location with ease

- communicate the data to other computers, printers and other output devices speedily and accurately.

This last facility has greatly increased the usefulness of computers, and has led to the rise of networking between desk-top computers within a particular location (such as Kellaways' Head Office) and of external data services, such as the Internet. A firm like Stokkit may also have direct data links with its main suppliers and customers.

CONSTRAINTS

> **!?!** Computers are systems. All systems, including those which generate information in an organisation, can be defined as a group of elements and/or activities that are interrelated.

For the most part, a system only works properly if the related activities and elements are carried out in a systematic way, i.e. according to standardised procedures. Humans are able to cope with flexible (or even disorganised) systems, and with ambiguous information because they possess both intelligence and a base of knowledge and experience from which to exercise it. Computers, as yet, have neither of these, despite intensive research and development efforts. They remain unintelligent machines which, however, can store, process and output an infinite variety of data in an infinite variety of ways, on two conditions:

1. they must be told precisely what to do (i.e. they must be equipped with a comprehensive set of instructions in the form of software)

2. the data must be input in the form(s) specified by the software.

Computers thus impose disciplines on their users, the first requirement being a systematic approach.

A system does not necessarily imply using a computer. An organisation that records details of its expenses in a purchases ledger and produces an analysis and summary four times a year is using a system. At this simple level, an information system may contain just three elements and three processes:

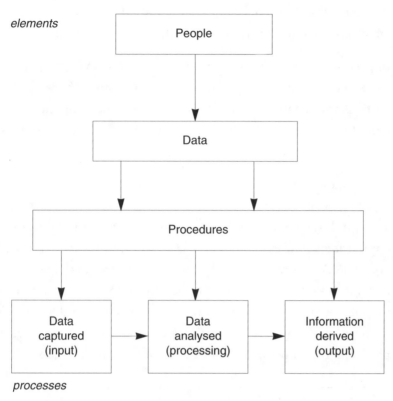

FIGURE 2.7: A simple information system.

In this model, the potential for data analysis is small. If there are few data to work on, little additional information can be derived from them.

Where computers are used to process information, the model becomes somewhat more complex, since elements now include software (programs) and hardware (the computer system). This is illustrated in figure 2.8.

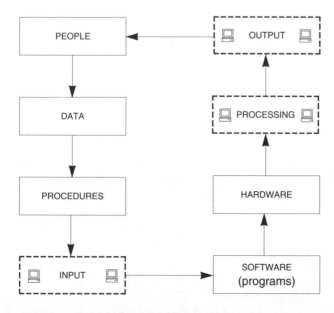

FIGURE 2.8: A computerised information processing system.

Both models are variants of the basic information processing system, which is called the input/process/output or I/P/O cycle.

In ensuring that a computer operates its I/P/O cycle as intended, rigid and systematic procedures are important. These apply in particular to the methods used for data input and validation of that data. Inconsistency and disorganisation here can produce the so-called garbage in-garbage out (GIGO) syndrome.

A computer cannot be presented with data such as that shown in figure 2.9, which once again comes from Stokkit's manual system. In a manual system, it would be possible for someone with the appropriate knowledge to make sense of this record, though it might take time. A computerised system would be unable to cope with it, as it stands; the data would have to be converted into a standardised format. For example, a single format for the date would be required if any processing is to be performed on that data field, e.g. if a particular report requires records to be printed in date order.

00035	21. 08. 95	Stephensons	36 cartons	Billie Dolls
00036	21. 08. 95	P&G	see del. note	cedar soap
00037	Aug 22		approx 1,000 (NB not counted)	misc.wooden items
00037		Rappoports	112 pkts candles	(ref0613778/55)
00038	22. 08. 95	Rappoports	Tiger Kites x 20 x45	
00039	22. 08. 95	Makeway & Parry	5,000 20 x28cm bags	mailing bags, brown (not for resale)
00040	23 Aug. 95	St/sons	480 (shrink-wrapped in 24s)	sun/moon mobiles
00041	23 Aug 95	Stephensons	3 gross (1x12-jar pack returned broken)	country jam

FIGURE 2.9: Stokkit's manual recording system.

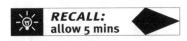

RECALL:
allow 5 mins

What are the two conditions we specified for the successful use of computers to handle data?

Computers operate strictly according to instructions, which among other things specify:

- the range and type of data that can be processed

- the order and form in which they are entered into the system (e.g. the format for dates)

- the kind of analysis that can be performed on them.

This, in turn, has implications for how the collection of data is organised, and how it is formatted for inputting. One consequence is the widespread use of data entry forms – standardised documents that ensure that each data record is constructed in a consistent way, with a 'slot' for each element of data to be recorded. A data entry form for standardising data like those in figure 2.9 is illustrated in figure 2.10.

Data records like that in figure 2.10 would clearly benefit from a more disciplined approach, including a standard format for entering dates, describing suppliers and goods, coding special notes, etc. However, the computer software can help, e.g. by permitting only one date format, or by entering the current date automatically. It can recognise suppliers' names from simple four-digit codes, thus saving data entry time and reducing clerical errors (e.g. 0044 = Stephensons). The system could also check with databases (see session 3) listing what goods come from which supplier. If, having entered 0044 as the supplier code, the operator entered a goods code that was not a 'permitted' Stephensons item, an error message would appear. The system would also prevent clerical errors such as the double use of the delivery code 00037. The data in this form would be used to update the main stock record file; any queries would be processed separately and corrections made in due course.

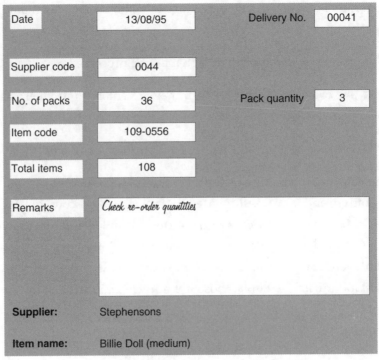

Date	13/08/95	Delivery No.	00041
Supplier code	0044		
No. of packs	36	Pack quantity	3
Item code	109-0556		
Total items	108		
Remarks	*Check re-order quantities*		

Supplier: Stephensons

Item name: Billie Doll (medium)

FIGURE 2.10 A simple data entry form for Stokkit.

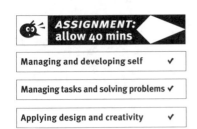

ASSIGNMENT:
allow 40 mins

Managing and developing self	✓
Managing tasks and solving problems	✓
Applying design and creativity	✓

ACTIVITY 13

Megacar Insurance uses a computer system to calculate quotations for motor insurance on the basis of information given by customers over the phone.

Your task is to draw up a data entry form for use by telesales staff. It should provide a comprehensive and systematic record of the data needed to work out the price for insuring a customer's car. The specific layout is not important, but the information should be grouped in a logical way.

The price quoted will depend on a number of 'risk factors', which Megacar considers to be the following:

- relative risk of accident: age, model and make of vehicle, previous convictions for speeding, reckless driving, etc., certain occupations

- relative risk of theft: model and make of vehicle, area where customer lives, parking in garage/street, business use.

It is the company's policy to reject applicants who have serious motoring convictions (such as banned for drink driving); who have previously been refused insurance; and who suffer from certain medical conditions including epilepsy. Applicants who have another kind of insurance policy with Megacar (such as personal or domestic) are entitled to a discount.

You need to complete this activity on separate paper, though you may wish to use the box below for notes. First list all the elements of data that the form will need to contain, and then draft the form out neatly. Try to limit it to one A4 page.

Methods of data capture

This section deals exclusively with computerised data, but we will distinguish between data that is input automatically (e.g. by bar code scanning or other scanning devices), and data entered manually by humans (e.g. using a keyboard or mouse).

Everyone is now familiar with the computer keyboard as a means of entering data into a computer and of interacting with it. Words, numbers and instructions are easy to input in this way, and few people lack the skill needed to touch a series of keys in the right order. The speed at which an individual can do so, however, is another matter, and many people who use computers do not have the high speed and accuracy that a thoroughly trained data processing clerk would have. Even where trained staff are employed to input data in large quantities – data from income tax returns, for example – the procedure is relatively inefficient: computers are capable of receiving data at speeds hundreds of time faster than a keyboard could ever provide (there is a mechanical as well as a human limit on keyboarding speeds).

The keyboard, however, is not the only means by which humans can 'interface' with the computer and data be supplied to it.

EXERCISE:
allow 20 mins

Working with and relating to others ✔

Managing tasks and solving problems ✔

ACTIVITY 14

What other methods of inputting data or instructions to a computer can you think of? For what purposes is each method best suited?

You may need to take time out to observe computer users at work, and to study popular computer magazines where many different input devices are discussed, advertised and illustrated. Group your examples under headings below:

Input method: Best suited for:

(a) manual input:

(b) automatic data capture:

(c) accessing existing bulk data:

Commentary...

Input methods fall into two groups: manual input and automatic data capture.

Manual input involves direct interaction between the operator and the computer:

- Keypads are a practical way of entering numerical data only.

- Handheld terminals can accept a mixture of text and data; some types are fully portable and contain memory, so that data can be collected on the move and downloaded into a computer later.

- The mouse, touch-sensitive screens and datapads are useful primarily for giving instructions; they are seldom a practical means of data input.

- The human voice is potentially much quicker than keyboarding, especially for inputting text, but the software has proved very difficult to develop; applications at present are very limited.

Automatic data capture uses sensors to 'read' the data:

- Laser scanners and light-pens (handheld or fixed) that read bar codes are an important part of transaction processing systems (TPSs) at supermarket check-outs, etc.

- Page scanners can be used to input existing printed or typed text faster than could be done by re-keying it. They are also useful for inputting all kinds of graphic images.

- Automatic tellers (otherwise known as 'hole in the wall machines') read data from magnetic strips on cash cards. In other parts of Europe, 'smart cards' containing a microprocessor are used for the same purposes.

- Sensors and counters of various kinds can also be used to collect data, as in manufacturing process control and environmental control systems.

Accessing existing bulk data relies on data that has already been stored on a computer:

- Floppy disks, tapes, hard cartridges, CD-ROMs and other 'portable memory' media can be used to transfer existing data into computers at electronic speeds.

- Networks enable computers to draw on databases and other computers to which they are directly connected, usually within a limited physical area.

- Communications links over 'dedicated' lines or via a telephone modem into the public telephone system can be used to transfer bulk data in or out, and over unlimited distances.

Information overload

Since the IT revolution and the 'information age' began, the volume of data being recorded about people, processes and things of all kinds has multiplied enormously. This in turn has multiplied the volumes of information which can be – and are – derived from the data. Not only this, but other forms of information have also multiplied. In Britain alone there are:

- dozens of TV channels (including satellite and cable channels)

- scores of radio channels

- hundreds of national and local newspapers, some published daily

- thousands of journals and magazines covering every possible topic

- more than 50,000 new books published each year, the majority scientific or technical in content.

If English-language publishing in other countries (the USA, Canada, Australia, etc.) is included, the figures in the last two categories increase four-fold.

In addition to these established information sources, new ones are developing rapidly. One popular package called Autoroute enables any driver to check (and time) the best route between A and B anywhere in the British Isles, taking account of variations in traffic density and road types and the time of day to travel. Others allow individuals to check their tax liability and complete tax forms. The range of information published on CD-ROMs for use on desk-top computers is also increasingly rapidly, as a glance at the software advertisements in any computer magazine will reveal. Some CD-ROMs contain astonishing amounts of information, for example:

- the complete works of Shakespeare with illustrations

- multimedia encyclopedias (e.g. Microsoft's Encarta)

- the complete BT telephone directories.

Over the years, many organisations have built their own computerised information listings. Commercially marketed databases include: all the doctors in the UK, coded by speciality and region; all universities; all subscribers to particular publications. Other databases may be much more specialised:

- university departments have compiled technical and reference databases for every imaginable subject

- all books and scientific articles published in Britain are listed on the British Library's databases

- organisations like the Royal Society for the Protection of Birds maintain databases of sites of special scientific interest (SSSI), and of planning applications, so they can keep watch over developments that may affect wildlife.

Increasingly, it is becoming possible for anyone owning a computer to access these databases, either by direct links or via the global information communications network called the Internet. To join the network requires modest expenditure on hardware (a device called a modem which links the computer into the telephone system) and software, but usage charges are generally low. So many information services are available via the Internet, and their number is growing so rapidly, that it is impossible to keep track of them.

The same technology is increasing the scope of personal communications. Networks within organisations, and beyond, allow individuals to 'electronically mail' messages, letters, documents and other data to each other, replacing traditional paper-based communication.

COPING WITH INFORMATION

People in developed countries are daily bombarded with much more information than they can possibly assimilate or interpret. Fortunately, in ordinary life we can ignore or reject a great deal of it – 'junk mail', for example. People working in organisations are not so fortunate. Typically, jobs now entail a much higher information content than in previous eras. Managers, for example, are typically the target of large flows of information from many sources:

- written reports on operational performance, management problems, new projects, competitors, markets and many different aspects of business development

- tabular reports, e.g. on financial performance, budgets, forecasts, cost analyses, print-outs of product sales

- oral information delivered in meetings, large and small

- technical data

- proposals and submissions from potential suppliers

- recruitment data

- letters, memos, minutes and messages

- background reading, e.g. the technical and business press.

Computer-generated information is significantly increasing these flows, but there is a difficulty here. Research by Henry Minzberg (1973, The Nature of Managerial Work, New York: Harper & Row) showed chief executive officers spending nearly two-thirds of their time in meetings, talking and listening to others (listening takes up two-thirds of this time). A mere 22 per cent of their time was spent at their desks. Rosemary Stewart (1967, Managers and Their Jobs, Macmillan) reported that over a four-week period managers had, on average, only nine periods of 30 minutes or more during which they were uninterrupted.

Managers therefore have limited time for reading, and little opportunity to concentrate on complex material. Yet computer-generated information is intended to be read.

? **SAT:** allow 10 mins

Managing tasks and solving problems ✔

ACTIVITY 15

What conclusions would you draw from the statements in the last two paragraphs as to the way in which computer-derived information should be managed?

Commentary...

An increase in the volume of computer-generated management information risks being counter-productive, because the managers will not have time to study it. This was the risk at which we hinted when we discussed the proposal to computerise Anxia's donations book. If the new kinds of management information are to fulfil the expectations which we rightly have of them, then great care will be needed to ensure that:

- the volume of information provided is not so great as to be counter-productive

- the information produced is relevant to people's real needs

- its value justifies the resources invested in generating it

- it is presented in such as way as to be quickly and easily assimilated.

summary

▶ Data can be defined as 'recorded facts and figures'.

▶ Individual data are of little value; when grouped together as data records (defined as 'related data') they become more useful. In many organisations, the main data records are created and stored by transaction processing systems (TPSs).

▶ Data records can be processed to answer a wide range of questions relevant to the operational and strategic management of the organisation. Management information is derived from data by computer processing, mostly of a simple kind.

▶ The information derived from the processing of TPS data, such as the productivity of one individual, is most useful when there is something relevant with which to compare it, e.g. the average productivity of staff performing similar tasks.

▶ Manual systems can cope with simple analysis of limited numbers of records. Complex analysis of large volumes of data only becomes possible when computers are used.

▶ Since computers are inflexible and require precise instructions, they impose a strict discipline on the way data are collected and entered into the system. Data entry forms are commonly used to organise the data appropriately.

▶ Data input is often a labour-intensive area, with costs to match; however, a wide and growing range of input methods is available. These may be both faster and less error-prone than keyboarding.

Meeting an organisation's information needs

THE BULGING IN-TRAY

INFORMATION MANAGEMENT
IN ORGANISATIONS

MANAGEMENT INFORMATION
SYSTEMS

DECISION SUPPORT SYSTEMS

PERSONAL INFORMATION
SYSTEMS

INFORMATION FLOWS

Objectives

After participating in this session, you should be able to:

▶ **explain why it is possible to have too much information**

▶ **describe some techniques used to reduce information flows to manageable proportions**

▶ **list and define the six subsystems that may be found within an organisational information system**

▶ **explain how spreadsheets, models, databases and planning software can be used within a decision support system**

▶ **draw up suitable criteria, objectives and performance requirements for the development of a management information system**

▶ **trace information flows within an organisation and indicate how these are filtered and focused in the light of the organisation's goals.**

In working through this session, you will practise the following BTEC common skills:

Managing and developing self	✔
Working with and relating to others	✔
Communicating	✔
Managing tasks and solving problems	✔
Applying numeracy	✔
Applying technology	
Applying design and creativity	

The bulging in-tray

Managers need information to plan and control the progress of activities. The less information available, the worse the management decisions are likely to be, but beyond a certain point, increasing information flows does not necessarily help.

SAT:
allow 10 mins

Managing tasks and solving problems ✔

ACTIVITY 1

Consider what we have said so far about information and assess whether the following statements are true or false? Give your reasons in each case.

1. More information on a subject allows better decisions to be made.

2. Twice as much relevant information means that the decisions based on it should be twice as good.

3. Providing more information reduces the time needed to reach decisions.

4. Providing more information simplifies the task of reaching a decision.

5. Within modern organisations, most operational and financial information is collected and processed automatically, and can therefore be considered 'free'.

Commentary...

In theory, more information allows better decisions to be made, provided that the information is relevant.

But, doubling the amount of information does not double the quality of the decision. Information tends to follow the 80:20 rule – 80 per cent of the value comes from 20 per cent of the information. Adding more information can add a few percentage points to its total value, but it seldom (if ever) doubles it.

On the contrary, the more information provided, the longer the time needed to reach a decision, because the decision maker has to spend more time perusing the information.

More information does not simplify the task: on the contrary, it makes it more complex, since the amount of 'information processing' that has to take place in the manager's mind is greatly increased.

Information is seldom cost-free. Automatic data collection and processing systems are expensive to establish, and need to be maintained and supported by qualified people. Where non-routine information is collected and analysed for a specific purpose, the costs can be high.

INFORMATION AND THE QUALITY OF DECISIONS

A 'good' decision can be thought of as a combination of three main factors: 'rightness', speed and economy. Up to a certain point, increasing the amount of relevant information improves decision quality, since increasing rightness outweighs decreasing speed and economy. Beyond an optimum point, rightness increases much less rapidly (this is the 80:20 effect) while speed and economy begin to fall rapidly. If the information flows become overwhelming, rightness may also decline. Figure 3.1 shows a theoretical 'utility curve' based on these considerations.

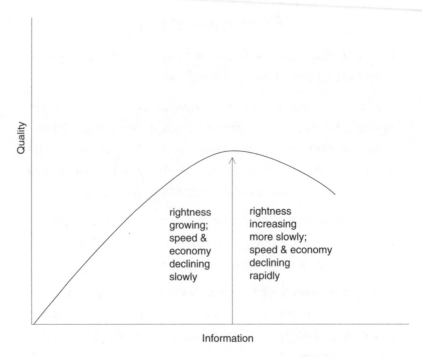

FIGURE 3.1: Effect of increasing information flows on decision quality.

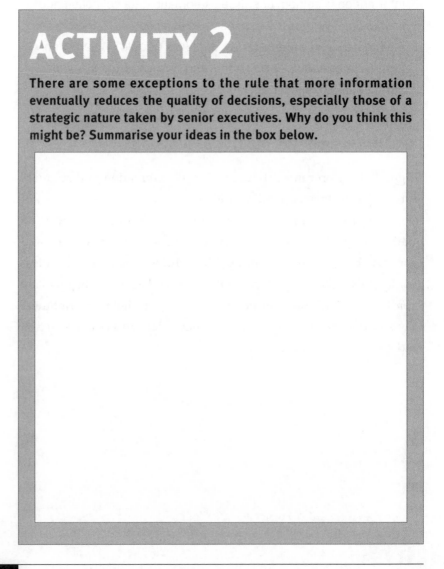

ACTIVITY 2

There are some exceptions to the rule that more information eventually reduces the quality of decisions, especially those of a strategic nature taken by senior executives. Why do you think this might be? Summarise your ideas in the box below.

Commentary...

The diminishing returns rule mainly applies to ordinary management decisions, where speed is of the essence. Strategic decisions are different in three key respects:

- they apply to the long term

- the financial impact of even a small increase in the quality of the decision can be considerable

- speed (and even cost) are therefore relatively less important than rightness.

Senior executives commonly seek out a very wide range of information, and commission information such as market and opinion surveys. They may also invest in special information-management tools such as business models and simulations before reaching a strategic decision.

The problem of too much information is a common one for managers. It greatly increases their workload and complicates their tasks. Here is what Stephen Gage, the European sales manager of Pefgo Flooring plc, found in his in-tray after returning from a week-long business visit to France and Spain:

STEPHEN GAGE'S IN-TRAY

1. 20-page monthly sales report (covering all market and product sectors)
2. six internal memos on various subjects
3. copies of Stephen's own correspondence
4. some old notes that Stephen no longer needs
5. weekly production report and forecast (six pages)
6. sales reports from agents in Greece and Italy
7. sales/activity report from subsidiary in Finland
8. weekly sales reports from Stephen's five European representatives
9. Stephen's expenses sheets
10. Stephen's diary/visits plan
11. an airline timetable
12. agendas for three forthcoming meetings
13. holiday rosters for Stephen and his staff
14. document about a change in the company pension scheme
15. progress report on new product development project
16. monthly all-Europe market share and competitor activity survey
17. advertising literature from various organisations
18. three trade magazines (one in German)
19. magazine articles about business conditions in Eastern Europe
20. note about a forthcoming visit of customers from Hungary
21. first draft of Stephen's three-month sales activity plan
22. copy of a long letter from legal advisers about a negligence claim
23. proposal from a management training consultancy
24. draft copies of the latest company brochures for Stephen's comments
25. disputed invoice from a translation agency
26. memo reporting an attempt to obtain a bribe from one of the sales team
27. five short-listed application forms for a new administrative assistant
28. document on Stephen's position in the staff share purchase scheme
29. Stephen's own monthly sales report and budget for completion.

This in-tray is fairly typical. It contains a mixture of operational, personal and background information, plus problems to be dealt with and other matters requiring action. Some of the information is also available in more detail on the computer.

Like most managers, Stephen has only very limited time available for reading (about 10 per cent of his time, compared with two-thirds spent in meetings and discussions). He therefore needs be efficient in managing the information in his in-tray, which ranges from the irrelevant to the vitally important.

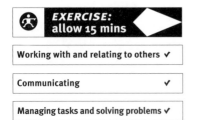

EXERCISE:
allow 15 mins

Working with and relating to others ✓

Communicating ✓

Managing tasks and solving problems ✓

ACTIVITY 3

In groups of four, discuss the best way to approach the large pile of reading matter in Stephen's in-tray. You may find it useful to ask some people in management roles what strategies they adopt for dealing with the many documents they have to read and act upon.

In your groups, make a note of the approaches, strategies and techniques that you think will be most useful.

Note which items in the list contain tasks and problems that Stephen needs to deal with personally.

Summarise your findings in the box below.

Commentary...

Stephen follows typical management practice by scanning the contents of the in-tray rapidly and sorting them into groups according to their importance and/or urgency. Table 3.1 shows how he begins to sort the material into four groups.

Group	Importance urgency	How handled
1.**Unwanted material** (e.g. items 4 and 17)	nil	Destroyed immediately
2.**Background information** that may be useful (e.g. items 14,18, and 19)	low	Put aside to be read later, or filed with other relevant documents for processing at the relevant time
3.**Information of operational relevance** that Stephen needs to study and understand (e.g. items 1, 8 and 16)	medium	Placed in Stephen's briefcase to be read as soon as possible
4.**The action file**: material that needs his personal attention, and possibly action (e.g. items 9,10, 20, 21, 24 and 25)	high	Placed in 'action' file

TABLE 3.1: Sorting information according to importance and urgency

All the items in the in-tray can be sorted in the same way. Obviously, Stephen must have a well-organised filing system so that documents like those in group 2 can be retrieved quickly when they are needed.

The action file contains items that Stephen must deal with personally. His next action is to sort them into priority order. He will deal with each item as soon as possible, but some of the non-urgent items may stay in his file for days or even weeks, as yet more urgent items arise and take priority over them.

Stephen has learned speed-reading and scanning techniques to help him deal with printed documentation more rapidly; see Sutcliffe, G.E. (1988) Effective Learning for Effective Management, Prentice Hall. Other information and task-management strategies that he uses include:

- making lists of tasks that he needs to carry out over the next few days; these may include studying some of the operational data in group 3 or reading background information in group 2

- asking his assistant to scan reports and draw anything of significance to his attention

- delegating some tasks to his assistant or other colleagues.

Other managers employ different methods to manage incoming information, but the general approach is always to focus attention on the priority issues and to de-prioritise as much as possible. Computerised systems offer a number of ways of reducing the burden of information-management tasks that are common to almost all managers.

Information management in organisations

We have just looked at the information management problems of one individual, in a system which is largely paper-based. In organisations that use information technology on a large scale, the opportunities for obtaining information are greatly increased, but so is the problem of overloading information users.

Managers may come to regard information as a problem because it increases demands on their time, increases complexity, and makes it more difficult to decide on priorities for action. From the perspective of the organisation, cost is also an important issue. So, while organisations are eager to ensure that their managers and other staff have all the information sources and tools they need, they try to be selective in providing them. Thus when planning information systems, they ask themselves the following questions:

- What information is it essential to provide?

- What non-essential information would it be useful to provide?

- What is the cost of providing each of these kinds of information?

- What should our priorities be in providing information?

- How do we prevent our staff from being overloaded with information?

These questions are asked in respect of each distinct level of information-user in the organisation. The answers depend on three aspects of the particular organisation:

1. the nature of its activities

2. its goals

3. its internal structure.

SYSTEMS FOR INFORMATION MANAGEMENT

Using the high-speed processing power of computers, digital communication (often through local networks) and a variety of software programs, organisations are now designing full-scale information systems which operate on a number of levels. These are often known as management information systems (MIS), but we prefer to use the global term organisational information systems (OIS) for two reasons:

1. Not all information in the system is intended solely for managers: administrators, technical staff and senior executives also use it.

2. Within a given organisation, there may be up to six distinct subsystems, one of which is properly called the management information system; it is helpful to distinguish between this MIS and the overall OIS.

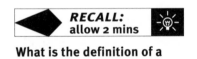

RECALL:
allow 2 mins

What is the definition of a system?

The organisational information system and its various subsystems bring together many kinds of information and facilities to provide a flexible and multidimensional view on a particular topic.

Within an OIS, Kroenke and Hatch (1994, Management Information Systems, 3rd edn, Mitchell/McGraw-Hill,) have identified up to six distinct information systems which interlock but also serve separate purposes in distinct ways. Three of these are essential:

1. The office automation system (OAS) is primarily a communications structure, based on local area networks (LANs). These networks link numerous computer users within an organisation, allowing individuals and work groups to share facilities and to communicate using e-mail, voice mail, image transmission and direct exchange of data. Networks often have 'gateways' to external communications networks and databases. The OAS provides the environment within which the other systems are operated.

2. The transaction processing system (TPS), which we introduced in session 2, records data about the organisation's basic operations, and is thus the prime source of management information.

3. The management information system (MIS) processes operational data recorded by the TPS to generate the information needed to support operational management. Some of this information is also used by higher management.

Any computerised organisation is likely to have an OAS, TPS and MIS as we have described them. The next two subsystems are however optional; if taken to their full potential they can be expensive both to install and to operate.

4. A decision support system (DSS) is distinct from MIS and ESS (see below) in that it does not consist of information flows but of systems and tools for modelling and testing the impact of decisions taken in the light of this information.

5. An executive support system (ESS) is designed to channel information from a variety of sources to the organisation's senior executives. Summaries of management information are included, plus a variety of 'headline' financial figures, such as daily takings, gross profitability, cash position, gearing and market share. Some of this information will be reported daily.

Finally, the technology allows individuals to establish a small subsystem to meet their particular needs.

6. Personal information systems (PIS) are the information structures that individuals within an organisation connect with, customise or create themselves in order to meet the particular needs of their work and role. They may contain information that is available to no one else in the organisation.

Figure 3.2 shows how these subsystems relate to each other within the overall OIS. The connections within the systems and the different groups are made by the OAS. The other subsystems are explicitly shown on the diagram.

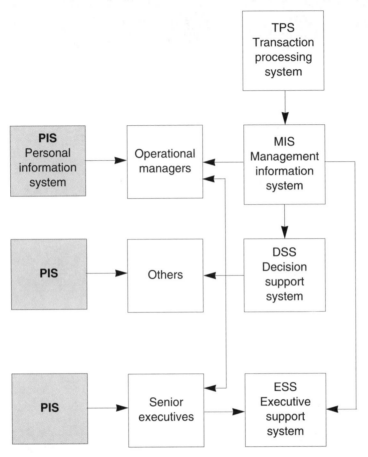

FIGURE 3.2: Subsystems within the organisational information system.

A SECOND LOOK AT TRANSACTION PROCESSING

Before going on to look at MIS, DSS and PIS in some detail, first let us remind ourselves of the vital role played by the TPS at the bottom of the pyramid of information applications.

Transactions are the basic units of operational activity: a retail sale, a booking for a package holiday, a donation received by a charity, the sending out of a Council Tax bill, a stock movement, an inquiry dealt with by a Citizen's Advice Bureau, an insurance policy taken out, a machine assembled, and so on.

ACTIVITY 4

Give three reasons why organisations must record these transactions, and make notes suitable for developing flip chart pages or overhead projector slides, so that you can, if necessary, give a short presentation on the subject.

Commentary...

First, the transactions must be recorded for the sake of operational efficiency. Without records, queries cannot be dealt with, and severe operational problems may arise: the retailer may run out of stock; the cinema and the holiday company may overbook; the factory may find itself either overstocked or unable to fulfil orders.

Second, the keeping of accurate records of financial matters such as sales turnover, expenses, stock levels, materials consumed, is required by law, directly or indirectly:

- they feed into the organisation's annual financial statements (profit and loss account, balance sheet and cash flow statement) and if these are not accurate the organisation will be in breach of its statutory duties under the Companies Acts, Stock Exchange Listing Rules and other financial legislation

- the Inland Revenue authorities, who collect Corporation Tax and National Insurance payments, require accurate records to be kept for these purposes

- HM Customs and Excise requires accurate and up-to-date records to be kept for VAT purposes, and inspect VAT-registered organisations to ensure that this is being done.

Many non-profit-making organisations are subject to the same regulations; charities are in addition supervised by the statutory Charities Commission, which insists on the accurate recording of donations and of how they were spent.

The third reason for keeping transaction records is so that managers can manage. Without the information contained in these records they cannot tell if the organisation's activities are proceeding according to plan, and whether they should take corrective or preventive action.

An organisation's TPS is absolutely fundamental to effective management, because it is the source of almost all the information used for operational management, and a great deal of what is needed at the strategic level. Without a TPS, a MIS cannot exist.

Management information systems

> !?! A management information system (MIS) can best be defined as 'an information system that facilitates management by producing structured, summarised reports on a regular and recurring basis' (Kroenke and Hatch, 1994, Management Information Systems, 3rd edn, Mitchell/McGraw-Hill).

Managers are responsible for planning and controlling routine operations and projects to ensure that they proceed smoothly. They must make sure that operations are in line with the requirements of the organisation's ultimate goals. They must be thoroughly familiar with the activities for which they are responsible, and maintain close contact with the people who perform them. However, managers are generally not required to know every detail of what is going on, or to supervise every process personally. This is the job of supervisors, charge-hands – and increasingly, as organisations try to devolve responsibility and encourage initiative – the staff themselves. The manager's role is to ensure that progress generally conforms with the plan, by acting preventively or correctively, and by dealing with the specific problems that arise.

Managers therefore need to know:

- how activities are progressing, compared with plans, budgets, operating standards, targets, etc.

- where problems that require a decision are emerging or have emerged.

In complex organisations, the progress of activities cannot simply be observed. If by a given stage of a project 6,000 km of cabling are due to be installed, a manager cannot check this by looking out of the window. Nor can a visual inspection of a vast storage facility show check whether a planned 2 per cent reduction in stock levels has been achieved. This kind of information depends on the accumulation of numerous separate records, interim reports, checks and, of course, data processing, culminating in management reports.

Management reports are not an invention of the computer age. For example, before its stock systems were computerised, the compilation of management reports was one of the main tasks undertaken by Stokkit's accounts department. Table 3.2 shows the main regular reports that were produced.

Report	Content	Frequency	Date of appearance	Distribution
Cost analysis	• Direct (purchase) costs of goods sold • gross profit per cent	Quarterly	6 weeks in arrears (ie. by second board meeting after end of period)	All directors and senior managers with financial responsibilities
Overhead analysis	• Indirect costs, excluding wage costs, analysed against the budget codes used in the Profit & Loss Account and broken down between five cost centres	Quarterly	6 weeks in arrears	As above
Sales analysis	• Total sales for period: (a) items sales by product group; (b) broken down by supplier; (c) broken down by customer	Monthly	Target: 18 days after month end	As above
Stock report	• Listing of all stock items, with average stock holding and stockturn ratio	Quarterly	4 weeks after end of period	Operations and warehouse managers; finance director
Productivity report	• Staff numbers and wage costs per cost centre and in total; and as a proportion of each cost centre's total indirect costs	Monthly	Target: 18 days after month end	All directors and departmental managers

TABLE 3.2: Management reports produced at Stokkit prior to computerisation.

The analyses were very comprehensive. The sales analysis, for example, was produced in three forms:

1. Sales of all items within each product group

2. Sales by supplier

3. Sales by customer.

Furthermore, each version showed the monthly and cumulative position of actual sales, budgeted sales and variances. Table 3.3 shows a small extract from the item sales by product group report.

MONTHLY ITEM SALES ANALYSIS PRODUCT GROUP 312: POSTERS, FRAMES, MIRRORS Actual and cumulative sales against budget							MONTH: APRIL DATE OF ISSUE: 20th May		
Item code	March £			April £			Cumulative (March onwards) £		
	actual	budget	variance	actual	budget	variance	actual	budget	variance
013	1,250	1,200	50	855	1230	(375)	2,105	2,430	(325)
014	631	665	(34)	711	675	36	1,342	1,340	2
015	793	795	(2)	899	810	89	1,692	1,605	87
016 etc.	2119	2355	(236)	1,948	2,475	(527)	4,067	4,830	(763)
Total (all items in group)	71,895	75,225	(3,330)	66,195	77,850	(11,655)	138,090	153,075	(14,985)

Notes: 1. Negative variances are shown in brackets.

2. The 'total' line includes the figure for items 001–012 and 017–060, which are not shown here for reasons of space.

TABLE 3.3: Extract from Stokkit's item sales report.

In all, 43 product groups were analysed in the item sales by product group report, with one A4 sheet to each, plus a two-page summary; the sales per customer report consisted of 17 pages, sales per supplier of 22 pages. The sales reports alone therefore amounted to 84 pages of figures every month. Most of the other analyses shown in table 3.2 were somewhat less extensive, but the stock report, produced on computer from manually input data, amounted to over 200 pages of print-out.

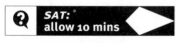

SAT:°
allow 10 mins

Managing tasks and solving problems ✔

ACTIVITY 5

In its time, Stokkit's reporting system was much admired. What comments would you make on it, in the light of our RARTAC criteria?

Make comments under the six RARTAC criteria:

- relevant

- accurate

- reliable

- timely

- accessible

- comprehensible.

Commentary...

Our comments in the light of RARTAC are as follows:

- Relevant: The reports generated by Stokkit appear to be relevant, but the directors seem to be receiving too much detailed information.

- Accurate: We do not have enough information to judge their accuracy, but where manual clerical methods are used, some errors are certain to appear.

- Reliable: Again, we can assume that the records are derived from reliable sources (e.g. time sheets, invoices and goods-in notes would all be subject to their own checking procedures).

- Timely: Clearly the reports are not timely. Even 'monthly' reports only appear 18 days after the month end. If a significant change occurred in the first week of a month, it would be at least six weeks before this was reported–

far too late to act on it. The reporting system is very weak in this respect.

- Accessible: Clearly it is not accessible. Managers were obliged to study hundreds of pages in order to identify any significant information.

- Comprehensible: Again, it is clearly not comprehensible. Even with practice, endless pages of tables are extremely difficult to assimilate.

We can summarise this system by saying that while it produced extremely thorough reports, the sheer bulk of information was likely to be counter-productive. The reports must have been extremely costly to produce, and their tardy appearance reduced their practical value considerably.

In 1989 – in the interests of improving operating efficiency, and of reducing the cost of providing management information – Stokkit's whole stock control system was computerised, at a cost of £1.35 million. The new system revolutionised the work of operational management overnight. Now transaction data is captured instantaneously and is processed within 24 hours. More management reports can now be produced, in enormous detail, and as often as required (weekly, and even daily).

At first, managers were enthusiastic about the prospect of being able to react immediately to operational situations, but within a month the system was in crisis: key managers were spending so much time poring over piles of computer print-out that their efficiency was actually falling.

Consultants rapidly recommended (at additional expense) major changes to the structure of the system. A network was established, so that all relevant staff would in future receive (and distribute) most of their information via desk-top computer terminals. An information technology (IT) unit was put in place to manage the information system, to maintain the network hardware and software, and to support system users.

The consultants designed a revised MIS for Stokkit incorporating a new range of reports for operational management and a new range of standard financial management reports. The new system of operational management reports is based on the following:

1. Complete analyses are updated daily, but are not distributed in hard copy. Managers are able to access the reports through

their desk-top terminals, searching for item, product, customer and supplier codes as required and calling the relevant information to their screens. One copy of each complete report is printed out each week, as a safeguard against computer failure.

2. A two-page summary of each analysis is produced weekly. It is on computer but managers are also sent a hard copy.

3. A more detailed trend analysis report is prepared and issued in hard copy each month. Designed for discussion at regular management meetings, this includes 12-month forecasts against budgets, plus extracts from the financial information (see below). Of the 11 pages in this report, five contain tables, and the rest consist of graphs and charts.

4. In addition to the existing productivity report (now computer-generated), a new labour management system installed in the warehouse provides a wider range of information about work rates, efficiency and costs.

5. An exception reporting facility on the system saves managers having to look through large amounts of data in order to spot anything needing their attention (exception reporting is described below).

6. Graphical software enables users to view information as graphs or charts where desirable.

The new range of standard financial management includes additional reports, updated daily and made available to password-holders over the network, with weekly hard copy summaries. This information details:

- valuation of stock held

- totals of cash payments in and out

- cash balance (the 'cash position')

- projected cash flow (a short-term forecast to warn whether more working capital would be needed to fund cash flow)

- total debtors and total creditors, plus analysis by age

- the following financial ratios:
  direct costs : sales revenue (gross profit)
  overhead costs : sales revenue

all costs : sales revenue (net profit)

labour costs : sales revenue

stockturn

capital tied up in stock : sales revenue

net profit : total capital employed (pre-tax profitability)

MANAGEMENT BY EXCEPTION

A major part of a typical manager's role is to prevent and correct deviations from the plan. As with doctors, who concentrate on the minority of sick people and largely ignore the healthy majority, most managers prefer to focus their skills and efforts on the 'differences that make a difference'. This is sometimes called management by exception, and it is a highly practical example of how managers use information. Using this approach, the manager's main objective is to identify the significant differences (i.e. exceptions, variances and deviations from plan) among a mass of unexceptionable information.

Traditionally, as in Stokkit before computerisation, managers had to pore over extensive management reports, spotting variances and deciding whether the deviation was significant.

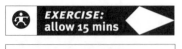

EXERCISE:
allow 15 mins

Managing and developing self ✔

Working with and relating to others ✔

Managing tasks and solving problems ✔

ACTIVITY 6

In groups of four, discuss how the revised system compares with the original pre-computerised system and the initial computerisation, which was a failure. Write brief answers to the following questions.

○ Why was the initial attempt to computerise a failure?

○ Why is the revised system much more satisfactory?

○ What new ways of inspecting information does the revised system make available?

○ One important factor for the effective operation of the system seems to have been ignored in both computerised versions. What is it?

Commentary...

The initial attempt to computerise failed because it swamped managers in information without focusing and filtering it to make it manageable. This merely exacerbated the faults of the pre-computer system.

The revised version solved this problem by reducing the output of reports to a minimum, while allowing managers access to the full range of data and information whenever they need it. It also provides valuable new information: the trend analysis, the reports from the new labour management system, and all the financial information.

New ways of inspecting the information are provided by the graphics software and the exception reporting system.

The factor that seems to be missing is the provision of training for managers and other staff in how to use the system with all its new facilities. Repeated experience shows that without adequate training and support the most impressive systems can easily fail to achieve its goals.

SAT:
allow 10 mins

Managing tasks and solving problems ✓

Applying numeracy   ✓

ACTIVITY 7

Look again at table 3.3. In this report, the deviations from the plan are called variances – they show where actual sales have under- or over-performed compared with the budget.

Using the data in table 3.3, work out the percentage variances (variance as a percentage of budget figure) in March, April and the cumulative figures for the item codes 013 to 016 and for the total items in the group. Present your results in a table.

Which variances would you consider large enough to merit possible action by managers? What overall comment would you make about these results shown in this analysis?

Commentary...

The percentage variances are shown in table 3.4.

Item code	March variance%	April variance %	Cummulative variance %
013	4.17	(30.49)	(13.37)
014	(5.11)	5.33	0.15
015	(0.25)	10.99	5.42
016	(10.02)	(21.29)	(15.80)
TOTAL (all 60 items in group)	(4.43)	(14.97)	(9.79)

TABLE 3.4: Variances in Stokkit's sales performance against budget.

Interpretation of these results is a matter of judgement and experience, but it is possible to draw up a few simple rules:

- Small variances in a single month (under 10 per cent) can be ignored as they may well be recouped in the following month.

- Variances in the range 10–25 per cent in a single month should give cause for concern particularly if the cumulative variance is also high.

- Cumulative variances should tend to settle down as more monthly figures accumulate. Thus after three months, a cumulative variance of 5 per cent may be considered 'small' and not cause for concern, but after nine months, 5 per cent might take on rather more significance.

- Variances of more than 25 per cent in a single month need to be investigated and explained.

- In sales figures, negative variances are obviously more serious than positive variances, but substantial and recurring positive variances should be investigated. There may be an error; if not, managers will want to know the reasons for their unexpected success.

The overall picture painted by the analysis in table 3.4 is of substantial under-performance across the whole product group. This is a cause for concern.

Where sales variances are at significant levels, they should be considered in parallel with cost variances.

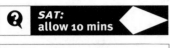

✔ Applying numeracy

ACTIVITY 8

An alternative to spotting variances by studying tables is to treat the data graphically. Figure 3.3 shows monthly sales and direct costs, both budgeted and actual, over a six-month period (not cumulated). What conclusions can you draw from it?

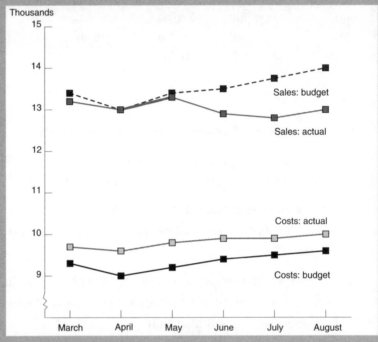

FIGURE 3.3: Monthly sales and direct costs – actual results and budgets.

Commentary...

Figure 3.3 shows a consistent negative variance for sales and a positive variance for direct costs (cost of sales). This has several serious implications:

- Sales performance is below par, which means that revenue is too low.

- Costs are not being controlled satisfactorily.

- The gap between revenue and costs is narrowing.

- A narrower gap between sales and direct costs means lower gross profit (since sales less direct costs equals gross profit).

- It also results in falling profit margins.

Management action is clearly needed here; the trend should have been obvious as early as April, and certainly by May.

It is relatively difficult to identify deviations from plan (in this case, from budget) by examining printed tables of figures; graphical presentation makes the task much easier, but if the graphs have to be prepared manually, not much is gained. Computer systems are capable of producing graphic versions of information at the touch of a few keys, but as we shall see in session 4, this too can be unsatisfactory when large numbers of different items need to be studied. However, computers provide an excellent alternative by generating 'exception reports' automatically.

EXCEPTION REPORTS

Where the relevant information is computerised, the task of combing through it, calculating variances and assessing their significance can be automated. The system will need to be told what to do, but this presents little difficulty. Here are some typical instructions:

- Search for instances where sales exceed budget by more than 10 per cent or fall below budget by more than 5 per cent.

- Search for any stock item whose stockturn has fallen below 3.75 for four or more weeks consecutively.

- Search for any item where physical stocktake figures vary from book figures by more than 3.5 per cent.

The process of identifying the exceptions, even among Stokkit's 20,000 stock records, is very quick. The system then highlights them in various ways, for example by:

- retaining the exceptions in the main file but 'flagging' them in some way, so that the user can either work manually through the file noting relevant items as they appear or move quickly from one to another by pressing a particular key

- copying the exceptions into a separate 'exceptions file', where they can be examined and analysed further, and printed out if required.

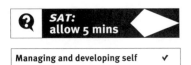

SAT:
allow 5 mins

Managing and developing self ✔

Managing tasks and solving problems ✔

ACTIVITY 9

Imagine yourself in the role of a manager who has to deal with exceptions identified in large volumes of data, and considering what we have said earlier about handling information, which of the options described above would you find most satisfactory?

State your reasons briefly.

Commentary...

The answer will depend on circumstances and personal preferences, but most users would consider that the 'separate exceptions file' approach would save time, be more convenient (because a printed record could be made) and would reduce the risk of missing some of the items.

In general, exception reporting provided by computerised systems is a highly efficient way of performing information management tasks that would present an intolerable burden if performed manually.

Decision support systems

Decision support systems (DSS) are distinct from management information systems, being primarily tools and facilities to help managers (and others) rather than information flows.

RECALL:
allow 10 mins

Define:

- an organisational information system (OIS)

- a management information system (MIS)

- a decision support system (DSS).

Decision support systems do not in themselves solve problems or provide decisions: they help people make better decisions on the basis of information at their disposal. Take one of the problems dealt with in Section 1, Session 5: how to price a product for optimum sales. This problem is fairly complex, but can be solved, given enough information and time. A decision support system could help us solve it more easily.

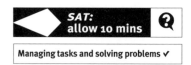

SAT:
allow 10 mins

Managing tasks and solving problems ✓

ACTIVITY 10

List the information that is needed to decide the optimum price for a product, i.e. the price that will result in the largest absolute amount of profit.

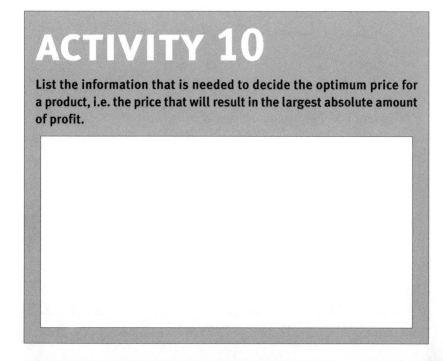

Commentary...

We need to know:

(a) the cost of the product (this should be fairly easy to establish, although cost may well vary according to the volume produced)

(b) how the price will affect sales levels (the price sensitivity of demand).

Price sensitivity of demand is a more difficult problem. It requires an understanding of how demand is affected by changes in price. For that, we need extensive knowledge of the market, competing products and the effectiveness of sales outlets, etc. If we have sufficient knowledge and experience to assess how sales will change as the price rises or falls, we can use a spreadsheet (or, even better, a statistical software program) to map out this relationship and calculate the total profit generated at each point on the curve. The optimum point is the one where total profit, rather than total revenue, is maximised.

If this situation is a one-off, we probably have no choice but to tackle it the hard way, creating a complex series of calculations, projections, graphs and tables. But if similar exercises are undertaken regularly, it may be worth buying and/or developing decision support tools:

- A statistical software package may provide a range of typical price demand curves, avoiding the need to work out complex equations. Costing and estimating packages also exist. At a minimum we would need a good-quality spreadsheet program.

- Company-relevant costing data and costing systems may already be available on the computer system.

- Examples of actual price/demand curves (established by test marketing of other company products, for example) may be available.

- Best of all, someone may have already developed a company-relevant price/demand 'model', drawing on past data and experience, and offering a range of options and forecasts at the touch of a key.

This presents a typical picture of a decision support system – special software, past data for reference and comparison, and models incorporating previous experience. This would amount to what is sometimes called an expert system, but it is still only an aid to decision making. The computer system can provide a great deal of insight into the problem, but the decision itself (and responsibility for that decision) rests with the manager.

DECISION SUPPORT SOFTWARE

Spreadsheets are mainly used for modelling a particular situation, but they often lie at the heart of complex models that link together a large number of costs, revenue and economic variables within a more complex structure. So although large-scale business financial models are available commercially, better spreadsheet software is making it easier for organisations to create their own models.

Other specialised software that can help support decisions. Examples include:

- statistical packages such as Arcus Pro Stat and MiniTab

- Estimator Plus and Floorplan Plus, which help to automate decisions about building design, techniques and costs

- Business Plan Builder, a valuable resource for creating business plans and proposals

- project management software, such as Microsoft Project, which contains extensive planning and analysis facilities

- Employee Appraiser and Workwise Evaluator, whose purposes are self-explanatory.

There is, in addition, a wide and growing range of software applications as diverse as sales activity planning, journey planning, 'organising time, activities and people', creating forms and preparing presentations.

Project management packages are a good example of decision-support software. Among other facilities, they allow users to enter data such as the time targets, interim deadlines and expected duration of the various subsidiary tasks which make up the project. The program then helps the user decide:

- the most sensible order for these subsidiary tasks

- which tasks can be carried out simultaneously, and which must be sequential

○ whether the total time needed for subsidiary tasks adds up to more than has been allowed for the whole project.

Database programs are not always relevant to decision support situations, but for particular decisions it may be useful to maintain:

○ lists of major customers

○ lists of staff, with details of their skills and experience

○ records of physical assets belonging to the organisation

○ details of contacts in the press and other influential positions

○ databases of 'authorised suppliers', with details of their capabilities, specialities and track record.

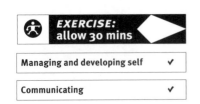

EXERCISE: allow 30 mins	
Managing and developing self	✔
Communicating	✔

ACTIVITY 11

Using a current issue of one of the major computer magazines such as Microcomputer World or Computer Buyer, look through the advertisements, articles and reviews and make a note of ten different software programs that could be used in a decision support role.

Select one of these ten programs and write a short report (of not more than 400 words) describing how it could usefully be applied in the organisation in which you work or study.

Summarise your key points in the box below.

In most organisations, there will be individual managers who use decision-support tools (mainly off-the-shelf software) supplemented by data collected in the past and modest decision models. Occasionally, however, an organisation will put substantial resources into developing a decision-support function, employing specialist IT staff and seconding specialists from other departments.

Naturally, this is a costly exercise, but where the improved quality of decisions is reflected in better financial and operational performance, the investment may well be justified.

EXECUTIVE SUPPORT SYSTEMS

Management information systems typically make a considerable amount of detail available to managers, split between routine reports and accessible data. Executive support systems (ESS), which are also known as executive information systems (EIS) have a different character. All managers are short of time, but senior executives most of all; also their time is the most valuable. We do not discuss ESS/EIS in detail here, but executives and directors who are controlling large organisations and making strategic decisions need information with the following characteristics:

- a wide variety, covering the organisation's operations and financial status, forecasts of economic trends, market research, opinion data, studies of competitors, product development reports, etc.

- in summary form, consisting of indexes, ratios, totals and 'executive summaries' based on the organisation's operational transaction data and management information, but avoiding complex tabulations and long written reports

- of high quality – executives make high-value decisions and must have high-quality data, so it is worth investing relatively large amounts of time, skill and money in collecting and analysing it

- in easily assimilated form – there is a strong preference for graphical presentation, and where the information is delivered through computers, for colour and even animation.

Finally, senior executives need to be able to query information and obtain alternative forms of analysis; the ESS must therefore be backed in depth with supporting information, and should be designed for flexible and user-friendly handling.

Personal information systems

An organisation-wide management information system can provide a vast range of information and facilities, but each individual in the system will have his or her own distinct personal and job-related needs.

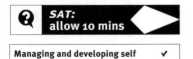

SAT:
allow 10 mins

Managing and developing self ✔

ACTIVITY 12

Consider the range of information that you need to organise your own studies, work and personal time. Note down what information you need to record, and the various ways in which you normally do so.

Commentary...

- Most people need to record dates and times of holidays, lectures, meetings, appointments and special events. This implies they need a diary, or even a detailed time-planner.

- Most people refer to addresses, telephone numbers, restaurants, books to read, etc. This implies keeping lists.

- Most people record and refer to financial data such as bank balance and value of cheques issued. This implies filing documents and making calculations.

The increasing need to make calculations, check the time, and communicate with other people means that individuals are increasingly equipping themselves not just with watches and calculators, but with extensive 'personal organisers', electronic organisers (which perform similar functions), mobile phones, lightweight 'notebook' computers and even portable fax/modems.

Such aids are useful for people on the move. People at work can use similar facilities provided through their desk-top computers. Windows software, for example, provides a diary, an on-screen calculator with both numerical and statistical functions, and a small-scale database, which can be used for recording addresses, etc.

One step up are integrated packages for desk-top computers, combining word processor, spreadsheet, database, 'communications' and sometimes 'drawing' (i.e. graphics) programs. Examples include Microsoft Works, Claris Works, WordPerfect Works. Some of these packages also contain facilities for making high quality visual presentations.

ONE MANAGER'S PERSONAL INFORMATION SYSTEM

Stephen Gage of Pefgo Flooring has a desk-top computer in his office, and a portable 'notebook' computer which can be linked to it via telephone modem from anywhere in the world. He can send or receive data and electronic mail, and access data and software from the company network. His only paper-based information aids are a small personal organiser containing the minimum of essential information in case his powerful 'notebook' computer fails or is lost.

On computer he has the following software, which is separate from what is available on the network, and which constitutes his personal information system:

- a 'works' package combining spreadsheet, word processor, database and communications (modem and fax) features

- a simple graphics program and a store of 'clip-art' images for use in brightening up his documents

- a sophisticated 'organiser' package, which he uses for planning his travels and meetings

- some simple project management tools for planning new sales and market research initiatives

- a program for drawing flowcharts

- a five-language 'phrasebook'.

plus copies of all kinds of recent reports, documents for reading, personal files and notes. He stores three important databases:

1. the customer database listing significant customers and 'leads' in Europe

2. those parts of the personnel database detailing his sales and support staff

3. Pefgo's product database containing all product, technical and sales data issued by the company, plus details of products under development and reports on competing products.

This is a very professional approach to PIS, designed by a serious and dynamic individual. It would be fair to say that most PIS holders include a selection of more personal and even trivial material in their systems.

Information flows

Earlier in this session we listed key questions that need to be asked when designing an information system. We explained that the answers depend on three particular aspects of the organisation concerned:

1. the nature of its activities

2. its goals

3. its internal structure.

We also explained that these aspects need to be considered in relation to departments, roles and management levels within an organisation, since each of these has different information needs. We now illustrate the point about management levels by returning to Kellaways, the blue-chip UK retailing business, which has a strong hierarchical organisation.

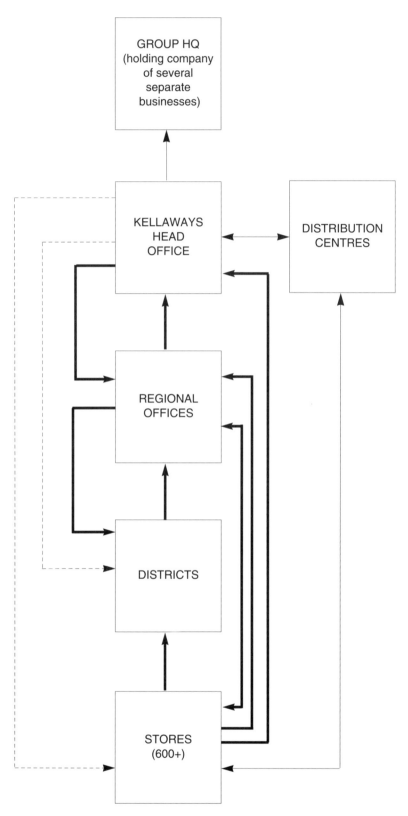

FIGURE 3.4: Kellaways' organisational structure and information flows.

Although the company consists of hundreds of geographically separated units, a MIS links the whole structure together. It is supplemented by DSS and ESS facilities where appropriate. In figure 3.4, the thickness of the lines shows the volume of the information flows.

The stores are the main source of information. Their TPSs generate the vast majority of the financial and operational information used in the company; the other main sources are the distribution centres and the Head Office purchasing function.

Much of the operational information is used for operational management at store level, and does not enter the company-wide MIS. The main information that the stores record and provide for the MIS is as follows:

1. volume of sales by item

2. value of sales

3. stock orders

4. goods received

5. delivery errors, shortages, breakages and goods returned

6. number of transactions (mainly customer purchases)

7. stock 'shrinkage' due to theft, wastage and error

8. staff costs, hours worked and productivity

9. other direct costs (cleaning, security)

10. progress of staff training

11. 'incidents' (anything which a higher level ought to know about, from complaints to accidents).

② SAT:
allow 10 mins

Managing tasks and solving problems ✔

ACTIVITY 13

Some of the information listed above is collected at close of business every day and processed overnight so that summaries can be shown to senior executives at Head Office and in the regions the following morning.

Highlight those items in the list that you think it would be appropriate to process in this way.

Commentary...

In a retail business, which operates on high volumes and low margins, cash flow and gross profit margins are of vital importance. Senior executives want to know how many transactions are taking place (item 6), how much money is being taken (item 2), what the average transaction is worth, and the gross profit resulting (these are both calculated by Head Office computers from the data provided). Head Office watches for adverse trends so that it can take immediate company-wide or region-wide action. Thus, if the number of transactions falls below target, the company may within days launch a national advertising campaign to attract more customers into the stores.

Sales and transaction information (items 2 and 6) is fed to district, regional and Head Office daily; costs and other data less frequently. Regional offices use the information primarily to analyse the comparative performance of districts and stores. Summary reports on this also travel upwards to Head Office in due course, but is mainly designed for use by district managers. Some less immediately important data, such as progress on training plans, also travel up the hierarchy via district and region before reaching relevant managers at Head Office in summary form. Stores send stock orders and report delivery errors and details of returns direct to the distribution centres

MAINTAINING MANAGEMENT FOCUS

The Kellaways hierarchy generates and consumes a large amount of information, but filters and focuses it carefully to ensure that managers at different levels receive only the information that is relevant to their roles. Thus much of the extensive TPS data generated at store level stays there for operational use; the store level information that enters the MIS is progressively reduced and concentrated as it moves upwards (with the exception of sales results, which go direct to the top).

The purpose is to avoid distracting any level of management with unnecessary information, and to keep it strongly focused on its key tasks. Thus district managers, who are each responsible for the performance of around 20 stores, receive the information they need to achieve their three key result areas:

1. to instruct and motivate store managers and their teams in how to achieve their operational objectives

2. to study and compare results from their stores, identifying under-performance and other problems, and intervening rapidly to try to overcome these

3. to perform personnel management roles for the store managers and management trainees in their district, as well as carrying out certain general management functions (this includes a good deal of trouble-shooting of various kinds).

This role determines the information provided to district managers. They periodically see comparative results from other districts, but like store managers they are kept strongly focused upon operational matters. They receive strong flows of information from their regional office and from their stores. District managers are completely dependent on information: they live and breathe it, and their working lives are dominated by data print-outs, reports and budgets. The same pattern is repeated at regional offices. Here management is mainly concerned with performance of the districts. It does not normally concern itself with events in individual stores – that is the district manager's job.

Head Office focuses on company-wide summarised information, which it uses for identifying adverse trends and taking rapid action to correct them, and for planning medium- and long-term strategies.

This brings us back to the concepts outlined in Session 1.

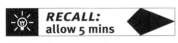

RECALL:
allow 5 mins

State the two main purposes for which information is used in organisations

What are the three main levels of decision making at which it plays a significant role?

Organisations need information if they are to function effectively in achieving their goals. Information plays a particular role in decision making: on the one hand, in planning the strategies, resources and activities that will lead to the goals; and on the other, in managing the progress of operations. The three decision-making levels are: strategic, managerial and operational. As our description of information use within Kellaways shows, these levels are likely to overlap, since lower levels of management may look to higher levels for advice, support and confirmation of their decisions, and higher levels may seek to devolve decision making where possible.

The significance of this structure, with its levels and overlaps, for the design of information systems is that:

- different kinds of information are needed for different levels of decision making

- where huge amounts of information are available, it has to be filtered carefully to prevent individuals from being swamped in irrelevant material.

Now that the technology available is capable of delivering so much more information, analysed in so many different ways, organisations are having to reconsider their approach to information management. In the past, organisational information has been a hotchpotch of uncoordinated databases, programs, processes and departmental structures. In the future, the pressure of costs and the increasing capacity and flexibility of IT facilities means that the emphasis will be on the development of advanced organisational information systems. If we can understand these developments, we will be able to influence the development of IT and ensure that the systems meet our needs, and that we can obtain full value from our systems.

SPECIFYING AN INFORMATION SYSTEM IN A SMALL ORGANISATION

We end this session with a substantial assignment for you to complete. It takes us back to the small charity Anxia. The charity does not have a coherent information system at present. It collects and records data and processes these into information by a mixture of manual and computerised methods.

A proposal has been made to install a local area network (LAN) incorporating six existing and four new computer terminals, with a new central microprocessor unit acting as a file-server (a powerful data storage and processing unit) to support the terminals. Output would be through existing printers. Once the LAN is running, all financial, membership and inquiry processing would be transferred to the system. All operational activities and the processing of all management information would then be handled by computer. Anxia's objectives in taking this step are shown in table 3.5.

Priority	Objective	Explanation
1	Control overhead costs	To halt the growth in administrative costs, thus increasing the net sums available for spending on charitable activities
2	Improve services	Provide more rapid response to inquiries and communications from members
3	Increase revenue from donations and grants	By better analysis of donors, leading to better targeting of marketing campaigns
4	Increase revenue from mail-order trading	By more effective use of member and inquirer databases
5	Improve management information	So as to produce financial and performance information more quickly, and analyse it in more useful ways, while minimising paperwork

TABLE 3.5: Anxia's objectives for installing computer network for operational and information processing functions

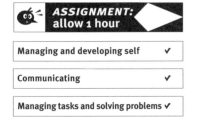

ACTIVITY 14

Your task is to build on the information in table 3.5 by outlining an organisational information system that will meet Anxia's objectives. You should approach it in three stages:

1. State in broad terms what information systems you believe Anxia will require, and their functions.

2. List any specific software packages that you believe will be appropriate.

3. Draw up a short list of criteria which the information systems should meet.

Prepare your report on separate sheets of paper. Summarise your main findings in the box below.

summary

Managers need information to help them to make correct decisions, but too much information can actually reduce the quality of decisions. Given that limited time is available for reading, managers need to adopt an effective strategy for sorting incoming information into categories and identifying high-priority items.

▶ OISs may contain up to six subsystems: the office automation system (OAS), a transaction processing system (TPS), a management information system (MIS), decisions support systems (DSSs), executive support systems (ESSs), and personal information systems (PISs).

▶ In practical terms, the TPS is the bedrock on which information management rests. The MIS is a system for extracting information from these data. All such systems are only made possible by modern information technology, especially computers.

▶ An especially important aspect of information management is exception reporting, which draws managers' attention to 'differences that make a difference', so that they can take preventive or corrective action as early as possible.

▶ Decision support systems are designed to help managers and others make better decisions, by providing tools such as spreadsheets, databases and models, and by drawing on past data to illuminate present problems.

▶ Executive support systems aim to give busy senior managers rapid access to key data, usually in highly summarised form, so as to help them exercise more effective strategic and organisation-wide control.

▶ Personal information systems are the collection of software tools, facilities and databases that individuals develop to help them perform their particular role.

In organisations, information flows are planned to ensure that key information reaches the right people as quickly as possible. Organisations also seek to protect managers from excessive amounts of information, by filtering and focusing the material passing through the system.

Using information technology

DATABASES

SPREADSHEETS

ACQUIRING DATA

PRESENTING INFORMATION EFFECTIVELY

Objectives

After participating in this session, you should be able to:

▶ explain and use the key features and commonly used functions of relational databases

▶ explain and use the key features and commonly used functions of a spreadsheet package

▶ identify the principal methods by which data can be acquired

▶ use spreadsheet and database graphing facilities to present information visually.

In working through this session, you will practise the following BTEC common skills:

Managing and developing self	✔
Working with and relating to others	
Communicating	
Managing tasks and solving problems	✔
Applying numeracy	✔
Applying technology	✔
Applying design and creativity	

Databases

Databases are 'collections of facts'; see Rothwell, D.M. (1993) Databases: An Introduction, McGraw-Hill. They are lists which have been organised according to particular criteria. The British Telecom telephone directory is a database; it contains lists of facts, organised according to the following criteria:

- entries are limited to a particular geographical area (e.g. Leicester)

- entries contain surname, initials, address (but not postcode) and telephone number

- entries are arranged in alphabetical order

- customers who have requested 'ex-directory' status are excluded from the published directory (though the telephone company includes them in its own confidential lists of all subscriber numbers).

In Britain, the Post Office publishes directories of addresses that include postcodes, and many other kinds of directories are also available in print.

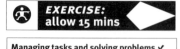

EXERCISE: allow 15 mins

Managing tasks and solving problems ✔

ACTIVITY 1

Using your workplace, home or college library to give you ideas, list ten printed 'collections of facts organised according to particular criteria'.

Look carefully at the entries in one or two of your examples. What do they have in common?

Commentary...

Our search revealed the following:

- recipe books

- Wisden's cricket almanac

- a stamp catalogue

- a reference guide to 'E-numbers' (food additives)

- various dictionaries

- an A–Z of garden plants

- the AA Hotel Guide

- an internal telephone directory

- an Argos catalogue

- a directory of holiday properties for rent.

Some of these publications contain only short factual entries, while others mix facts with 'soft' information, commentary and images. Some arrange the data into subgroups (such as India, Pakistan and Burma in the stamp catalogue). Nevertheless they all have two things in common:

- the data they contain all focus on a particular subject or group of related subjects

- the data entries are compiled in a consistent and standardised way.

This focus, consistency and standardisation is convenient for the user, but even more so for the publisher, because such publications are now generally produced from computerised databases. Computers need unequivocal instructions and data must be entered in a strictly specified way. Database management programs provide the former; the latter is decided by the system user, who must:

- define an appropriate format for the individual records of which the database will consist

- ensure that when data are entered, each attribute is placed in the right field.

Private individuals use databases, of course. Most people keep some kind of address/telephone/key dates list. Others list the books they have read, the CDs in their collections, the wines in their cellar, and so on. These are useful, and sometimes essential, but the biggest users of databases are organisations, many of which are dependent on them.

Here are some examples of databases held by the organisations we have met previously in this workbook:

Stokkit:

- stock items (part of the stock control system)

- staff (the personnel records system)

- customer data

- supplier data

- accounts.

Kellaways:

- stock items

- staff

- suppliers

- real estate assets (details of stores and other sites rented, leased or owned)

- inventory of equipment, computer terminals, store fixtures, etc.

Anxia:

- staff

- donors

- organisations to which appeals for funds can be made

- members

- doctors working in general practice (purchased from a specialist supplier).

Pefgo:

- staff

- suppliers

- customers and potential customers (sales contacts) in Britain and Europe

- shareholders – Pefgo is a PLC, with thousands of individual shareholders, with whom it must communicate periodically.

> **RECALL:**
> **allow 10 mins**
>
> When a manual record system is computerised as a database, what is usually the primary motive?
>
> What extra benefits can be obtained from computerisation?
>
> What methods or systems can be used to enter data into a database automatically?

What databases contain

In this section, we use the database facility within Microsoft Works as an example. This is one of the database systems available for personal computers. Other databases, such as Paradox, dBase, Symantec Q&A and MS Access behave in an essentially similar way.

To make full use of this session you will need access to a personal computer with a database package. Databases are an organised and systematic way of storing data so that it can be readily accessed and updated. These data typically consist of facts and figures, but modern databases also offer space for free-form notes, and some, like Blackwell's Idealist, can also handle images and graphics.

ACTIVITY 2

List four circumstances in which it would be useful to have the kind of database which could include photographs, drawings and other graphic material.

Commentary...

Personnel and security databases would clearly benefit from including a photograph of the individuals concerned. Drawings or photographs would also enhance technical databases, such as parts lists. Scientific databases, recording processes and compounds, could usefully include formulae and flow-diagrams. The databases from which mail-order catalogues and holiday brochures are compiled would also be more useful if they could contain photos of the goods, hotels etc. on offer, and maps and explanatory 'icons' where appropriate.

The disadvantage of including graphics, and especially photographs, is that they use a large amount of computer memory and processing power, which can slow down the pace at which the computer can operate. However, as computers become more powerful, this is becoming less of a problem.

Database design includes three basic types: flatfile, hierarchical and relational. These terms refer to the structure of the database.

FLATFILE DATABASES

Flatfile databases are held in a single file, in which all records share the same pattern of data items. For example, a personnel file would contain one record per employee; each record would have fields containing details of that employee, e.g. name, address, hourly rate of pay, tax code, etc. At least one field would be chosen as a 'key' field (e.g. surname) so that reports could be printed with the records in that order.

Figure 4.1 shows a simple flatfile, holding information used by the switchboard of a company. Data appears in the file in the same order as it was originally entered, i.e. not in any apparent order. If both surname and extension number are defined as key fields, two different reports could be produced: one listing the data in alphabetical order of surname; the other listing extension numbers in sequence.

Employee surname	Employee list name	Extension number
Jones	Julie	4279
Agate	Sandra	1994
Martin	John	2294
Smith	Paul	1449

Report 1:

```
Agate, Sandra      1994
Jones, Julie       4279
Martin, John       2294
Smith, Paul        1449
```

Report 2:

```
Smith, Paul        1449
Agate, Sandra      1994
Martin, John       2294
Jones, Julie       4279
```

FIGURE 4.1: A simple flatfile database.

However, flatfile databases can prove wasteful on space. For example, if a personnel file includes details of courses attended by each employee, a decision would have to be made about the number of courses each employee might attend and enough fields allocated for this data in every record. An employee record of someone who has only attended one course would take up as much space as someone who has attended the maximum number of courses. If someone attended more than the maximum number of courses anticipated during the design of the database, not all of this person's data would fit into their record.

A flatfile can be useful for computerising a simple card index, but its single level structure limits its use to the simplest of data handling problems. It would be difficult (if not impossible), in the above example, to obtain a list of all employees who had attended a certain course.

Most 'free' databases supplied with computer systems are of this flatfile type, and while they are not as sophisticated as the other structures, they provide a useful introduction for new users.

HIERARCHICAL DATABASES

Hierarchical databases solve some of the problems which cannot be solved using flatfiles. The data is split into two types: header and transaction data. In the personnel file discussed above, the header record would contain the information about an employee that occurs just once, i.e name and address. Transaction records are then used to hold data which may occur more than once for any employee, e.g. courses attended. Several different transaction records (holding different information) can be generated for each employee, e.g. payroll record, sick leave record, jobs held and so on.

Figure 4.2 shows how these different records are linked in a 'tree' shape.

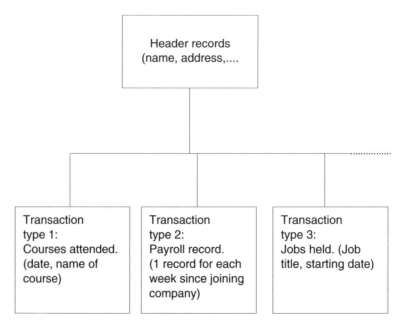

FIGURE 4.2: Scheme of a hierarchical database.

One field within the header record is chosen as the 'key' field, e.g. the employee number. All transaction records are linked to the header records by the key field; this appears in every transaction record, so we know whose data it is.

Figure 4.3 shows how the records of one transaction type are linked to the header records, by the key field. It is then possible for each employee to attend as few or many courses as necessary, and for all this data to be recorded – without wasting space. (Note however that the data within these two flatfiles would not usually be stored in the order shown. Data would be added to the header records as new employees join the company. Data would be added to the 'courses' transaction file in date order of the courses attended – not in employee number order as shown.)

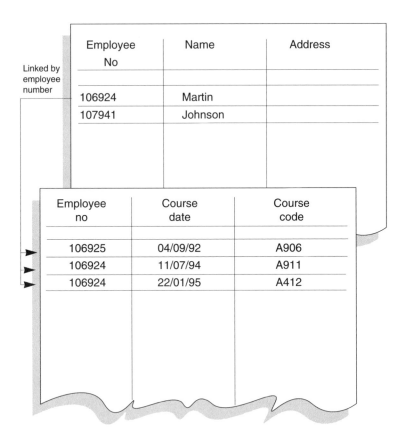

FIGURE 4.3: A transaction file and header record, linked by a key field.

Hierarchical databases have one major disadvantage. Careful design is needed to ensure the data is stored sensibly (i.e. to allow access to whatever is required) by identifying what should be in the header record and what should appear in transaction records. However, even then, new questions arise which cannot be answered. For example, the question 'Which managers have attended the first-aid course?' needs data from transaction types 1 and 3 to be linked. With hierarchical databases, it is not possible to perform functions that involve more than one transaction type at a time. However, relational databases solve this particular problem.

RELATIONAL DATABASES

A relational database is similar to a hierarchical database in that it stores all data items in a series of tables; these are usually called forms. Like hierarchical databases, these forms are linked, using key fields. However, in relational databases many links are allowed between forms, and this allows a greater flexibility when interrogating the database.

In designing relational databases, rather than identifying one header record and several transaction types, it is only necessary to identify groups of related items of data and put these on separate forms. Relationships can then be defined between the forms which allow data to be 'looked up' from one form to another.

The designer of the database can control access to information presenting users with a 'user view' to match their needs. For example, a personnel database may be used in several departments. The accounts staff would be given access to information relating to pay; the training department would be given access to data about course attendance but would not be able to access information about pay.

There are many extra benefits of relational databases. The first is that it is easy to include additional forms, and to link them to existing forms. For example, if a company decides to provide cars for certain employees, an additional form would be needed to record the details of the vehicles, and this would be linked to the form holding details about the employees to whom cars are issued. This reduces the amount of data entry in setting up the new application (because employee data is already on the database) and avoids 'data duplication' because having an employee's name appearing twice is wasteful on space. It also reduces the possibility of 'data inconsistency'. If data has to be changed (e.g. an employee moves house) there should be only one field in which this data is stored and hence only one data entry that has to be amended. Having to amend data in several places risks either not doing it, or making mistakes in the process.

In view of the great flexibility offered by relational databases, this type of database has become the standard. Any problem that could be solved using a hierarchical can be solved using a relational database;

and there is no worry of new questions arising which might cause design headaches. The actual design of the relational database – setting up all the forms and the relationships between them – can be time-consuming and requires a degree of flair. However, once this is done, using the database becomes easy.

LINKED DATA – AN EXAMPLE

Figure 4.4 shows how the stock, customer and supplier data are linked in Stokkit's system.

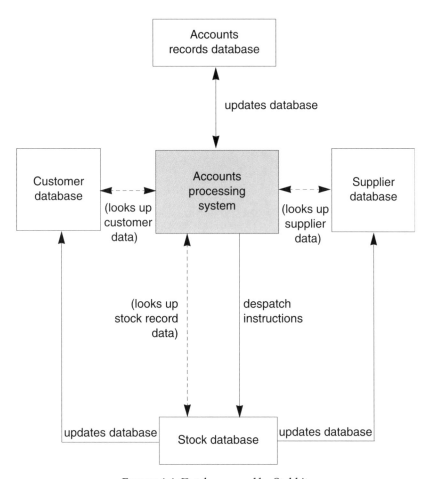

FIGURE 4.4: Databases used by Stokkit.

The figure shows only a simplified version of the interactions. These can be summarised as follows:

1. When customer orders or supplier invoices are received the accounts department's processing system looks up details on the customer, supplier and stock databases

2. It then issues despatch instructions to the warehouse.

3. Following despatch, 'actual' despatch data are used to update the stock, customer and supplier databases and are then passed to accounts.

4. Accounts issues invoices or instructions for payment and updates the accounts database accordingly.

USING A RELATIONAL DATABASE

Using a database is simple; it involves three main functions:

- keeping the database up to date – entering new data, amending data and deleting data
- searching for information – called interrogation
- sorting and analysing data to produce reports.

Updating the database

It is often necessary to update information on database records – changes of address, new sales data, change in contact's title, etc. Database programs allow users to do this very easily. The form layout on the screen is chosen to look very much like the document from which the data is entered e.g. a sales order form. Alternatively new records can be added in 'list mode' where the records appear as a table on the screen with each new row representing one new record of information to be entered.

The database program can also be accessed remotely for updating purposes. Purpose-designed databases may allow instant automatic updating from on-line transaction processing systems (TPS), or by batch processing. In Kellaways, for instance, stock movement data is electronically 'polled' (i.e. gathered) from every store after close of trading and these data are processed 'as a batch' and used to update the stock database overnight.

Searching for information – interrogating the database

Database programs include a 'structured query language' (SQL) which allows the user to express enquiries in a way that the database can be searched and the required information found. (Check your database package; what is the name of the query language?) The SQL is similar to English and includes commands, e.g. a 'FIND' command may identify groups of records within a given form that share a particular attribute.

Code	Country	Type	Name	Role	Organisation	City/town	Address
1023	Hungary	Educ	Kekszakallu, Z.	Director	Szeged Polytechnic	Szeged 1300	Dozsa Gyîrgy ut. 61
1024	Czech R.	Mil	Mazepa, D.	Maj-Gen	COMZAVY btn	Plzen B355	Bolzanova 22
1026	Poland	Mil	Wozzek, A.F	Adjutant	Dept 3. Voin/minstr	Warszawa 2	Konstytucji 10
1027	Slovakia	Ind	Dvo ak, A.	Chairman	Stalorucji-Kosi e	Ostrava 25	Soulenicka 127
1028	Poland	Gov	Jankowski, D.	Adviser	Sports Ministry	Krakow 9	ul Westerplatte 51
1030	Hungary	Ind	Kodaly, Z.	Prod. Dir.	Estergom-FÅrdo	Gyîr 2121	Martirok ut. 100

TABLE 4.1: An example form

For example, using the form in table 4.1, the command 'FIND country=Poland' will list all records in which the country attribute is 'Poland' (i.e. records 1026 and 1028). The same method can be used to find:

- all contacts of a particular sales representative

- all military contacts

- all contacts who placed contracts in a given year, etc.

(Each different make of database will have slightly different lists of commands included in their SQL and different ways of expressing enquiries. Check the requirements of your database package and raise any problems with your tutor.)

Precise instructions in SQL will locate information very quickly. But if the user is not sure, e.g. if the spelling of a name is unusual, SQL allows 'wild cards' for the parts the user is unsure about. An asterisk (*) is a wild card meaning 'any number of other letters', and a question mark (?) is a wild card meaning 'any other letters in this position'. So, 'FIND name=SM*' will find all records in a form with the name field starting with the letter 'SM', and 'FIND name=SM???' will only list those having five characters starting with 'SM'.

The database will search for any data which matches the user's enquiry. The data can then be displayed on the screen, or printed as a report (see below). The user might also want to browse – looking through records to find the data he or she wants. Special key sequences will be available which make this process as effective as possible for the user. (Check with your tutor if you are not sure how this is done on your database package.)

Often someone needs to search the database in a more analytical way, in order to find, for example:

- the Hungarian contacts of a particular representative

- those Polish industrial contacts who placed contracts worth more than a certain amount in a given year

○ all contacts visited in the last three months, excluding military ones.

The database QUERY function allows users to incorporate, among other descriptors, the logical operators (AND, OR and NOT) and relational operators such as 'less than' or 'equal to or more than'.

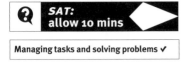

SAT:
allow 10 mins

Managing tasks and solving problems ✓

ACTIVITY 3

How many attributes are addressed in searching for:

(a) all the Hungarian contacts of a particular representative?

(b) Polish industrial contacts who placed contracts worth more than $5,000 in 1994?

Commentary...

In the first case, there are only two attributes: country (Hungary) and representative. The second case is more complicated, involving the following attributes:

○ country (Poland)

○ type (industrial)

○ contract dates with defined date range (1994)

○ contracts greater than $5,000

It is possible to identify contracts within a desired range of values through a feature of the QUERY command that allows users to ask whether a particular attribute is less than, equal to or more than a given value. Thus the system can also search for contracts worth more than, say $50,000, either alone or in combination with other attributes.

The system can also search for a single particular record.

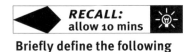

RECALL:
allow 10 mins

Briefly define the following terms:

- wild card

- attribute.

Describe how the FIND command (or its equivalent) in your database softwares operates.

Database reports

The sorting and searching functions of relational databases allow the user to bring together information and print out reports in three forms:

- full listings of all the records that match the desired criteria (e.g. a list of all data stored about all customers visited in the last month)

- selected listings, in which only some of the data fields are printed out (e.g. the name and country of all customers placing orders in the last month, together with order value)

- analysed reports, in which a collection of data is processed (e.g. total number of visits made, total and average value of orders placed, plus breakdowns by representative, country and customer category, and so on).

European Sales Report
Date: 7 July 1995

Summary	SALES ($000s)		Orders		Average order value	
	June 1995	1995 to date	June 1995	1995 to date	June 1995	1995 to date
Direct salesforce	104	367	5	16	20.80	22.94
Pefgo Gmbh salesforce	164	548	7	18	23.43	30.44
TOTAL	268	915	12	34	22.33	26.91

Sales by country:	SALES ($000s)		Orders	
	June 1995	1995 to date	June 1995	1995 to date
Austria	11	34.5	1	2
Belgium	26	61	1	3
Czech Rep	-	18	-	1
etc.				

Sales by Representative	SALES ($000s)		Orders	
	June 1995	1995 to date	June 1995	1995 to date
Anton	31	85	2	3
Carla	26	118	1	5
etc.				

TABLE 4.2: Extract of database sales reports issued monthly by Stephen Gage

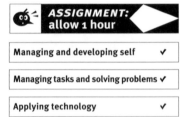

**ASSIGNMENT:
allow 1 hour**

Managing and developing self	✔
Managing tasks and solving problems	✔
Applying technology	✔

ACTIVITY 4

Your task is to design a database on the lines described above. If you have access to a computer and database software, use the system directly and print out your results. You will need to study the manual to find the correct procedure for setting up forms, but modern database programs make this an easy and user-friendly process. Otherwise treat this as a manual planning exercise.

The subject is customer complaints received by Kellaways. You need to organise the data so that the following can be recorded:

- details of person making complaint

- details of complaint

- details of store concerned

- action taken

- compensation paid, if any.

The company will want to be able to analyse complaints by category, scale of seriousness and cost in compensation, by region and by month, and you should take this into account.

Use separate paper to record your answer. If you complete the assignment using a database program provide a hard copy of your forms, queries and print-outs.

Spreadsheets versus databases

Databases, which are primarily to record information, and spreadsheets, which are primarily to make calculations with numbers, may overlap considerably. Thus a spreadsheet on Lotus 1-2-3 can be used as a very simple flatfile database, and the database and spreadsheet within Works 3 are visually similar and function in a similar way: the spreadsheet can be used to record, store and sort information, and the database can be used to carry out calculations. Thus a database that records visits made to a customer can also total the number of visits, or state the average number in a given period. If details of the customer's sales orders are also included, these can be summated and processed numerically.

Spreadsheets

Spreadsheets are probably more widely used than any business software application apart from word processing. They have taken over many processes that were once done painstakingly with paper and pencil, and have opened up new possibilities in management and planning. Spreadsheets work well because they lean heavily on the process that computers are best at – 'number-crunching'. They are popular because, as we show, they let users do things that are useful.

To make full use of this session you will need some hands-on experience of using spreadsheets. This section contains some activities which you should preferably carry out using spreadsheets programs. There are, naturally, minor differences in terminology and procedures between the various systems. We use the Microsoft Works 3 for Windows spreadsheet as an example, but much the same can be said of any of the popular spreadsheets on the market, such as Lotus 1-2-3, MS Excel, CA SuperCalc and Quattro Pro.

Spreadsheets consist of columns labelled A, B, C, etc., and rows numbered 1, 2, 3, etc., which intersect to form cells. Cells are identified by their column letter and row number, for example B15, T128, etc. The Microsoft Works spreadsheet contains 256 columns and 16,384 rows, making a total of 4,194,304 cells. This is 26,000 times more than can be shown on the computer screen at any one time, so in effect the screen acts as a movable window on the spreadsheet. Most spreadsheet users only use a small proportion of the available capacity.

Spreadsheets carry out four main processes:

- storing data in cells

- creating links between different cells

- performing calculations

- displaying their contents as tables, graphs or charts.

All the data and instructions required for these processes are entered into individual cells, in one of four forms:

- text

- numerical data

- mathematical formulae

- logical instructions ('functions').

A function is a built-in formula which carries out a process that would be cumbersome to define individually.

	A	B	C	D	E	F	G	H
1	Students	Bill	Carrie	Della	Eric	Raka	Total	5
2	study hrs	18	17	20.5	21	18	Total	94.50
3								
4		ave hrs	18.90					
5		most hrs	21					

FIGURE 4.5: A simple spreadsheet demonstrating the four kinds of cell contents.

In figure 4.5:

- cells A1 to G1, A2, G2, B4 and B5 contain text, which does not normally form part of any calculations; 'Students', 'study hrs' and 'Total', for example, are simply labels

- cells B2 to F2 contain numerical data, on which calculations are performed

- H1 contains a statistical function: =COUNT(B1:F1) which counts the number of cells (i.e. the number of students) in the range specified and displays the result

- H2 contains a formula: =B2+C2+D2+E2+F2 which adds up the values of cells B2 to F2 and displays the result; it would actually be quicker and simpler to do this using the logical function: =SUM(B2:F2)

- C4 contains a formula: =H2/H1 which divides the total hours worked (H2) by the number of students (H1) and displays the result (average hours worked); it would be simpler and quicker to do this using the statistical function: =AVG(B2:F2)

- C5 contains another statistical function: =MAX(B2:F2) which identifies and displays the highest figure in the range B2 to F2.

All spreadsheet packages offer a variety of functions, e.g.:

- date and time functions

- financial functions

- logical functions

- lookup and reference functions

- mathematical functions

- statistical functions

- text functions.

For details of the functions offered by your spreadsheet, see the appropriate user manuals.

The financial functions include calculations for net present value (NPV) and internal rate of return (IRR), which we described being calculated 'manually' in Section 1, Session 7. Indeed, many accountants and financial managers would now use a spreadsheet for performing this kind of calculation, in preference even to specialised financial software, which may take longer to set up.

The big advantage of spreadsheets, compared with handwritten analysis sheets, is that they are 'live' and active. Thus, when we change the values in row 2, or add new students and more data to the range, the spreadsheet automatically recalculates the outcome. Figure 4.6 shows what happens if we discover that Della studied for 22.5 hours, not 20.5, and correct this in cell D2.

	A	B	C	D	E	F	G	H
1	Students	Bill	Carrie	Della	Eric	Raka	Total	5
2	study hrs	18	17	22.5	21	18	Total	96.50
3								
4		ave hrs	19.30					
5		most hrs	22.5					

FIGURE 4.6: The modified student hours spreadsheet.

Spreadsheets are:

- precise – it is essential to enter data accurately, and to specify cells, formulae and functions correctly, or errors will result

- flexible – provided that your data, formulae and functions are correct, you can modify the spreadsheet greatly without disturbing them.

For example, we can insert more columns between column B and column F; see figure 4.7. This will turn column H into column I, but the new total (now in cell I2) still performs correctly, because the program adjusts it automatically (the function in I2 is now =SUM(B2:G2) and it will correctly calculate the new total). However, if the new columns are added before column B or after column F, the cell range in the formula will no longer be correct and the new values will not be counted.

	A	B	C	D	E	F	G	H	I
1	Students	Bill	Carrie	Della	Dennis	Eric	Raka	Total	6
2	study hrs	18	17	22.5	15.75	21	18	Total	112.25
3	Students	Usman	Helen	Inga	Jack	Kate	Lewis	Total	6
4	study hrs	17	19	17.5	21	20	23.25	Total	117.75
5									
6		ave hrs	19.17						
7		most hrs	23.25						

FIGURE 4.7: Student hours spreadsheet; expanded version.

More students have been added using two extra rows, as shown in Figure 4.7. There is a better approach to the design of this simple spreadsheet – see figure 4.8 discussed shortly.

SAT:
allow 10 mins

Applying numeracy ✔

ACTIVITY 5

Figure 4.7 shows an expanded version of the student hours spreadsheet, to which two rows and one column have been added. What changes to cells and formulae will be required to ensure that this new version works correctly?

Commentary...

Inserting the new column E (for Dennis) has effectively moved the data in previous columns E, F, G and H one to the right, so that they are now labelled columns F, G, H and I. However, because the new column was inside the range specified in the formulae from which the values in I1 and I2 are calculated, these formulae do not need to be changed.

Inserting the rows has however added new data outside the original range, and so new formulae have been provided for these rows: in I3 it is =COUNT(B3:G3), and in I4 it is =SUM(B4:G4). However, we now have two sets of totals which need to be brought into the calculations in C6, C7 and D7. The formula in C6 becomes =(I2+I4)/(I1+I3). The function in cell C7 becomes =MAX(B2:G2,B4:G4).

If, as seems likely, more students and data will be added in the future, then it would be better to redesign this spreadsheet in column form, as in figure 4.8. In this version, we have shown the formulae, rather than the values. We have also included a new column of data – an attendance register for a group study event (0 = absent, 1 = present).

	A	B	C	D
1		Student	Hours	Attendance
2		Bill	18	1
3		Carrie	17	1
4		Della	22.5	1
5		Dennis	15.75	0
6		Eric	21	1
7		Frank	18	0
8		Gerry	17	0
9		Helen	19	1
10		Inga	17.5	1
11		Jack	21	1
12		Kate	20	1
13		Lewis	23.25	0
14				
15	Total	COUNT (B2:B14)	=SUM (C2:C14)	Attendance %
16	Average Hours		=AVG (C2:C14)	=(SUM (D2: D14)/B15)*100
17	Highest	=MAX (C2:C14)	Lowest	=MIN (C2:C14)

Note: Row 14 has been left blank only to improve presentation.

FIGURE 4.8: Revised version of the student hours spreadsheet.

This version is easier to cope with: not only can new students be added (by inserting new rows), but the columns can be used for other data, such as a register (as shown above). This spreadsheet is both a working tool and a record of what has been occurring.

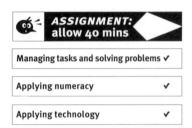

Managing tasks and solving problems	✔
Applying numeracy	✔
Applying technology	✔

ACTIVITY 6

Your task is to transfer the financial data given in account 4.1 in Section 1, Session 4 to a spreadsheet. Note that this task involves the analysis of Stokkit's profit and loss account, and there are numerous percentage calculations.

Use the dummy spreadsheet in Resource 2 at the back of the book to help plan your spreadsheet. Draw in extra columns if you need to. If you need to use any functions other than those we have already described, consult a spreadsheet user manual or other reference book.

Transfer the data from account 4.1 to a computer spreadsheet and provide a print-out of the completed profit and loss account. Include the dummy page completed to show the function, where needed, in each cell.

If you don't have access to a computer, fully complete the dummy spreadsheet page.

Summarise your findings in the box below.

LARGER-SCALE APPLICATIONS OF SPREADSHEETS

Most spreadsheet applications involve only relatively small blocks of data and limited numbers of calculations. However, spreadsheets work perfectly well for much larger and more complex sets of data and calculations, including scientific data such as readings from large numbers of instruments taken at frequent intervals.

More familiar to the organisational context will be the analysis of market research results, where numerous responses to a large number of questions might need to be recorded and evaluated. Kellaways, for example, used a spreadsheet to analyse the results of a 'standards audit' carried out in a sample of 30 stores, and consisting of ratings (on a scale of 1 to 10) of 44 different features, in seven groups. The spreadsheet both calculates the results and acts as a summary record of the exercise. An extract of this spreadsheet is illustrated in figure 4.9.

	A	B	C	D
1	Spreadsheet : Standards Audit			
2	Store no.	18	31	39
3	Date audited	May 6	May 6	May 8
4	Auditor	JEG	RM	JEG
5	Part 1: Housekeeping standards			
6	1A. Pavement	8	6	3
7	1B. Window	9	8	9
8	1C. W/display	8	7	6
9	etc.			

FIGURE 4.9: Spreadsheet results of Kellaway's standards audit.

It is also quite possible to build realistic models of a business, which have a more complex internal structure. These can then be used to test the effect of various changes. So, for example, the managing director of Pefgo Flooring plc and his team were able to create a rather sophisticated model of their business, as follows:

1. A 'table of variables' was constructed. This listed, among other factors, raw material costs, economic changes, interest rates, productivity indexes for different types of staff, machine capacities, maintenance frequencies, order levels, commission rates for sales staff, overtime pay rates and factors for competitor activity.

2. A detailed sub-model for each cost centre was designed (with both direct and fully absorbed indirect costs of executive, sales, marketing, administration, production and research) with linkages to the table of variables.

   To give an idea of the complexity of this model, the production cost centre included factors for:

   A. forecast of required production output (derived from sales data)

   B. quantity of raw material used per unit

C. maximum output per machine per hour

D. material wastage rates for different output rates

E. maintenance intervals (linked to output) and downtime

F. purchase cost of existing machinery

G. cost of purchasing replacement production machinery

H. capacity and staffing characteristics of new machinery (which can be expected to be more efficient, but more expensive)

I. expected lifetime of machinery

J. staffing levels per machine

K. shift durations (the factory normally worked double-day shifts, i.e. 0600–1400 and 1400–2200 hours)

L. production cost per unit

M. attribution of overhead costs to output units

N. total cost per unit

O. total actual output per machine

P. basic pay, overtime rates and shift allowances.

3. Similar sub-models at a similar level of detail were created for the other cost centres, and these were cross-linked where appropriate.

4. Cross-links in the model are sometimes quite complex. Thus a fall or rise in sales will have a series of knock-on effects, according to their extent. A fall will:

- reduce revenue

- reduce output and thus total raw material costs

- increase production unit costs (as the capital cost of machinery has to be absorbed by a smaller number of output units)

- trigger redundancies (but only if it persists for more than two months).

Conversely, a rise will:

- increase revenue

- bring forward the need to replace machinery

- increase overtime working

- lead to the introduction of a night shift, or of new machinery, or both, with effects on total labour employed and units costs.

Figure 4.10 shows one small group of interrelationships, relating to unit costs of materials or components. In cell H21 an IF function is used which can be expressed IF(condition, value if true, value if false). IF determines whether the condition is true or false, then gives either a 'value if true' or a 'value if false'. In this example, when the 'value' of cell I23 is less than 200 000 then the 'condition' is false and the 'value' of cell H21 is 1.0. The use of IF functions is a powerful tool in spreadsheets. Consult your spreadsheet user guide or other reference books for further information.

	F	G	H	I
21	(scaling factor) 1.0	(economic growth index) 1.0	(discounting factor) =IF(I23 > 200 000,0.95,1.0)	
22	(initial unit price) £3.255	(modified unit price) =F22*(F21*G21*H21)	(number of units) 65000	(total cost) =(G22* H22)
23				(total units in month) =H22 (includes other cells not shown here)

FIGURE 4.10: Examples of interrelationships between sub-models.

In this example, the unit price can be set at a 'normal' level in F22. It is then modified by other factors represented by cells F21, G21 and H21. Thus the scaling factor (F21) can be changed, for example to 1.025. This will test the effect of a 2.5 per cent increase in costs on the value in cell I22. The discounting factor depends on total units consumed on this and other projects per month (cell I23). If the total rises above 200 000, a discount of 5 per cent is obtained, and this is passed via G22 into I22.

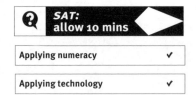

| Applying numeracy | ✓ |
| Applying technology | ✓ |

ACTIVITY 7

As Figure 4.10 stands, what is the value of:

- cell G22?

- cell I22?

If the value of cell I23 is 365 000, what will be the value of:

- cell G22?

- cell I22?

You may find it useful to work out this small model on a spreadsheet, if you have access to one.

Commentary...

As things stand, the value of cell G22 is £3.255, because cells F21, G21 and H21 are all 1.0 (so £3.255 x 1.0 x 1.0 x 1.0 = £3.255). The value of cell I22 is therefore £3.255 x 65,000 = £211,575.

If the value in cell I23 (which represents total units produced in a given period) rises above 200,000, it triggers a discount of 5 per cent in cell H21, whose value changes from 1.0 to 0.95. The value in cell G22 now becomes £3.255 x 1.0 x 1.0 x 0.95 = £3.09225, and cell I22 becomes £3.09225 x 65,000 = £200,996.25.

All the sub-models of the Pefgo business model feed data into the central section of the spreadsheet, which is a profit and loss account.

This includes some blank rows in which items which have been overlooked and contingencies can be added if necessary. All parts of the model work through to two 'bottom line' factors: total profit or loss, and share values (which are calculated by a complex formula).

The attraction of this model, which obviously functions as a decision-support and planning tool, is that although it takes a great deal of time and skill to establish and 'debug', it can be used to test out hypotheses of various kinds. This process is called sensitivity testing, and it answers 'what if?' questions:

- What if we replace existing machinery with more efficient types before the old machinery has reached the end of its useful life? What is the effect on capital spending, production volumes and production unit costs?

- What if we put more resources into sales? What are the cost implications of more sales people, more advertising expenditure, etc.? This may also impact on production output requirements.

- What if the value of an 'external variable' such as economic growth or bank interest rates rises or falls? How does this affect sales and profitability?

- What if some unexpected problem reduces output by, say, 50 per cent for a given period, say one month?

- What if we price a new product at £5.99 instead of £4.99? What effect will this have on sales/production volumes, turnover and profits?

Acquiring data

In the course of this workbook we have already described several ways in which data for analysis can be acquired. Transaction processing systems, which are designed to make data handling more efficient, are an important source for many organisations. Sometimes the data are input manually, sometimes automatically, and sometimes by a mixture of the two, as table 4.3 shows.

Process	Example
Manual	• **Telesales/enquiries**: when we call an insurance company for a quotation for car insurance, the person at the other end will ask for details verbally, and key them in immediately. The same happens when we book a holiday, a cinema seat, etc. • **Smaller commercial outlets**: e.g. shops that do not have electronic point of sale (EPOS) systems.
Mixed manual and automatic	• **Automatic tellers**: some data are read from the magnetic strip on the customer's card, while the customer keys in other data such as PIN number (in much of the rest of Europe, cards now use microchips to store customer data); similar systems are now available in some petrol stations. • **Market research and opinion surveys**: researchers complete coded forms by hand, but the forms themselves may be 'read' automatically by document reading machines. • Banks process cheques automatically using **docment readers** which can read the special print and ink identifying the customer and his or her bank and branch (but human beings have to verify and enter the handwritten details on the cheque).
Fully automatic	• **Barcode scanning**, as used by large supermarkets, automatically registers items purchased and their value, and these data automatically generate bills, credit card slips and receipts, and update stock records. • Data is captured by electronic and electro-mechanical **counters, sensors** and processed automatically in an increasing number of security, manufacturing process and environmental control systems.

TABLE 4.3: Input methods used for data collection

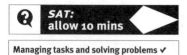

SAT:
allow 10 mins

Managing tasks and solving problems ✔

ACTIVITY 8

Stokkit is conducting some research into warehouse productivity, and is considering three different approaches to acquiring data. Which of the following methods of data collection is likely to prove the most expensive?

1. Analysing labour hours per customer order at different times of day and week (to see if performance differs between shifts or days of the week); this involves further processing of data generated by the computerised labour management system.

2. Checking picking routes provided by the computer against a physical map of the warehouse, to see if the optimum routes are being selected.

> 3. Confidential interviews with staff (conducted by an external consultant) to establish what problems they perceive and what improvements they can suggest.

Commentary...

The first approach is likely to be cheap, because the data are already being collected automatically by the labour management system.

The second approach is part-automatic (the production of picking routes) and part-manual (the checking process), and as such will be more expensive, since more time is involved.

The third approach is an entirely manual process, involving significant amounts of time:

- to design the survey

- to organise and carry out the interviews

- to code and sort them

- to analyse and report on the findings.

However, the fact that it is carried out (presumably for a fee) by an outside consultant does not necessarily mean it is more expensive than if it had been done by a suitably skilled employee.

The significance of this comparison is twofold:

- It underlines the fact that information has a cost, but that the cost is least when the information is being collected anyway.

    ● It shows that collecting and interpreting 'soft' information is often an expensive process.

SAMPLING AND QUESTIONNAIRES

Organisations often need to know more about human behaviour and attitudes. We have already referred to situations in which the attitudes of staff and an organisation's public image may be relevant to its performance. Similar information is also of considerable significance in the design, planning and marketing of products and services of all kinds. In these fields, knowledge is money.

To know what people think, and to predict what they will do (since the two are not necessarily identical), we have to ask them. However, this is not straightforward. It can be an expensive business. Take a company contemplating turning an empty warehouse into a cinema. As part of a business plan, it needs to know who the actual and potential filmgoers are in the area, how often they are likely to come to the proposed cinema, what sort of films they want to see and how much they are likely to spend. From this information, reasonable forecasts of likely takings can be made.

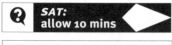

SAT:
allow 10 mins

Managing tasks and solving problems ✔

ACTIVITY 9

The would-be cinema owner needs to survey the market.

List the advantages and disadvantages of surveying everyone within travelling distance of the proposed cinema.

Can actual and potential filmgoers in the areas be identified so that they can be surveyed separately from the 'general population', and if so, how?

Suggest how such a market survey could be carried out in practice.

Note down to what extent might nationally available statistics on cinema attendance be useful.

Commentary...

A comprehensive survey would be extremely reliable, but the cost and the time-scale would be enormous. Segments of the population who seldom if ever go to a cinema (such as elderly people) would be included needlessly. In practice, almost all surveys are conducted among specific target populations, on the basis of sampling.

The specific target population is those people who actually or potentially go to see films in cinemas. National surveys show that these are predominantly in the 17–30 age group, so it would be possible for a researcher to approach people of that age group in the street, or to visit households and ask to speak to someone in that age group. Cinema-goers can, of course, be found at cinemas, so if there is one in the area, people entering, queuing or leaving could be interviewed.

Street surveys are easy to conduct, but the researcher must ensure that the sample is representative, by achieving a balance of males and females, and of ages within the 17–30 range. Postal questionnaires can be used, though since response rates are usually very low (well under 10 per cent) some inducement might need to be offered, such as a prize draw. Telephone surveys can be cost-effective, but it is more difficult to ensure that the target population is sampled reliably.

National statistics would indicate the proportion of cinema-goers among the general population and the frequency of their cinema visits. This can be extrapolated onto the local population, but:

- the local population may differ from the national population in some way

◉ specific local conditions, such as the presence or absence of an existing cinema, will need to be taken into account.

Surveys are an important source of management information, especially in a decision-support role, but experience, skill and resources are needed to ensure that quality information is produced. You can learn more about this subject in Market Relations, a companion workbook in this series.

Presenting information effectively

Communication is important for everyone in an organisation, but for managers, whose effectiveness is completely dependent on their ability to inform, influence and persuade others, it is a vital issue.

The large amounts of information that may be generated by modern IT systems go well beyond the ability of ordinary humans to assimilate in full. Thus while Stephen Gage could conceivably print out the full multi-page listing of his sales database as part of his monthly reporting, this would be highly inefficient in communication terms, and would be exasperating for his colleagues.

Stephen's approach is to communicate the minimum of information for the maximum of impact. He therefore produces:

◉ a one-page sales summary and forecast against budget

◉ a graphical version of the above

◉ a one-page breakdown of sales by country (this is for background information only, and is not graphed).

On the copies of the information that he distributes, Stephen highlights data that he considers to be significant, or that he intends to mention at the meeting. Stephen places this information on the management information system (MIS), so that it is generally available to management-level enquiries. He also takes his notebook PC to monthly management meetings so that he can look up any other information that may be requested.

Graphic presentation is most useful for communicating a broad issue simply and quickly. Human visual perception is much better than our ability to read and mentally analyse numbers, so a graph or chart will illustrate the magnitude of difference or the direction of trends much more clearly than a table of figures. However, visual presentation methods are noticeably less useful at providing detail, which is why the print-outs that Stephen provides include information in both graphic and tabular forms.

GRAPHIC PRESENTATION

All spreadsheet packages offer users a wide range of different ways of charting data: bar charts, line charts (graphs), pie charts, scatter charts (x-y charts), and variations and combinations of these, such as combined line and bar charts.

Some ways of presenting data are illustrated in figures 4.11 to 4.15. They are all based upon the data in table 4.4:

| Month | Sales by product type | | | | | | |
	C'floor £000s	H. Duty £000s	Sports £000s	EEZIGO £000s	Bricks £000s	TOTAL £000s	BUDGET £000s
Jan	29	24	12	58	5	128	125
Feb	16	67	8	62	7	160	150
Mar	4	32	10	68	4	118	150
Apr	12	27	8	41	7	95	100
May	38	20	12	33	8	111	105
June	12	44	12	46	3	117	110
July	38	58	10	37	9	152	125
Aug	44	39	16	48	12	159	125
Sept	25	51	19	66	4	165	125
Oct	8	39	15	58	5	125	140
Nov	20	40	14	63	8	145	140
Dec	14	30	20	43	2	109	115
TOTAL	260	471	156	623	74	1584	1510

TABLE 4.4: European sales data by product group at Pefgo Flooring

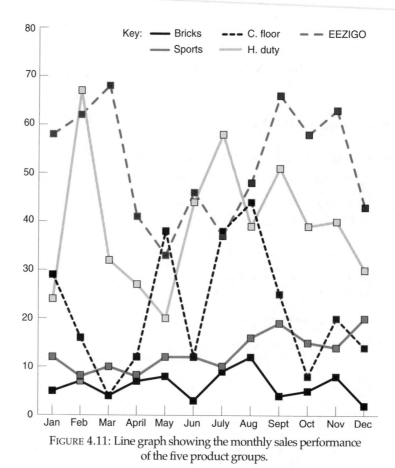

FIGURE 4.11: Line graph showing the monthly sales performance of the five product groups.

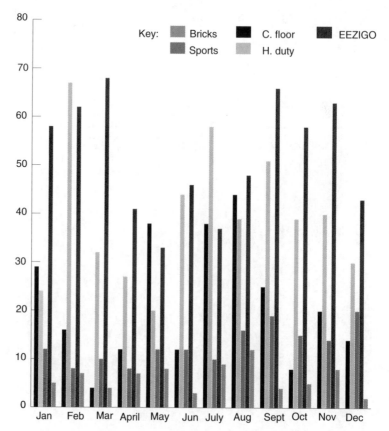

FIGURE 4.12: The same data presented as a bar chart.

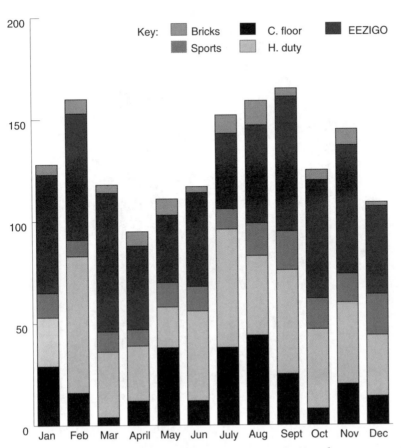

FIGURE 4.13: The same data presented as a stacked bar chart.

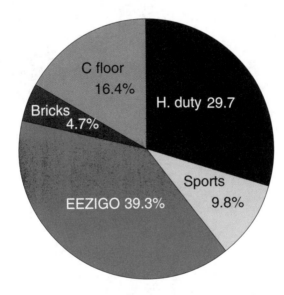

FIGURE 4.14: Pie chart showing each product's share of the year's total sales.

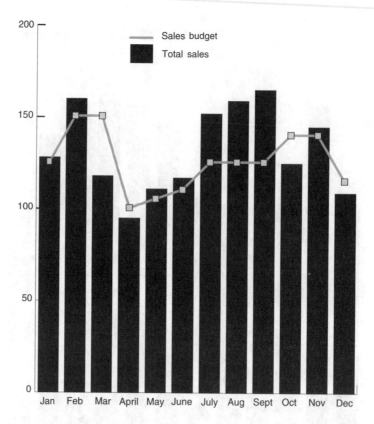

FIGURE 4.15: Mixed bar-line chart – the bars show actual total monthly sales, the line shows budgeted totals.

SAT:
allow 15 mins

Managing tasks and solving problems ✓

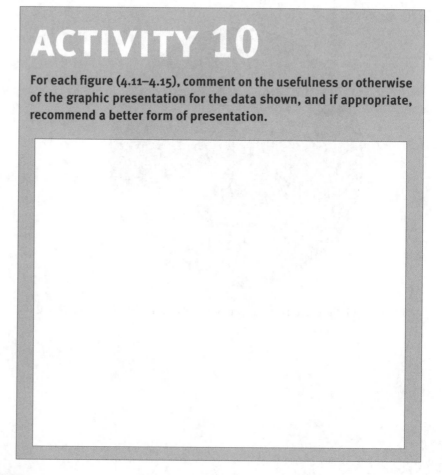

ACTIVITY 10

For each figure (4.11–4.15), comment on the usefulness or otherwise of the graphic presentation for the data shown, and if appropriate, recommend a better form of presentation.

Commentary...

Figure 4.11 contains a large amount of information, but the jumble of lines makes it virtually incomprehensible. Presenting just one or two product lines on the chart would be easier to assimilate, but on the other hand it would contain much less useful information. If the same data was totalled quarterly, or even better, annually over five years, the variability would be smoothed out, and any trends would be more visible. Figure 4.12 is little better: there is simply too much information here.

Figure 4.13 is an improvement, though the sales curve can only be visualised for the bottom segment ('C. floor'), so trends in sales of other product lines cannot be appreciated. However, this approach does at least show a total sales line.

Figure 4.14 is a good choice, clearly showing the relative importance of each product group, and also giving the percentage values. Figure 4.15 is also a good choice:

- it shows monthly sales against budget quite clearly

- it demonstrates a clear seasonal pattern.

It might be helpful to include a line showing the cumulative variance between budget and actual sales, but this would once again start to confuse the eye. This information should be shown on a separate chart.

A mixed type of graph can often be a good choice. Figure 4.16 shows the variance (actual sales against budget) as bars and total sales as a line.

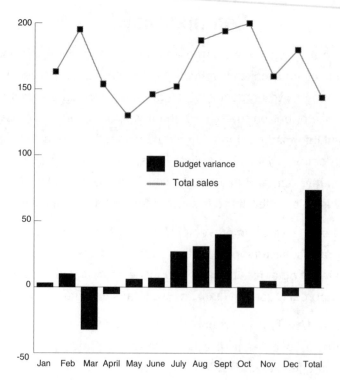

FIGURE 4.16: Sales variance and total sales.

This final example reminds us of the RARTAC criteria which we first explained in session 1. It sums up a great deal of information in a way that can be easily and quickly understood by the user: a picture is often worth a thousand words – or at any rate, a thousand numbers.

summary

▶ Databases are 'collections of facts' though they often contain soft information too. The term database is usually reserved for such collections of data held on computer.

▶ Three main kinds of computerised database are flatfile, hierarchical and relational. Relational databases are the most widely used, since they offer the greatest flexibility. Numerous database management programs exist for computers.

▶ Data records consist of a series of fields, each of which is used to record a particular attribute of the data. The records can then be searched by defining one or more of these attributes. Database users can identify and retrieve one particular record, or all the records meeting certain 'search' criteria.

▶ Relational databases consist of series of tables in which data are stored. Users can see a particular view of the data, by selecting fields from different tables, according to their information needs.

▶ Spreadsheets carry out numerical calculations. They consist of a large number of cells, which can be linked logically. Cells may contain text, numerical data, formulae or functions.

▶ Spreadsheets are 'live' and 'active', and when the numerical data in a cell are changed, any other cells that are linked with it change accordingly. This makes spreadsheets particularly useful for giving quick answers to 'what if...?' questions.

▶ All information systems depend on an adequate supply of data. Where this flows automatically, as with transaction processing systems, the cost is low. Where special steps have to taken to collect data (as in marketing surveys or research studies) the costs are much higher.

▶ Information must be presented and communicated effectively. Since the volumes of information are now potentially so large, the keys to success are compressing and summarising information and, where possible, presenting it in easily assimilated visual form.

Quality and reliability

HOW RELIABLE IS THE DATA?

HARDWARE AND SOFTWARE PROBLEMS

HOW INFORMATION CAN MISLEAD

EVALUATING FORECASTS

ERRORS OF ANALYSIS

EVALUATING WRITTEN REPORTS

Objectives

After participating in this session, you should be able to:

- identify the likely sources of data errors within an information system and describe ways of reducing them

- draw up procedures for minimising the impact of hardware and software faults

- explain some of the ways in which information can be used to mislead rather than to inform

- apply critical judgement to some aspects of forecasts, financial statements and the graphic presentation of information

- apply practical criteria for assessing the reliability of written reports.

In working through this session, you will practise the following BTEC common skills:

Managing and developing self	✔
Working with and relating to others	✔
Communicating	✔
Managing tasks and solving problems	✔
Applying numeracy	✔
Applying technology	✔
Applying design and creativity	

How reliable is the data?

Information is only as good as the data from which it is derived, but while it may be technically possible to obtain unfailingly accurate data, the cost of raising quality from, say, 96 per cent to 99 per cent may be disproportionately high. In practice, all organisations accept a compromise between information quality and cost. Where the compromise is pitched depends on circumstances.

- In business accounts and stock record systems, small discrepancies are ignored, on the basis that over time they tend to even out.

- Even where a slight loss of accuracy can have catastrophic consequences, as in railway signalling systems or nuclear power stations, there is a compromise, though in the latter case it is within a few fractions of one per cent.

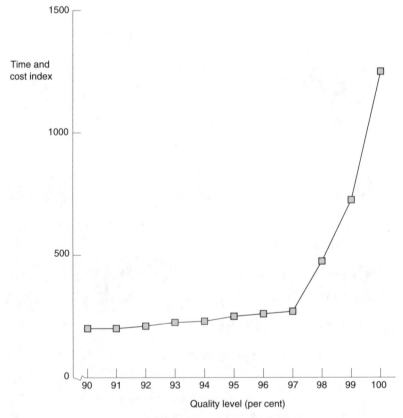

FIGURE 5.1: Time and cost versus quality.

Cost always places limits on quality: it may cost as much to raise quality from 96 per cent to 99 per cent as it did to raise it to 96 per cent.

Some degree of error and inaccuracy in information is therefore inevitable, but much can (and should) be done to make sure that the quality of information is as high as reasonably possible. Quality assurance procedures that are applied to production and service quality should also be applied to management information. This begins with the basic data from which information systems are constructed: if the data cannot be trusted, neither can any conclusions based on analysing them.

SOURCES OF ERROR IN DATA

In all the case studies that we have considered, organisations collect operational data, process them to create information, and then interpret them. Errors can occur in all three stages, but we will start with the collection of data.

At Stokkit, the information used in data processing and management information systems comes from three sources:

1. The order processing department: Most customers send their orders by telephone, fax, telex or (occasionally) post, and details are keyed into the system by order clerks. A small number of large customers send their orders directly into the system from their own computers (by modem / telephone link).

2. The goods-in section: Data about goods received from suppliers are used to update the stock control database and validate suppliers' invoices. Three input methods are used:

   (a) bar codes on packaging 'outers' are read by hand-held scanner

   (b) code numbers from outers are keyed in to hand-held terminals (generally when bar code scanning is not available for some reason)

   (c) details from delivery notes are keyed into the goods-in office computer terminal.

3. The picking and despatch section: Despatch notes stating what items, in what quantities, have been consigned to the customer, are sent both to the customer and to the accounts section so that invoices can be generated.

Note the complex chain of actions leading to the production of despatch notes.

1. Customer orders are passed electronically to the warehouse computer.

2. The warehouse computer generates a 'picking note'.

3. After the picking run is completed, the picking note is amended to take account of any items that were out-of-stock. These amendments, if any, are fed back into the warehouse computer.

4. The computer then generates a despatch note. At this stage the stock control program is updated and the actual despatch data is passed back to Accounts. Thus the despatch note is not necessarily identical to the customer's order.

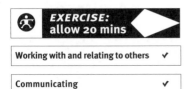

EXERCISE: allow 20 mins	
Working with and relating to others	✓
Communicating	✓

ACTIVITY 1

In groups of four, discuss the processes described above. Identify the stages at which errors might occur, and describe what sort of errors might be involved. Use a separate sheet of paper to record your ideas, arranging the errors under the headings:

(a) errors in processing customer orders

(b) errors at goods-in stage

(c) errors at the picking/despatch stage.

When you have finished compiling your list, go through it again and make a note of any errors that you think likely to be particularly common, or particularly serious.

Finally, compare notes between groups and write a brief summary of your conclusions in the box below.

Commentary...

There are many points where errors could occur:

Order processing errors would mainly be clerical, i.e. mistakes made when transcribing telephoned orders or when keyboarding details into the system. Errors occasionally occur during transmission by fax or telex (e.g. lines of text omitted) and during electronic transmission (although this is rare, because a checking mechanism is used).

The goods-in process is also error-prone, with the additional complication that theft and fraud may be taking place, e.g. by suppliers' drivers colluding with Stokkit's staff. Errors can occur in scanning bar codes, if the scanner is dirty or the bar code is torn or distorted. Keyboarding also takes place at this stage, and is always error-prone. Further errors occur where goods are incorrectly stored; the computer will show them present, but pickers will be unable to find them. They may be 'lost' until the next physical stock-take.

Picking and despatch errors include 'human errors' made by pickers – omitting items, picking the wrong items, picking the wrong quantity of the right items, etc. There may be loading errors, with consignments going on to the wrong lorry. 'Book' errors can occur when picking notes are reconciled with despatch notes.

The errors described above inevitably cause operational problems, ranging from disputes with customers to reduced management control. The latter in turn results in:

- decreased service standards as more items go out-of-stock unexpectedly

- more wastage as incorrectly recorded stock builds up

- increased losses due to theft (always associated with decreased control over goods in store)

- more management time used to investigate problems.

THE PROBLEM OF HUMAN ERROR

Where human beings have to perform a process, errors are likely to occur. Clerical errors include:

- incorrectly transcribing a detail given over the telephone

- pressing the wrong key during data entry

- failing to notice a mismatch on two related pieces of documentation.

Modern IT systems, like Kellaway's till-based transaction processing system, can record operator error rates, and also the number of transactions processed in a given period. Such information can be used to identify operators who need extra training or supervision.

This type of monitoring is a cost-effective way of increasing overall data-input quality. Other kinds of errors can also be reduced by a combination of training, supervision, audit and built-in error checking systems.

- Training should be carried out systematically against a plan which details the competences to be acquired, and the standard by which they will be measured.

- Supervision should concentrate on ensuring that work is carried out to standard. It should pay special attention to areas where problems have been identified.

- Internal audit procedures should be in place. The financial systems of many large organisations now contain built-in auditing structures, which can also be used by internal auditors to make non-statutory checks on the data collection and processing systems, production processes, stores records and so on.

- Automatic error-checking is commonly built into transaction processing systems, and goods-in, sales and order processing programs refuse to accept invalid entries. For example, supermarket tills allow operators to key in item codes if the scanner is not working. The till's microprocessor looks up the code in the master file of item codes. If there is a mismatch an error message is given, and the operator has to re-enter the code.

Similarly, a goods-in system may validate product codes against quantity codes and supplier codes. An incorrect product code will be rejected (unless it happens to match another valid product code for that supplier). This eliminates many, but not all, keying errors. The goods-in codes may be validated against the order which has generated them, and any non-matching items will result in an error or query message.

Hardware and software problems

Collecting good quality data is not the end of the story. It is still vulnerable to hardware and software problems, and to errors during processing. In reality, computer errors, in the sense of the hardware producing an incorrect result, are extremely rare. Faults are usually due to human error in setting up a program or selecting data for analysis. Yet data collection and processing equipment is not immune to errors, especially if it is not regularly maintained. New products are more likely to contain faults than established ones.

Hardware faults include:

- document readers taking two sheets together, thus failing to process the lower one

- communications links 'going down', with the loss of some data in transit

- outright machine failure

- hard disk failure in computers, peripheral storage devices and network 'file servers'.

The failure of data storage devices can be highly damaging. At best, access to data may be impossible until the system has been repaired; at worst, large amounts of data may be lost altogether. This is a significant risk where individual computer users are storing and processing important operational data, databases, spreadsheets and other business information which has been built up over a period.

REDUCING THE RISK OF LOSING DATA

ACTIVITY 2

Imagine that you are responsible for advising your organisation on the additional data back-up facilities now available for desk-top computers (over and above the built-in floppy disk drives).

Your task is to research the subject – you may, for example, want to refer to current computer magazines and IT books in the library – and to identify:

- at least three data back-up methods

- their approximate storage capacity in megabytes

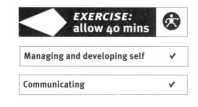

EXERCISE:
allow 40 mins

| Managing and developing self | ✓ |
| Communicating | ✓ |

> ○ the approximate cost of purchasing the necessary hardware for one desk-top computer.
>
> When you have done this, prepare a short presentation on the subject, in the form of notes suitable for display using a flip-chart or overhead projector. Summarise your main points in the box below.

Commentary...

All desk-top PCs have drives for removable floppy disks, which are commonly used to back-up working files. A 3.5 inch magnetic diskette can contain around 1.44 Mbytes of data, and as a rough guide, two of these would be needed to copy all the word processor and spreadsheet files that make up this workbook. Additional floppy disk drives can be bought quite cheaply, but while this is a reasonable back-up option for relatively small amounts of data, it is not practical for:

○ very large files (such as big databases)

○ very large numbers of files

○ backing up large software programs.

However, an increasing range of options for bulk data back-up is available, as you can see in any computer magazine. Capacities range from 100 Mbytes upwards on removable magnetic hard disks, and much more on optical storage disks. In both cases, the drive units may be built-in or free-standing, and the disks or cartridges can be usually removed and stored securely elsewhere.

The other principal option is a 'tape streamer' – a fast high-capacity magnetic tape system, which can also be internal or external to the computer, and contains a removable cartridge.

We will not comment in detail on prices, as they are changing rapidly as technology develops and the market expands. Floppy disks are cheap, and suitable drives are usually already present on the computer. Hard disks and magnetic tape have fallen greatly in price in recent years, but the biggest advances are in optical storage media. These are more expensive than hard disks, but because their capacity is usually much higher, the storage cost per Mbyte may be lower.

REDUCING THE RISK OF HARDWARE AND SOFTWARE FAILURE

Mechanical and electrical failure of computers and peripheral devices is an unavoidable hazard, but provided that data and programs are backed up, it should be manageable. Most organisations keep some hardware in reserve, and in a well-managed computer network, the inconvenience of losing one machine should be minimal. However, failure of major components of the network itself (cabling, control units and file servers) can be much more serious.

Where data links (for example from one working location to another) are a crucial part of a system, a communications fault will be a serious problem, and the IT department may arrange either a stand-by facility or an alternative means of communicating. In the most sensitive situations, the expense of maintaining parallel data links may be justified.

So, for example, a large supermarket chain might design its in-store transaction processing system to minimise the risk of a total system breakdown. (This would be very serious, since up to 70 electronic tills might be in use, and if all 70 were to 'go down' simultaneously the loss of data and disruption of sales operations would be enormous.) The system is split into two, with alternate check-outs linked to separate master computers, as shown in figure 5.2. A third master computer is kept on stand-by to replace either of the others rapidly if need be.

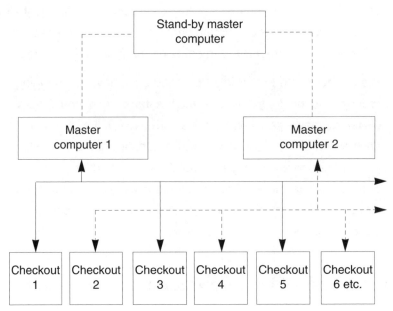

FIGURE 5.2: Precautions against system failure in a large supermarket.

SOFTWARE ERRORS

Tried and tested commercial software packages are unlikely to give problems, but newly released software often has minor faults and shortcomings. Purpose-designed software is much more error-prone, being essentially 'handmade' and sometimes inadequately tested.

Pefgo Flooring plc commissioned some special software for computerising its register of shares, but the package was soon abandoned in favour of the old manual register. There were three problems:

1. The software consultants had failed to understand the requirements of the system fully, so there were shortcomings in the program design.

2. The program when delivered contained a number of faults ('bugs') that were not immediately apparent.

3. Pefgo failed to allocate enough time and resources to briefing the consultants, to liaising with them during the development phase, and to testing and evaluating the program before implementing it.

When purpose-designed software is introduced, caution is advisable. It is typical for a new system to be run in parallel with the old one for months if not years, while software engineers monitor and adjust its performance. This is, of course, expensive but the alternatives are even more so.

ACTIVITY 3

Make inquiries about the experiences of the organisation in which you work or study, with respect to software. (This may involve talking to IT managers, operations managers, to the managing director in smaller organisations, or to college IT specialists.)

What problems, if any, have they encountered with commercial software programs?

What purpose-designed (or heavily modified) software have they employed, and what problems, if any, have arisen?

What precautions, if any, do they take when installing new software?

Report your findings in the box below.

How information can mislead

Information always seems more authoritative when it is set down 'in black and white' than when it is given verbally. This is especially true when it comes from respected sources such as managers and 'experts', and even more so when figures are involved. Yet it can pay to be sceptical about information: it may have been collected and interpreted carelessly or incompetently, and there may even be a deliberate intention to mislead.

In section 1, we worked on the assumption that financial information is reliable and accurate. In practice, a great many of the figures that appear in company accounts are a matter of judgement and policy rather than fact, and should be interpreted with caution. Company financial statements are a case in point.

RECALL:
allow 5 mins

List the three financial statements that companies must publish annually.

Company financial statements are used:

- to inform shareholders of the company's progress and financial status

- to demonstrate to other stakeholders (such as bankers, customers, suppliers and staff) that the company is healthy and in good order

- in the case of PLCs, to assist financial analysts and potential investors in deciding whether the company is a good investment risk.

Company directors naturally try to place their company's performance in the best possible light. However, there are numerous statutory and other controls to constrain their enthusiasm. Companies are required to follow strict rules about how their accounts are collected, presented and publicised. Brochures and marketing statements relating to the sale of shares in PLCs are also carefully policed.

The existence of such regulation is a direct reflection of the strong temptation for directors to mislead others about the true state of their organisations. It is fair to say that although the regulations are frequently tightened and loopholes abolished, there is still widespread concern about the truthfulness of company financial statements and the effectiveness of the accountancy profession in ensuring that a 'true and fair view' is given. For an entertaining and alarming review of this field, you should read Creative Accounting: How to make your profits what you want them to be by Ian Griffiths (Firethorn Press, 1986).

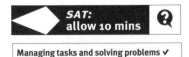

ACTIVITY 4

Imagine yourself in charge of a publicly accountable organisation. What pressures would you be under to enhance the organisation's financial results?

Commentary...

There are several reasons for wishing to enhance the financial position. The first three are common to managers in all organisations:

1. the personal need to appear successful

2. the need to achieve pre-set targets and objectives

3. the desire to maintain the confidence of lenders, customers and suppliers.

The fourth reason applies to profit-making organisations only:

4. the need to appear attractive to shareholders, potential investors and city analysts.

Many of the techniques used to 'window-dress' company results are too arcane and technical to describe here, but it is worth focusing briefly on profitability.

INTERPRETING PROFIT STATEMENTS

Profitability is naturally the most important piece of information for investors, because it is the main determinant of:

- the dividend they are likely to receive in return for their investment

- the likely rate of growth in the value of the shares (capital growth).

All things being equal, if firm A declares higher profitability than firm B, firm A is the more attractive investment – provided the declaration is true.

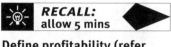

RECALL:
allow 5 mins

Define profitability (refer back to Section 1, Session 4).

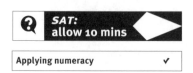

SAT:
allow 10 mins

Applying numeracy ✓

ACTIVITY 5

Work out the percentage return on capital (RoCE) in the cases below.

1. Teapot Ventures Ltd
   Total capital employed: £1.73 million
   Net profit after tax and interest: £216,000

2. Teapot Ventures Ltd
   Total capital employed: £1.73 million
   Net profit before tax and interest: £255,000

3. Milkjug Enterprises Ltd
   Total capital employed: £5.95 million
   Net profit after tax and interest: £650,000

4. Toastrack Investments Ltd
   Total capital employed: £4.45 million
   Net profit after tax and interest: £600,000

What is the percentage difference in profit between:

(a) case 1 and case 2?

(b) case 3 and case 4?

Commentary...

In case 1, Teapot's RoCE after tax and interest is 12.49 per cent. It is 14.74 per cent when calculated before tax and interest (case 2) – an 18 per cent difference. Companies can elect to show profit either before or after tax and interest, or both, but whichever course they choose they must state the fact.

In case 3, Milkjug's RoCE is 10.92 per cent. In case 4, Toastrack's is 13.48 per cent. However, the only difference between these two companies is that Toastrack leases assets worth £1.5 million rather than owning them, thus reducing its capital employed to £4.45 million. It pays leasing costs, which reduce its profit by £50,000 compared with Milkjug's, but the net result of this perfectly legal difference in policy is that its profits appear to be 23 per cent higher.

Other popular areas for creative accounting include:

- depreciation policy (which can be used to increase or decease apparent profits)

- the use of capital allowances

- the writing off of 'goodwill' following takeovers

- the valuation of the taken-over company's assets

- the handling of pension funds

- the treatment of bad debts

- the failure to mention factors that might cast the annual results in a different light.

As an example of the last point, in the financial year 1993–94 the accounts of Stokkit Ltd showed a profit of £263,000 (a RoCE of 21.16 per cent). However the accounts included £18,440 owed by a customer. When the auditors first saw the accounts, this debt was already over three months old, and Stokkit was on the verge of cutting off further supplies to the customer. The auditors argued that the accounts should be adjusted to show the £18,440 as a bad debt instead of revenue, but Stokkit's directors disagreed, saying that they were confident that the debt would be recovered.

Directors and auditors need to reach agreement about how a company's accounts are presented, and what they say. Auditors have a duty:

- to report fraud

- to issue qualifying statements where they disagree with some aspect of the published accounts

- to confirm that the business is 'a going concern'.

Sometimes organisations sack their auditors if they will not do what the directors want (the auditors are required to report this to their successors). More commonly, the two parties agree a change in accounting policy. This can have a significant effect on declared profits, and both the change of auditors and change of policy must be revealed in the Annual Report and Accounts. Thus an investor needs to read with care not just the financial statements, but the whole of the annual report.

USING GRAPHICS TO MISLEAD

Even where no public forecast is made, a company's annual accounts may be designed to encourage readers to imagine a rosy future. This may be supported by the 'creative' use of graphics.

ACTIVITY 6

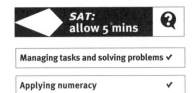
Here is a record of a company's profits (expressed as the percentage return on capital) for the last seven years. What can you say about this performance, based on the figures alone?

1988	1989	1990	1991	1992	1993	1994	1995
16.3	17.5	16.8	17.6	17.9	17.2	18	17.8

Now here is a graphed version of the same figures, including an extra line which represents a 'smoothed' version of the same data which is intended to illustrate the general trend of profit growth.

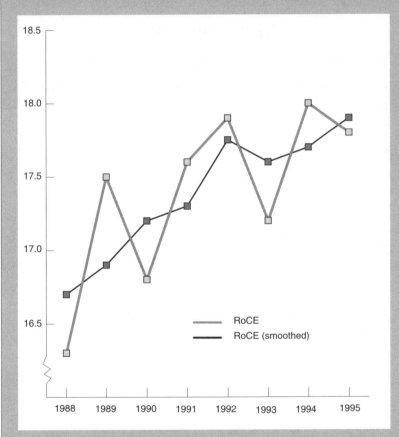

Would you now describe the profit performance differently? And if so, how?

Why does the graphed version of the information have this effect?

Commentary...

The figures alone can be interpreted as a modest but steady performance. The company is consistently returning 16.5–18 per cent on the owners' capital – twice as much as could at present be earned by putting the money in a bank. There is also evidence of a trend upwards.

The graphed version gives a much more dynamic impression (the zigzags in themselves have a positive psychological effect). The addition of the 'smoothed' line helps reinforce the sense of strong upward movement.

In fact, this effect is achieved by careful choice of scale: the scale on the graph has been deliberately selected to start at 16 and end at 18.5 – a very small range which greatly exaggerates the rate of growth. The same data graphed on a base of 10, gives a different impression: the dynamism has been removed.

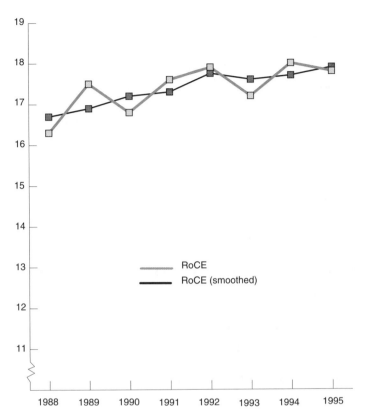

If we were to be completely honest and use a graph based on 0, the growth trend would be almost invisible.

A CHECK-LIST FOR ANALYSING FINANCIAL ACCOUNTS

Even when we have discounted the effects of window-dressing, published statutory accounts need careful evaluation. In particular, they only tell us about the past, whereas we actually want to know about the future – which is where investment decisions, long-term contracts, loan agreements, and profits have to be made. To judge whether satisfactory historic accounts point to a satisfactory future, we need to consider three things:

1. How does the historic performance compare with the performance of investments generally, and with other enterprises in the same economic sector?

   ◉ A business ought to provide a better return than a bank, because it incurs more risk.

   ◉ Different business sectors carry different levels of risk, and more profitability will be expected from a high-risk sector.

   ◉ Companies whose activities are diversified among several different sectors generally carry lower risk.

2. Is there anything in past published accounts to suggest that a problem may be developing?

  ◉ Is the level of debtors, overhead costs, directors' emoluments, or depreciation unusually high?

  ◉ Do the accounts contain non-routine items such 'special provisions', large redundancy payments, 'special reserves', etc., and if so, what do these imply?

  ◉ Have there been any accounting policy changes, have the auditors been changed, have auditors made qualified statements or other criticisms?

3. Is anything known about future trading conditions that may affect the company's performance adversely?

  ◉ Is the dominant technology about to change and, if so, has this business prepared for it?

  ◉ Is there a risk from statutory regulation (such as new pollution, safety or pricing controls)?

  ◉ Are new competitors likely to enter the market?

  ◉ Are the business's products or services reaching maturity and, if so, has the business prepared new products and new strategies to counter this?

A company like Stokkit, which is a small player in the multi-billion pound wholesaling market, may be vulnerable to:

  ◉ larger firms with more financial strength, which could afford to cut prices long enough to destroy Stokkit

  ◉ trends in supermarket retailing towards direct just-in-time delivery from manufacturers (this becomes more attractive financially as supermarket units grow larger)

  ◉ new technology. The largest and most efficient warehouses are now purpose-built with computer-controlled robotised picking systems. Can Stokkit ever find the capital needed to re-equip on these lines?

A more technology-based manufacturing company like Pefgo Flooring plc may also be vulnerable to competition, but the possibility of major technological change may present a bigger challenge.

ACTIVITY 7

Why may technological change threaten the profits of a company like Pefgo?

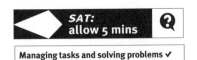
Commentary...

Technological innovation takes place under the pressure of competition, its purpose being to reduce production costs or to make new kinds of product, or both. It is therefore impossible for an existing manufacturer to stand by while competitors adopt new technology. The challenge is fourfold:

1. New technology makes old technology obsolete, and gives users of the new technology a big advantage in the markets.

2. Every business that intends to stay in the market must therefore invest in the new technology, the capital cost of which is usually very large.

3. New technology increases labour productivity, but also production capacity. Unless the markets also expand rapidly, this increase in capacity will increase competitive pressures even more.

4. The adoption of new technology often causes upheaval in a business, as major new installations take place and everyone concerned has to be retrained.

A superficial reading of the accounts may show that a company has declared healthy profits (and high dividends to shareholders) for many years. More careful analysis may reveal that this has been achieved at the expense of investment in new products and facilities. This will eventually manifest itself in a rapid decline in market share, with drastic effects on profits and share values. It may be that the directors have privately recognised that this will start to happen soon, but have kept it to themselves.

Company financial information cannot be taken at face value, in spite of all the controls and regulations that are in force.

Evaluating forecasts

Businesses operate in an atmosphere of uncertainty about future events, with decisions to be made in the face of this uncertainty. Educated choices about future events are more valuable to decision-makers who operate in a climate of uncertainty than are uneducated guesses. Thus the ability to predict future events with accuracy is a necessary part of managerial planning and control.

Jarrett, J. (1991) Business Forecasting Methods, 2nd edn, Blackwell

Forecasts are an attempt to predict the future development of an organisation's activities. There is an incentive to make forecasts as accurate as possible. However, forecasts:

- are not part of the statutory reporting structure

- are not liable to audit

- deal with the future, so they cannot be disproved in advance, though their accuracy and the reasoning behind them may be suspect.

Directors often make 'confident predictions' about future growth, to impress their investors, lenders and customers. Forecasts therefore need to be evaluated even more cautiously than statutory financial statements.

In its simplest form, forecasting takes past data and extrapolates them into the future. Here is a simple example.

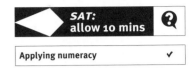

ACTIVITY 8

Plot the data for 1992–95 on the blank graph below, and draw a line connecting the points.

Now extend the line to create a forecast for 1996 and 1997. Fill in your predicted values for 1996 and 1997 in the spaces provided, and explain why you think your forecast may be under- or over-optimistic.

Past sales data (£million)				Forecast:	
1992	1993	1994	1995	1996	1997
196.5	197	198	200	___	___

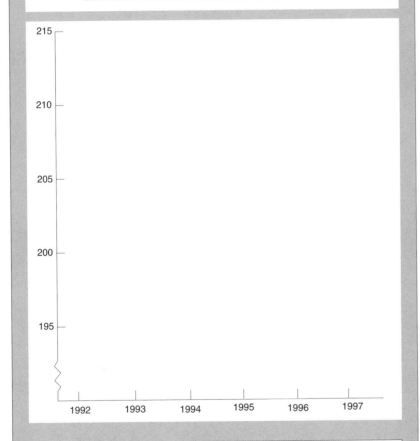

Commentary...

More than one result is possible. The graph below shows two of these possibilities, both of which have been produced arithmetically from the past years' sales data.

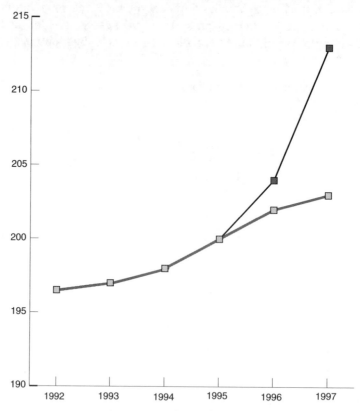

In the top line, the curve established by data for 1992–95 is extended on the assumption that the previous rate of increase will continue (the data show that the increase has doubled every year, from £0.5 million to £1 million to £2 million). While this is not impossible, in practice competitive pressures, unpredictable external events and product maturation effects make such impressive performance a rarity.

The straight-line extension of the line represents a different approach, under which the average growth for 1992–95 (0.5 + 1.0 + 2.0 = 3.5; 3.5 / 3 = 1.167) has been applied to the two following years. This, however, may be unduly pessimistic. In practice, the actual performance is likely to be somewhere between the two (though there is always a possibility that it will be higher or lower).

Which forecast is correct? With more detailed analysis we may be able to say that one outcome is more probable than another, but not that the outcome will definitely be one or the other. Ultimately, it is a matter of judgement, but we are entitled to ask whether the person who prepared the forecast is careless, prey to self-deception, or deliberately trying to give a misleading impression.

Here is a further example. Figure 5.3 shows two versions of Pefgo Flooring plc's five-year financial forecast. Version 1 was incorporated in a business plan that Pefgo showed to its bankers; version 2 was calculated by the bank's analysts.

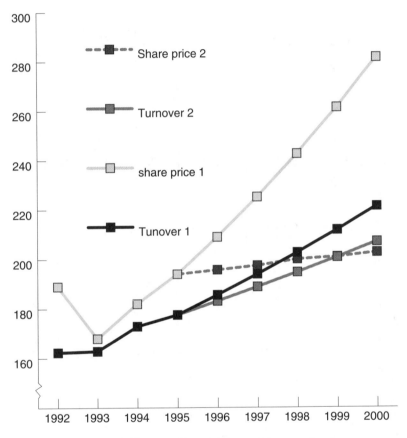

FIGURE 5.3: Five-year financial forecast (two versions).

Figure 5.3 shows two versions of the forecast share price (the upper pair of lines) and two versions of the forecast turnover (the lower pair). Up until 1995, the two versions are identical, because these are past data; the difference between the versions is accounted for by choosing a different base date for the forecast.

Table 5.1 shows how these two very different forecasts were constructed.

VERSION 1: GROWTH BASED ON % INCREASE 1993-95
This version ignores 1992 and uses the years 1993-95 to calculate the percentage growth factor used in the forecast.

	% growth 1993-95	1992 (actual, not used)	1993 (actual)	1994 (actual)	1995 (actual)	1996 (forecast)	1997 (forecast)	1998 (forecast)	1999 (forecast)	2000 (forecast)
TURNOVER (£millions)	4.51	162.35	162.86	172.93	177.55	185.56	193.93	202.67	211.81	221.37
NET PROFIT	13.27	7.31	5.05	6.05	6.39	7.24	8.20	9.29	10.52	11.91
% PROFIT ON TURNOVER	8.06	4.50	3.10	3.50	3.60	3.89	4.20	4.54	4.91	5.31
CAPITAL EMPLOYED		55.30	59.22	55.39	51.04	48.04	51.06	51.11	51.12	51.62
RoCE		13.22	8.53	10.92	12.52	15.07	16.06	18.18	20.58	23.07
SHARE PRICE (pence)	7.74	189.00	168.00	182.00	194.00	209.01	225.19	242.61	261.38	281.61

VERSION 2: GROWTH BASED ON % INCREASE 1992-95
This version uses the years 1992-95 to calculate the percentage growth factor used in the forecast.

	% growth 1992-95	1992 (actual)	1993 (actual)	1994 (actual)	1995 (actual)	1996 (forecast)	1997 (forecast)	1998 (forecast)	1999 (forecast)	2000 (forecast)
TURNOVER (£millions)	3.12	162.35	162.86	172.93	177.55	183.09	188.80	194.70	200.77	207.04
NET PROFIT AFTER TAX	-4.20	7.31	5.05	6.05	6.39	6.12	5.87	5.62	5.38	5.16
% PROFIT ON TURNOVER	-6.67	4.50	3.10	3.50	3.60	3.36	3.14	2.93	2.73	2.55
CAPITAL EMPLOYED		55.30	59.22	55.39	51.04	48.04	51.06	51.11	51.12	51.62
RoCE		13.21	8.53	10.92	12.52	12.74	11.50	11.00	10.52	10.00
SHARE PRICE (pence)	0.88	189.00	168.00	182.00	194.00	195.71	197.44	199.98	200.93	202.71

TABLE 5.1: Pefgo's five-year financial forecast

ACTIVITY 9

The difference between the two versions of the forecast is brought about by the choice of base year – 1993 in version 1, 1992 in version 2.

Study table 5.1 and write a brief explanation of why this difference comes about.

Note down anything else that strikes you as suspect about the information provided in table 5.1.

Commentary...

The difference between the two sets of forecasts depends entirely on which year is chosen as the base for calculating the growth percentage: 1993 was a bad year, but 1994 and 1995 were much better. The average growth rate measured over the years 1993–95 appeared much higher than in version 2, in which 1992, a relatively good year, was included.

The table shows a reduction in capital employed from 1994 onwards. This, of course, has the effect of boosting RoCE (calculated as net profit as a percentage of capital employed), and is thus a significant factor in making the forecast look attractive. In the absence of any explanation, we may suspect that this reduction in capital was achieved by a manoeuvre such as the sale and lease-back arrangement referred to earlier. This would not then represent a genuine improvement, but only another example of window-dressing.

We should point out that while Pefgo's directors were inclined to window-dress their forecast to impress the bank, the bank was eager to choose the most cautious option, so as to argue for better lending terms from its own stand-point. Organisations (and their managers) tend to be influenced by their self-interest when making judgements of this kind. A more neutral analyst might have selected a forecast midway between the two, based on a longer series of years (say 1985–95).

WHY FORECASTS ARE DEBATABLE

Although improved statistical techniques (including multiple regression analysis, ARIMA and Box-Jenkins methods – see Jarrett, 1991) have improved the inherent accuracy of forecasts, they all have one fundamental weakness. They use the past to predict the future, and the future is naturally open to uncertainty. Thus when interpreting forecasts, we need to ask four questions:

1. Is the forecast based on reliable data?

2. Is the forecast produced by reliable methods?

3. What do we know or suspect about future conditions that may have a bearing on the forecast?

4. What, if anything, might the forecaster expect to gain by selecting this particular forecast (out of the many other possibilities)?

Only when we have considered these issues can we decide whether, in the circumstances, the forecast is reasonable.

Errors of analysis

Errors of analysis range from arithmetical errors and mistakes in formulating spreadsheets to a broader failure to understand the nature of a problem or the analysis methods needed to deal with it.

A common example is in the use of averages. This is a simple and often useful technique. If customer A's orders are worth £5,000 a month on average, and customer B's are worth £1,500, this is worth knowing. It may lead us to change the amount of sales resources we devote to either, or both. However, any basic text on statistics (see Susan F. Wagner, 1992, An Introduction to Statistics, HarperCollins

College Outlines) tells you that the average (or mean) is not always the most useful of the 'measures of central tendency'. Certainly averages can be misleading, as the example below shows.

A PROBLEM WITH AVERAGES

The average number of enquiry calls received by Kellaways' customer service department has been measured over several weeks and the data are shown in table 5.2.

Hour Day	9–10am	10–11am	11–12noon	12–1pm	1–2pm	2–3pm	3–4pm	4–5pm	5–6pm	Daily average per hour
Monday	36	40	45	59	98	50	32	30	43	
Tuesday	25	23	16	27	44	31	20	17	26	
Wednesday	27	24	20	28	51	33	24	19	28	
Thursday	22	22	15	18	39	21	17	15	24	
Friday	16	12	13	18	29	15	10	9	12	
Saturday	8	12	13							
Hourly total										
Hourly average										

TABLE 5.2: Calls received by Kellaways' customer service department

ACTIVITY 10

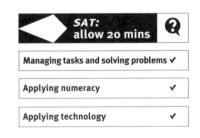

SAT: allow 20 mins

Managing tasks and solving problems ✔

Applying numeracy ✔

Applying technology ✔

Table 5.2 shows the average number of calls received per working hour in each day of a standard week. On Saturdays the office is closed from 12 noon. Preferably, you should enter the data into a spreadsheet and use spreadsheet functions to calculate the results and produce graphs.

Work out the following and enter the figures in the table:

(a) the hourly totals and hourly averages (the bottom two rows on the table)

(b) the daily average per hour (the right-hand column on the table) and enter these figures in the blank cells in the table.

Now draw two graphs, using the grids below.

On grid 1, draw graphs to show (a) the average calls per hour, (b) the actual hourly figures for Monday, and (c) actual hourly figures for Saturday.

On grid 2, draw a graph to show the daily average calls per hour.

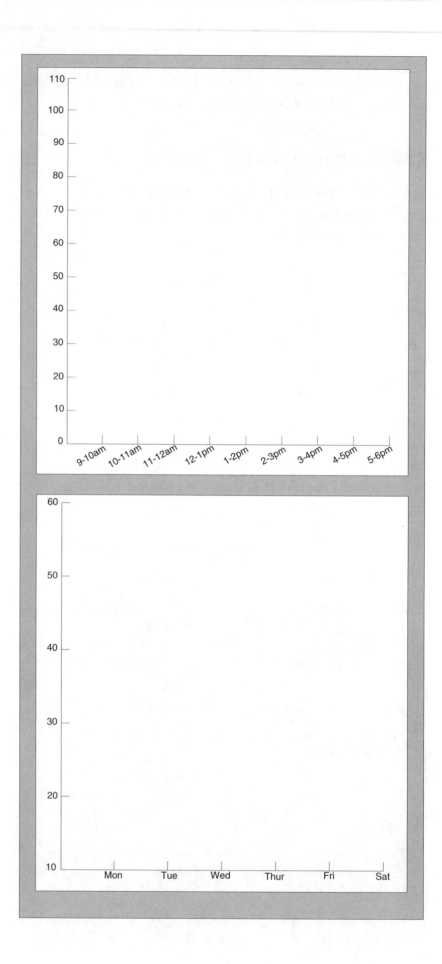

Commentary...

When you have completed the table, the following figures should appear in the right-hand column: 48.11, 25.44, 28.22, 21.44, 14.89, 11.00. These are the daily averages. The total figures per working hour should be 134, 133, 122, 150, 261, 150, 103, 90,133, and the averages should be 22.33, 22.17, 20.33, 30.00, 52.20, 30.00, 20.60, 18.00 and 26.60.

Your two graphs should look like those illustrated in figures 5.4 and 5.5.

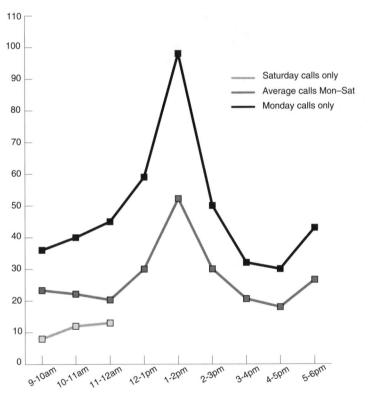

FIGURE 5.4: Average calls per working hour plus
actual calls on Monday and Saturday.

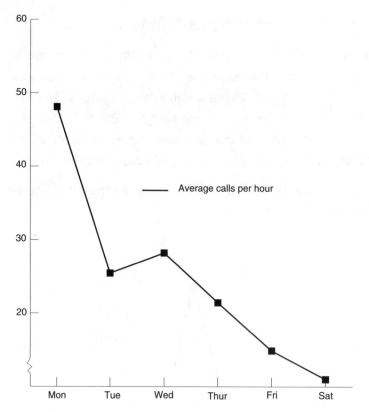

FIGURE 5.5: Average calls per hour, Monday to Saturday.

Kellaways expected to use these data as a basis for deciding the optimum staffing levels for their customer service department (i.e. the smallest number that can provide the required service). The following data are also relevant:

- The service standard is that each call should be answered within 4 rings.

- The employees in the department work a full-time 40-hour week Monday to Friday (Saturday work is overtime).

- Each person can deal on average with 20 calls per hour (call average three minutes).

- Each person is entitled to a one-hour break, either from 12 noon to 1 p.m. or from 1 p.m. to 2 p.m.

ACTIVITY 11

Managing tasks and solving problems ✓

Applying numeracy   ✓

Using the averages that you calculated in the previous activity, plus the data given above, answer the following questions.

1. How many full-time staff are needed to maintain the service at the level required?

2. How many staff would be needed to provide this level of cover on Fridays?

3. To what extent does a knowledge of average call rates and answering data help to solve this problem?

4. How could Kellaways reduce the cost of this operation?

Commentary...

The number of full-time staff needed is not determined by average levels of calls, but by the maximum level for which cover is needed – 98 calls between 1 p.m. and 2 p.m. on Mondays. This is nearly twice the weekly average for this hour (52.2 calls), and is more than three times the rate for the quietest day (Fridays).

The number of staff needed to cover a peak of 98 calls an hour is 5 (98 divided by 20). However, because each staff member can take one hour off duty either from 12 noon to 1 p.m. or 1 p.m. to 2 p.m., five staff is not enough to cover a peak of 98 occurring in these hours.

		12 noon–1p.m.	1–2 p.m.
(1)	Actual calls on Monday	59	98
(2)	Number of full-time staff theoretically needed to answer 98 calls	5	5
(3)	Staff at lunch	-3	-2
(4)	Staff actually working during this hour	2	3
(5)	Calls unanswered	19	38

Two more full-time staff members would suffice to deal with the 19 unanswered calls between 12 noon and 1 p.m. and the 38 unanswered calls between 1 p.m. and 2 p.m. However, they too would be entitled to a break, so the actual requirement is for three more, i.e. eight altogether.

Using the same approach to calculate staffing needs for Friday, we find that with only 18 and 29 calls to be answered in the hours in question, only three staff are needed.

Reliance on averages in this situation is bound to lead us astray. The figures for calls received in given hours on given days are themselves averages, which may disguise a considerable variation. On some Mondays the peak may be not 98 but 120 calls. The number of calls that an individual can answer in an hour is also an average, but sometimes the calls may turn out to be longer than this, and a few particularly complicated calls may distort the pattern considerably. Finally, the incoming calls are unlikely to arrive at conveniently spaced intervals: sometimes several dozen callers may try to ring in simultaneously. The total number of full-time staff required might therefore be at least double the eight so far suggested. Average figures simply do not help to solve this particular problem. (It needs a considerably more sophisticated analysis using statistical techniques that are beyond the scope of this workbook.)

There are three possible ways of reducing what now looks like a costly and inefficient operation. First, Kellaways might reduce its service standard. At present it states that all calls must be answered promptly. However, it could decide to let calls 'stack up', or to be given the engaged tone.

The main problem is that the customer service staff often have little to do. Two obvious alternatives suggest themselves:

1. Staff the department up to capacity with full-timers, but give them other useful work to do when not answering customers' calls.

2. Cease staffing the department exclusively with full-timers. Two full-timers can cover all except the two peak hours, and the hours 11 a.m. to 12 noon and 2 p.m. to 3 p.m. on Mondays. Part-time staff can be employed to provide cover at these busier times.

Evaluating written reports

As we saw from Stephen Gage's in-tray in session 4, managers often have to read and evaluate reports written by colleagues, consultants and others. Like analysing accounts, this calls for a clear head and a critical eye.

How reliable is the information and the analysis contained in the report? We can start to assess this by using a check-list and a rating scale. Figure 5.6 illustrates a check-list and rating scale.

	score 1 (low) to 5 (high)				
	1	2	3	4	5
A. How reliable is the writer?					
● What is this person's track record for accuracy and reliability?	☐	☐	☐	☐	☐
● Does this person have enough skill and experience to give the report credibility?	☐	☐	☐	☐	☐
● Is he or she free of personal bias that may affect reliability?	☐	☐	☐	☐	☐
● Is he or she able to set aside any personal self-interest that may affect reliability?	☐	☐	☐	☐	☐
B. How reliable is the information?					
● Did the writer draw on an appropriate range of sources?	☐	☐	☐	☐	☐
● How reliable are these sources?	☐	☐	☐	☐	☐
● How thorough and comprehensive is the coverage of the report?	☐	☐	☐	☐	☐
● Do the conclusions correctly reflect the evidence?	☐	☐	☐	☐	☐
OVERALL RELIABILITY	☐	☐	☐	☐	☐

FIGURE 5.6: Reliability rating scale.

It is important to consider whether the writer used all the sources available, or only some of them, and to identify any areas where he or she has glossed over topics, or dismissed them too rapidly. It may also be useful to 'validate' a report against other sources to which we have access.

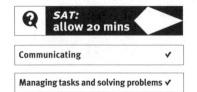

SAT:
allow 20 mins

Communicating ✔

Managing tasks and solving problems ✔

ACTIVITY 12

Stokkit is planning a major extension to its warehouse, and expects opposition at the forthcoming planning enquiry. A junior executive has drawn up a report that shows that although 2,228 households lie in the area potentially affected by building noise, increased traffic, etc., only 15 have written letters complaining to the company. In summing up his findings he states: 'It therefore appears that local opposition to our development is minor in scale, with a mere 0.7 per cent expressing any concerns'.

(a) What reasons might there be for querying this conclusion?

(b) How could the writer's judgement about the low level of opposition be tested and validated?

Write a short 'memo'-style report of no more than 150 words, and summarise your key points below.

Commentary...

The obvious point to query is whether writing to Stokkit is the only form in which opposition is likely to be expressed. It should also be noted that people who are literate and angry enough to write letters may only be the tip of a much larger iceberg of opposition. The report should have considered this.

The way to validate the report's conclusions is to seek out more evidence that may confirm, modify or refute it:

- Residents may also have written protest letters to the local Council, the MP, local newspapers, and the planning authorities. The scale of this may well exceed letters sent direct to Stokkit.

- Local councillors, the MP and the editors of local newspapers may have expressed their own opinions publicly. This can be checked.

- An organised campaign against the development may have been proposed, or even launched. Has the writer checked this?

- Are there any objective tests of public opinion on the subject (i.e. surveys and opinion polls)?

- Other experienced and well-informed people in the company may have useful information that should be considered.

- Consultants and advisers can be asked to comment.

- Any record of similar issues in the past can be consulted.

In evaluating all kinds of information, from news stories to stock record print-outs to management reports, it pays to be sceptical. Data generally contain errors, and when these rise above a certain level, any information derived from them must be considered highly suspect. High error rates also generate endless operational problems. When data are lost, damaged or interfered with, this may invalidate the sophisticated analysis techniques that we can use to analyse them.

Much of what purports to be information also needs to be approached with caution. We tend to assume that facts and figures set out in black and white – and especially when they appear in expensively produced annual reports – are the simple truth. But a great deal of so-called information is in fact designed to misinform, or at least to give a slanted impression.

Finally, we need to consider our analytical tools and skills. Information may flow through our organisations with ever-increasing vigour, but unless we learn the techniques of analysis and develop the expertise to evaluate the outcomes, we will never be able to make full and effective use of this elusive but crucial resource.

summary

▶ The first determinant of information quality is the quality of the data from which it is derived. Data are never entirely error-free, because this is too costly to achieve.

▶ Human error is perhaps the main source of error. Training, supervision, audit and automatic error-checking systems can all help to reduce error and assure quality.

▶ Problems can occur with hardware and software, and precautions need to be taken against any failure of either that may result in damage to or loss of data. Back-up procedures and stand-by hardware are principal safeguards.

▶ Printed information often gives the appearance of being authoritative, but this can be misleading. Such information may have been produced carelessly, incompetently or using faulty data.

▶ There may be a deliberate intention to mislead, particularly where financial statements and forecasts are concerned. The pressures to 'window-dress' results are great, despite extensive regulations to prevent it. Financial statements need to be analysed with care.

▶ Financial statements should be evaluated by considering the historic performance of the organisation and comparing it with others in the same field. Search the published accounts for any hints of problems and consider the organisation's prospects in the light of what we know about the future.

▶ Graphics can also be used to give a misleading impression, for example by altering the scale of diagrams. Since graphics are a powerful means of communication, they should be looked at with caution.

▶ Forecasts call for particular caution, since they cannot be proved or disproved in advance, and there are usually several ways of calculating them, all of which will generate different outcomes.

▶ Written reports, like financial statements and forecasts, also require repay careful evaluation. They are particularly prone to bias, unproven assumptions and faulty reasoning on the part of the writer.

Resources

Resources

PERCENTAGE RATE OF DISCOUNT

years	1	2	3	4	5	6	7	8
1	0.990	0.980	0.971	0.962	0.952	0.943	0.935	0.926
2	0.980	0.961	0.943	0.925	0.907	0.890	0.873	0.857
3	0.971	0.942	0.915	0.889	0.864	0.840	0.816	0.794
4	0.961	0.924	0.888	0.855	0.823	0.792	0.763	0.735
5	0.951	0.906	0.863	0.822	0.784	0.747	0.713	0.681
6	0.942	0.888	0.837	0.790	0.746	0.705	0.666	0.630
7	0.933	0.871	0.813	0.760	0.711	0.665	0.623	0.583
8	0.923	0.853	0.789	0.731	0.677	0.627	0.582	0.540
9	0.914	0.837	0.766	0.703	0.645	0.592	0.544	0.500
10	0.905	0.820	0.744	0.676	0.614	0.558	0.508	0.463

years	9	10	11	12	13	14	15	16
1	0.917	0.909	0.901	0.893	0.885	0.877	0.870	0.862
2	0.842	0.826	0.812	0.797	0.783	0.769	0.756	0.743
3	0.772	0.751	0.731	0.712	0.693	0.675	0.658	0.641
4	0.708	0.683	0.659	0.636	0.613	0.592	0.572	0.552
5	0.650	0.621	0.593	0.567	0.543	0.519	0.497	0.476
6	0.596	0.564	0.535	0.507	0.480	0.456	0.432	0.410
7	0.547	0.513	0.482	0.452	0.425	0.400	0.376	0.354
8	0.502	0.467	0.434	0.404	0.376	0.351	0.327	0.305
9	0.460	0.424	0.391	0.361	0.333	0.308	0.284	0.263
10	0.422	0.386	0.352	0.322	0.295	0.270	0.247	0.227

years	17	18	19	20	21	22	23	24
1	0.855	0.847	0.840	0.833	0.826	0.820	0.813	0.806
2	0.731	0.718	0.706	0.694	0.683	0.672	0.661	0.650
3	0.624	0.609	0.593	0.579	0.564	0.551	0.537	0.524
4	0.534	0.516	0.499	0.482	0.467	0.451	0.437	0.423
5	0.456	0.437	0.419	0.402	0.386	0.370	0.355	0.341
6	0.390	0.370	0.352	0.335	0.319	0.303	0.289	0.275
7	0.333	0.314	0.296	0.279	0.263	0.249	0.235	0.222
8	0.285	0.266	0.249	0.233	0.218	0.204	0.191	0.179
9	0.243	0.225	0.209	0.194	0.180	0.167	0.155	0.144
10	0.208	0.191	0.176	0.162	0.149	0.137	0.126	0.116

years	25	26	28	30	35	40	45	50
1	0.800	0.794	0.781	0.769	0.741	0.714	0.690	0.667
2	0.640	0.630	0.610	0.592	0.549	0.510	0.476	0.444
3	0.512	0.500	0.477	0.455	0.406	0.364	0.328	0.296
4	0.410	0.397	0.373	0.350	0.301	0.260	0.226	0.198
5	0.328	0.315	0.291	0.269	0.223	0.186	0.156	0.132
6	0.262	0.250	0.227	0.207	0.165	0.133	0.108	0.088
7	0.210	0.198	0.178	0.159	0.122	0.095	0.074	0.059
8	0.168	0.157	0.139	0.123	0.091	0.068	0.051	0.039
9	0.134	0.125	0.108	0.094	0.067	0.048	0.035	0.026
10	0.107	0.099	0.085	0.073	0.050	0.035	0.024	0.017

RESOURCE 1:

Present value (discount) factors

RESOURCE 2:

Over page...
Spreadsheet grid for use with Activity 6, Section 2, Session Four.

	A	B	C	D	E	F	G	H
1								
2								
3								
4								
5								
6								
7								
8								
9								
10								
11								
12								
13								
14								
15								
16								
17								
18								
19								
20								
21								
22								
23								
24								
25								
26								
27								
28								
29								
30								